Using Music to Enhance Student Learning

Integrating musical activities in the elementary school classroom can assist in effectively teaching and engaging students in Language Arts, Science, Math, and Social Studies, while also boosting mental, emotional, and social development. However, many elementary education majors fear they lack the necessary musical skills to use music successfully. Future elementary school teachers need usable, practical musical strategies to easily infuse into their curriculum. Written for both current and future teachers with little or no previous experience in music, *Using Music to Enhance Student Learning* offers strategies that are not heavily dependent on a musical background. While most textbooks are devoted to teaching music theory, this textbook is dedicated to the pedagogical aspects. The ultimate goal is for elementary school children to leave the classroom with an introductory appreciation of music in a joyful, creative environment.

Special Features

- **Listening Maps** help listeners focus on music selections through clear visual representations of sound.
- **Group Activities** reinforce the social aspects of music-making, as well as the benefits of collaborative teaching and learning.
- **A thorough integration of music** in the curriculum establishes that music is essential in a child's development, and that the incorporation of music will significantly enhance all other subjects/activities in the classroom.
- **Learning Aids** include "Tantalizing Tidbits of Research," which provide the justifications for why these activities are important, and helpful "Teaching Tips," "Thinking It Through" activities, "Suggestions for Further Study," and a list of recommended student books.

The *Using Music* Package

- **Audio CD** offers listening selections from the Baroque, Classical, Romantic, and Contemporary Periods.
- *Get America Singing. . .Again! Volume 1* (published by Hal Leonard) contains 43 songs that represent America's varied music heritage of folksongs, traditional songs, and patriotic songs.
- **Appendices**:

  – A songbook with an emphasis on Hispanic folksongs
  – A recorder music songbook
  – Samples of key assignments and lists of music-related books for children and for teachers

- **Companion website**: www.routledge.com/textbooks/9780415878234

Dr. Jana R. Fallin is Professor of Music and Division Chair of Music Education at Kansas State University, and serves as Coordinator for the Faculty Exchange for Teaching Excellence (FETE) at Kansas State.

Mollie Gregory Tower taught elementary music and served 21 years as a music supervisor for Austin ISD. She now teaches in the School of Music, Texas State University-San Marcos.

Using Music to Enhance Student Learning

A Practical Guide for Elementary Classroom Teachers

Dr. Jana R. Fallin

Kansas State University

Mollie G. Tower

Texas State University

 Routledge
Taylor & Francis Group

NEW YORK AND LONDON

Senior Acquisitions Editor: Constance Ditzel
Senior Editorial Assistant: Denny Tek
Marketing Manager: Chris Bowers
Copy Editor: Janice Baiton
Cover Design: Jayne Varney

Development Editor: Nicole Solano
Production Manager: Mhairi Bennett
Text Design: Keystroke
Proofreader: Sue Cope
Companion Website Designer: Marie Mansfield

Credits and acknowledgments borrowed from other sources and reproduced with permission appear on the appropriate page within the textbook.

First published 2011
Taylor & Francis Group
711 Third Avenue, New York, NY 10017

Simultaneously published in the UK
by Routledge
2 Park Square, Milton Park, Abingdon, Oxon OX14 4RN

Routledge is an imprint of the Taylor & Francis Group, an informa business

© 2011 Taylor & Francis

The right of Jana R. Fallin and Mollie G. Tower to be identified as authorsof this work has been asserted by them in accordance with sections 77 and 78 of the Copyright, Designs and Patents Act 1988.

Typeset in Melior by
Keystroke, Station Road, Codsall, Wolverhampton

Images on pp.vii, ix, xv, 1, 3, 12, 25, 55, 57, 75, 94, 105, 107, 121, 137, 150, 177, 182, 186, 203, 210, 238, 251, 255, 274 used courtesy of Shutterstock®, http://www.shutterstock.com. Images on pp.38, 83, 192, and 193 used courtesy of the Open Clip Art Library, http://openclipart.org/.

Appendix 1—McGraw Hill
"A la rueda rueda"; "Acitrón"; "Bate, Bate"; "Campanas vespertinas"; "Chíu, Chíu, Chíu"; "De allacito carnavalito"; "Dry Bones"; "Head and Shoulders, Baby"; "Mi Cuerpo"; "Si me dan pasteles; reprinted with permission. Courtesy of Macmillan/McGraw-Hill.

Appendix 2—Recorder Songbook
Pages 203–213 reprinted with permission. Courtesy of Kay Greenhaw.

Appendix 7—Listening Maps
Pages 263–271 reprinted with permission. Courtesy of Susan Snyder/arts education I.D.E.A.S.

Library of Congress Cataloging in Publication Data
Fallin, Jana R.
    Using music to enhance student learning : a practical guide for
elementary classroom teachers / Jana R. Fallin, Mollie G. Tower.
        p. cm.
    1. School music—Instruction and study—Activity programs. 2. Education, Elementary—Activity programs. 3. Music in education. I. Tower, Mollie G. II. Title.
    MT1.F15 2011
    372.87'044—dc22   2010021020

ISBN 13: 978–0–415–87823–4 (set)
ISBN 13: 978–0–415–89473–9 (pback)

DEDICATION

To our wonderful elementary music students in Austin, Texas, and our marvelous Elementary Education students and Music Education Majors at Kansas State University and Texas State University . . . thanks for the inspiration you provided.

CONTENTS

PREFACE

This textbook has been written for the future teacher in Elementary Education who has had little or no previous experience in music. The biggest challenge with teaching a music course for Elementary Education majors is the amount of material to be covered in one semester. A course such as this has to offer musical knowledge and training to these students in addition to giving them pedagogical information. *Using Music to Enhance Student Learning: A Practical Guide for Elementary Classroom Teachers* is different from most texts used to teach music to Elementary Education majors. Most are much more devoted to teaching music theory and skills than providing pedagogical skills. We are dedicated to keeping the focus on the teaching aspect of music, rather than refining music skills. The ultimate goal is for elementary school children to leave the classroom with an introductory appreciation of music in a joyful, creative environment . . . perhaps wanting to broaden their understanding.

Our belief is that future elementary school teachers need usable, practical musical strategies to infuse into their curriculum. If college students already know how to play the piano, that will serve them well, but trying to get novices to a proficient level during one semester at this point in their careers is not a wise goal. To expect them to refine their music theory skills to performance standards is both unrealistic and counterproductive. A more achievable goal is to give them strategies to incorporate music into their classrooms that are not heavily dependent on their musical skills. This book offers a comprehensive over-view for non-musicians in order to help them grasp the importance of incorporating music into their classrooms. It highlights intuitive pathways to including music that most pre-service teachers have experienced in some form. The realistic music lessons will in turn help their elementary students learn more efficiently. This is what our book offers.

A major goal for our work was to create a textbook that pre-service teachers would continue to consult after completion of the course. Therefore, this book is also very applicable to teachers who are already working in the elementary classroom. In addition, it will be helpful to elementary music teachers and early childhood teachers.

Current Challenges in Elementary Education Addressed in *Using Music*

- The issue of standardized testing that squeezes music out of the curriculum and the importance of making musical connections to the academic curriculum.

- The issue of future teachers who need ideas and strategies for teaching students in diverse contemporary classrooms.
- The escalating population of non-English-speaking elementary students.

How This Text is Organized

The "Getting Started" section begins by involving students in musical activities and songs that could be used at the beginning of the year in an elementary classroom, while looking at the developmental aspects of children that must be addressed in a lesson. Next, easy-to-understand snapshots of major contributors to the field of education are offered. The ideas of Gardner, Bruner, Eisner, and Piaget provide a conceptual framework for the rest of the book. Presenting this information also provides connections from General Education to Music Education. In addition, the work of Hunter and Ladson-Billings are explored in connection with the practical aspects of teaching. Finally, we look inside music to break it down into its core elements. These are presented in a succinct manner, and taught in connection with a hands-on learning experience with the recorder for students.

Section II, "Doing What Musicians Do," provides excellent examples of how to use listening, singing, playing, moving, and creating in the elementary classroom. As students explore the various types of activities that can be used with children, they develop skills and confidence in using these avenues for involving children in music activities in their future classrooms.

Section III, the heart of the book, provides practical ideas for integrating music into each subject in the school day. Good suggestions present ways teachers can expand on the activities and personalize these for their individual teaching situations and populations. The chapters include comprehensive, approachable, and accessible explanations of the topics. Many hands-on activities are included. There are a wealth of practical ideas and easy-to-find resources.

The "Coda" for the book, Chapter 12, contains our "Favorite Teaching Tips." Excellent ideas for working successfully in the classroom are given based on our 80 combined years of working in the field of elementary education. Some things have not changed through all these years. Children today still love to listen to music, play instruments, and sing songs. Astute teachers will use the natural childhood love of music to their advantage, and let it help them teach with more success.

Special Features

- *Listening maps* This book includes listening maps for use in the college course, and future use when teaching students in the classroom. Listening maps help listeners focus on music selections through a clear visual representation of sound. A good map provides representation of important musical elements such as melody, rhythm, form, dynamics, tempo, and so on. They may also contain historical and/or cultural information reflected in the images used on the map. We created these for one of our other books, and users have told us they are a helpful and welcome resource.
- *Group activities* Another strength of this book is the emphasis on group activities—to allow students to build community in a class, and also to provide safety for those who are less sure about their musical abilities. We have found that students feel more comfortable in trying new things when working in groups, and it reinforces the social aspects of music-making, as well as the benefits of collaborative teaching and learning.
- *Integration of music* We feel that *Using Music to Enhance Student Learning: A Practical Guide for Elementary Classroom Teachers* does an excellent job of establishing the value of music in education. It is important that the students understand the "why" in addition to the "how to"—or they will not attempt to use music in their future classrooms. This book establishes that music is essential in a child's development, and that the integration of music will significantly enhance all other subjects/ activities in the classroom.
- *Learning aids* Each chapter has many learning aids:

  - "Tantalizing Tidbits of Research" explain why these activities are important.
  - "Teaching Tips" are wonderful suggestions to enhance teaching skills.
  - "Thinking It Through" offers topics to explore in order to expand learning.
  - "Suggestions for Further Study" and "Recommended Student Books" provide useful resources at the end of each chapter
  - Key music activities are tagged for immediate recognition in the margins with icons for singing ♫, listening ◠, playing ♀, moving ⚡, and creating ✏. Watch for these icons throughout the text.

The *Using Music* Package

There are several special resources for both students and teachers:

- A CD specific to *Using Music*, with listening selections from the Baroque, Classical, Romantic and Contemporary periods. A strong listening program is a special feature of the ancillary package.
- *Get America Singing. . .Again! Volume 1*, which is a songbook developed in association with the Music Educators National Conference (MENC) and other music organizations. It contains 43 songs that represent America's varied music heritage of folksongs, traditional songs and patriotic songs.
- The appendices:

- A songbook with an emphasis on Hispanic folksongs.
- A recorder music songbook.
- Samples of key assignments and lists of music-related books for children and for teachers.
- Listening Maps to enhance the listening experience.

- The companion website: www.routledge.com/textbooks/9780415878234

- List of links to education resources.
- Instructors' resources (described below, under *To the Teacher*).

To the Teacher

We hope that teaching with *Using Music to Enhance Student Learning: A Practical Guide for Elementary Classroom Teachers* will make your instruction more effective yet your load lighter. The book provides ample comprehensive materials to use in your classroom. It was designed to be valuable to those who have taught elementary music classes, as well as to those who have never had that experience. It will be easy to tailor the materials for your particular course requirements.

We would have preferred a more rounded-out representation of world music and popular music, but we, along with the publisher, wanted to price the book lower than any on the market. The permission costs for including more contemporary music would have made a big difference in price. Moreover, it is our feeling that traditional Western art music and American folk music provide excellent examples for successful teaching, and this is, after all, not a music appreciation course, but an attempt to use musical examples to illustrate concepts.

The reviewers commended our emphasis on practical uses of music in the elementary classroom over music theory skills. In fact, some even wanted to take the element of music theory completely out of the book. We feel we have reached a perfect balance between the two sides of the issue by teaching basic music skills through the use of the recorder, an instrument that is quite simple to learn. Many classroom teachers will have students who will study recorder in their own elementary music classes. Our students have commented that it will be very helpful to be able to play the same instrument their students are learning.

The website for the instructor includes resources that will simplify your life: sample syllabi, quizzes ready to use over each chapter, students, handouts, assignment rubrics, recorder teaching suggestions, as well as a complete list of recommended materials to teach the course. The book and ancillary materials have been inspired through years of successfully teaching the music for elementary education major college course, and are designed to increase student learning (college level and elementary) by means of successful teaching strategies in music.

To the Student

As educators with wonderful years of experience teaching music to children in the public schools and training future teachers at the university level, we wanted to write a book that would help beginning teachers be successful in their teaching. Music is a marvelous tool to help children learn. However, many elementary education majors fear they lack the needed musical skills to use music successfully. This textbook has been written to put the Elementary Education student who has had little or no previous experience in music at ease. You will find a plethora of good teaching techniques and materials that you can easily use to energize learning experiences for children.

Our students have shared with us from their own elementary learning experiences that music can be an especially important part of a child's education. For some, success in music activities filled them with confidence to tackle things that were more difficult. Others noted that music is a socially interactive activity that can bring the class together with a feeling of community, and help shy students open up and "come out of their shells." Music can also help those students who might have a difficult time sitting still and listening. Music time can be a positive outlet for their energy. Finally, the word "joyful" was used by many of our college students to describe their elementary experiences with music. The goal of this book is to help you find ways to use music to successfully teach the elementary curriculum and to find the "joy" of teaching.

Jana R. Fallin and Mollie G. Tower
April 2010

ACKNOWLEDGMENTS

We would like to thank the reviewers who were instrumental in shaping our concept. In addition to several anonymous reviewers who appraised our book proposal and manuscript, we would like to specifically thank:

Katie Carlisle, University of Massachusetts-Lowell
Penny Dimmick, Butler University
Margaret Schmidt, Arizona State University

We also want to express our great appreciation to the following Master Teachers who contributed to the book:

Janet Armstead, Elementary Music Teacher, St. George, Kansas, Kansas Music Educators Association Teacher of the Year
Dr. Timy Baranoff, Ph.D., Director of Elementary Education, Austin Independent School District
Glenda Carnes, School of Music, Texas State University
Kristyn Crow, 2008 BCCB Blue Ribbon Book Author, Utah
Debra Erck, Elementary Music Teacher, Austin ISD, Texas
Jacque Fowler, Elementary Music Teacher, Austin ISD, Texas
Kay Greenhaw, Elementary Music Teacher, Austin ISD, Texas
Dr. Connie Hale, Winthrop University, South Carolina
Dr. Susan Holmberg, Elementary Music Teacher, Savannah, GA
Meredith Knapp, Elementary Music Teacher, Emporia, Kansas
Melody Long, Elementary Music Teacher, Austin ISD, Texas
John Maklary, Instructional Technology Coordinator at K-8 Parochial School, Sugar Land, Texas
Sheryl Maklary, Kindergarten Teacher, Katy ISD, Texas
Diane Steele, Elementary Music Teacher, 1999 Austin ISD Elementary Teacher of the Year, Austin, Texas
Dr. Robin Stein, School of Music, Texas State University
Debbie Tannert, Elementary Music Teacher, Austin ISD, Texas
Mary Ellen Titus, Multiage Elementary Classroom Teacher, Manhattan, Kansas
Dr. Christopher White, Music Faculty, Radford University, Radford, Virginia

In addition, we would like to thank Macmillan/McGraw Hill publishers for allowing us to reproduce Spanish songs from the publication *Musica para todos*.

Finally, we can't thank the marvelous editorial team at Routledge enough:

Constance Ditzel, Senior Editor
Mhairi Bennett, Production Manager
Denny Tek, Editorial Assistant

SECTION I | **GETTING STARTED**

Why We Should Involve Our Students in Music Activities

"Teach all aspects of the child—his mental, physical, emotional and social development must be considered in every lesson. Music can assist a teacher in each one of these areas."

Dr. Timy Baranoff, Director of Elementary Education, Austin Independent School District[1]

The recipe for biscuits calls for two cups of flour and three teaspoons of baking powder. The amount of flour is much larger, but the leavening agent—the baking powder—is critically important. Without baking powder, the biscuits will not rise. They will bake into hard, flat objects that are not tasty for eating. This analogy is applicable to the arts in the elementary classroom. When a teacher uses music and the other arts throughout the curriculum, a leavening or rising occurs. Much as baking powder interacts with other ingredients when stirred, kneaded, cut and baked to make delicious biscuits, blending music with other subjects makes the curriculum more interesting and inviting to students. The arts mix joy into the learning environment, enabling young students to interact with the subject matter in ways that enhance and foster the learning process.

A common characteristic among successful classroom teachers is the ability to capture and hold their students' attention. Music can help keep students' attention high and build motivation for the subject at hand.

Information in this book will provide future elementary teachers with concepts and methods for integrating music into their curriculum and for using music to enliven their teaching. Enjoying singing a song together or listening to CDs can provide release from stress, calm wiggly students, energize a fatigued class, provide exercise, ease transition times, and promote learning in all subjects. Any teacher can find ways to tap into the amazing educational benefits of using music in the classroom.

Teachers willing to infuse music into their curriculum will discover it is not only a possibility, but also becomes imperative. What starts as the rare experience will become the norm as teachers see the tremendous results for their students. Music becomes an important tool to enhance learning and bring joy and excitement to their students.

Individual Student Activity

Reflective Essay[2]

Write a Reflective Essay on your most influential classroom and music teachers. Begin with your elementary school years and move up. Think about how these teachers have influenced your decision to become a teacher. Discuss whether music activities were important in your education.

CHAPTER 1 | ORGANIZING FOR SUCCESSFUL TEACHING

Why We Should Involve Our Students in Music Activities

"A teacher who is attempting to teach without inspiring the pupil with a desire to learn is hammering on cold iron."

Horace Mann, American Education Reformer[1]

"It is the supreme art of the teacher to awaken joy in creative expression and knowledge."
Albert Einstein, Nobel Prize Winner in Physics[2]

"I believe that every person is born with talent."

Maya Angelou, Presidential Medal of Arts Winner[3]

"Learning improves in school environments where there are comprehensive music programs. Music increases the ability of young people to do math. It increases the ability of young people to read. And, most important of all, it's a lot of fun."

President Bill Clinton, P.S. 96, New York City, June 16, 2000[4]

"The 'back-to-basics' curriculum, while it has merit, ignores the most urgent void in our present system—absence of self-discipline. The arts, inspiring—indeed requiring—self-discipline, may be more basic to our national survival than the traditional credit courses."

Paul Harvey, American Radio Broadcaster[5]

"The arts can help students become tenacious, team-oriented problem solvers who are confident and able to think creatively. These qualities can be especially important in improving learning among students from economically disadvantaged circumstances.

Arne Duncan, US Secretary of Education[6]

Music is the Aural Art

Learning to listen,
Learning to hear,
Being aware of the sounds around us,
The music of life.

This saying was displayed throughout the year on the border above the chalkboard. The letters were cut out of colorful paper, designed to grab the attention of the students.

The honored spot among bulletin boards, reserved in most elementary classrooms for the revered alphabet, was devoted to a thought about listening to the sounds in our world. It reminded the students that engaged listening is learning to be *aware* of what we are hearing. Engaged listening in the classroom is critical to learning, and a wonderful way to improve engaged listening skills is through music, the *aural* art. As the alphabet is to words and reading, listening is to sounds and music.

Our world is noisy, and probably as a defense mechanism we learn to mask out sounds. Students learn to focus on the dialogue in the TV show, even though Mom is on the phone in the kitchen and the stereo is playing rather loudly. This practice of ignoring sound carries into the classroom, where experience tells us that over half of a child's school day is spent in listening.

The teacher who helps students learn to attend aurally is giving them a gift that will foster success throughout their school careers, and perhaps throughout their lives. We know that listening plays a key role in communication with others, and is vital in the learning process.

The following sections of this chapter give just a taste of the types of music activities that meet Dr. Baranoff's challenge to meet the mental, physical, emotional, and social development needs of students. Many, many more will be presented in the book.

Music and Mental Development: Improving Listening Skills

Focusing on listening will be of great assistance to the classroom teacher. For example, by teaching students to listen carefully for directions, the elementary classroom teacher can eliminate undue frustrations. The following scenario occurs far too often in the elementary classroom:

LISTENING

> After listing the directions on the board and telling the students what to do, the teacher turns around to see a child whose hand is raised. When recognized, the child asks, "What are we supposed to be doing?"

By developing listening skills, students will begin to *hear the first time,* rather than ask those off-task questions.

By using music activities to help students learn to listen more actively and accurately, focus and attention will be sharpened, and the teacher's life will become less frazzled. It is amazing what music activities can do in the elementary classroom!

LISTENING

Teaching Tip

Skilled teachers know to involve their students to make sure they hear the directions. Ask one student to recall and state one of the directions. Repeat the question to other students until all the steps have been remembered and restated.

Another technique is to involve everyone by having them respond using thumbs up for "yes" and thumbs down for "no." Answer yes or no: Step one is to get out the paper, Step two. . . etc.

Play the Echo Game

LISTENING

The Echo Game is an excellent tool to use to get students' attention and improve listening skills. The simple form of the game involves long and short sounds clapped in four-beat patterns. Students should listen to the teacher's pattern, then "echo" it exactly. Try the examples in the boxes below. Perform each box top to bottom. Use loud and soft claps.

long long short-short long	short-short short-short long long	long short-short long long	short-short long short-short long	short-short long long long
long short-short short-short long	long long long long	long long short-short short-short	long short-short long short-short	short-short short-short short-short long

To vary the game, use different body percussion sounds—patting, snapping, stamping, loud and soft handclaps, etc. For a more difficult game, the teacher can continue with a new pattern while the students echo the first pattern, and so on. One way to help students be more successful in this challenging game is to change the body percussion sound for each new pattern. This advanced game involves concentration and careful listening.

Music and Physical Development: Performing Singing Games and Chants

Partner hand-clap games are a strong part of the American folk music heritage. They also provide an enjoyable way to have students stand up and move in limited space.

SINGING

Using *Rote* Teaching Method with a Singing Game

Simple songs are best taught by *rote*. Rote is the "I-sing-you-sing" teaching method. Some songs, such as "Miss Mary Mack," can be taught with the whole-song approach. The whole-song approach can be used when the melody is very simple and repetitive. Simply sing the first verse a few times while asking students to answer questions about the words. Then have the class sing the song. Put the other verses on the board or a chart.

Most of the time, the rote method will use the phrase-by-phrase approach. This is the process of dividing the song into short sections, or phrases, and having students echo back or repeat what is sung. For example:

SINGING

(*Teacher sings*) Hey there neighbor, what do you say?
(*Students sing*) Hey there neighbor, what do you say?
(*Teacher sings*) We're gonna have a happy day.
(*Students sing*) We're gonna have a happy day.

And so forth. After singing the song with one phrase repeated, then sing it with the students repeating two phrases at a time.

(*Teacher sings*) Hey there neighbor, what do you say? We're gonna have a happy day.
(*Students sing*) Hey there neighbor, what do you say? We're gonna have a happy day.

Finally, sing the entire song, and have students repeat. Clarify and practice any parts that are not repeated accurately. When students can sing the song correctly, then add the motions. For older students, it can be fun to reverse the teaching order and teach the motions first. Then they can add the melody as the teacher moves and sings each phrase for them to repeat.

Effective Use of *Audiation* with Singing Games

Audiation,[7] a term coined by Dr. Edwin E. Gordon, is the process of mentally hearing music when no sound is present. One effective use of audiation is at the end of a singing game. For the final performance of a song or chant with motions, have the students audiate (mentally sing) while still performing the movements. This will be an excellent challenge, while also leading to a very quiet classroom where the teacher's new directions to students can be heard.

Try these wonderful singing games and chants that are great for use at the beginning of the school year. "P" and "I" mark which songs are more appropriate for primary grades, for intermediate grades, or both. Faster performance or more difficult hand-clap games can take a singing game from primary to intermediate. Experience rote learning, audiation, and movement in a limited space with folk music singing games.

Small Group Student Activity

Rhythmic Activities[8]

Divide into groups of six or eight. Each group learns one or two of the chant/singing games to teach to the class.

MOVING
AND
SINGING

Songbook Selections

Appendix 1

P & I	"Miss Mary Mack" African American Clapping Game Song	191
P & I	"Head and Shoulders, Baby" African American Street Game	197
P & I	"Hey There, Neighbor" Traditional	190
P	"Bow Wow Wow" Traditional	192
P	"Bate, Bate" Mexican Game	194

Music and Emotional Development: Singing Good Morning Songs

Singing is a great method for establishing community within a classroom. Many teachers find that a wonderful way to start the school day is to have students sing a positive, up-beat song together. With younger students, using the same "hello" song can have a calming effect—when they sing the song, they know that class has officially begun. With older students, it can be fun to use lots of different songs—general "good morning" songs, songs to link to a theme for the day or week, songs to link to a culture to be studied in Social Studies, and so forth. Enjoy singing these positive message, "good morning" songs.

SINGING

Songbook Selections

Get America Singing. . .Again!

I	"Oh, What a Beautiful Mornin'" (*Oklahoma*) by Rogers and Hammerstein	32
I	"Blue Skies" by Irving Berlin	11
P & I	"Zip-A-Dee-Doo-Dah" (*Song of the South*) by Wrubel and Gilbert	46
P & I	"De colores" Mexican folk song	13

Another great way to begin the day is to build up excitement for learning by adding movement to a familiar song. "My Bonnie Lies Over the Ocean" can be used in this manner. Instruct students to sing the song while looking or listening for words that begin with the letter "B." Start with students in their seats, and then direct them to stand or sit as they sing each "B" word—stand on the first "B", sit on the second "B", etc. The fun comes in the refrain—"Bring back, bring back, oh, bring back my Bonnie to me, to me!" When performed correctly, students should be seated to show the final "B" word in the song. Try it!

SINGING

Songbook Selection
Get America Singing. . .Again!
P & I   "My Bonnie Lies Over the Ocean" Scottish folk song   31

LISTENING

Establishing a Positive Learning Environment

Music can have a powerful effect on the learning environment. Researchers have found the use of instrumental music[9] as very quiet background music to be helpful in encouraging and maintaining a positive learning environment for students of all ages. The music by composers such as Handel, Mozart, Bach, Vivaldi, and Pachelbel seems to work best. The key is to have the music playing so softly that it can barely be heard when the room is silent. This idea is especially effective when students are doing quiet seatwork, or when children first enter the room. It is important to choose "calm" music as opposed to "exciting" music.

Sources for the music can be the CD with this textbook, as well as free classical music selections that can be heard on the Classics for Kids website (www.classicsforkids.com). This website has excellent music selections as well as lesson plans, information about composers, etc.

Note: It is important to maintain a "quiet corner" with earplugs available for students who prefer silence to do their work. A good rule is to limit the use of background music to 30 percent of total class time each day.

Music and Social Development: Promoting Successful Student Interaction

One way to promote social–emotional development in young students is to help them identify and label their feelings. Read *My Many Colored Days* by Dr. Seuss[10] to students aged 3 to 8.

This rhyming story is a wonderful way for teachers to talk with young students about their emotions. Each day is described in terms of a particular color and animal, which in turn is associated with specific emotions. The unique book covers a wide range of moods and emotions.

MOVING AND SINGING

To enhance the learning experience, add music by using *My Many Colored Days CD* and scarves kit (www.aeIdeas.com), or by finding music from your own CD collection. Have students move to short music excerpts while showing the feelings described—bodies and faces should be very expressive.

To reinforce vocabulary words learned in *My Many Colored Days*, have groups of students make up new verses for "If You're Happy and You Know It," using the words *sad, scared, lonely,* etc.

Partner Singing Games and Chants. . .Again!

Research points to a second important reason to use singing games and chants in the classroom. Frances M. Carlson[11] has written repeatedly about the introduction of positive, appropriate touch into the classroom having a "dramatic and immediate effect on the level of aggression in a classroom." The use of touch in partner singing games and chants is an excellent way to promote appropriate touching between students, and to provide opportunities for students to interact physically with each other.

MOVING AND SINGING

The goal of these games should be that each student interacts with as many other students as possible. Using inner and outer circles to shift partners for each verse is one way to attain this goal.

Individual Student Activity

Social Skills Songs

Look on teacher websites listed in Appendix 4 to find "piggyback" songs (new words written to familiar tunes) to teach social skills (manners, listening, sharing, and friendship). Bring one to share with the class.

Music Activities as a Part of Effective Classroom Management

Classroom management plans should be based on specified high expectations (with motivators for success included), lesson presentations full of energy and enthusiasm, good communication skills, daily routines, and respect for every student. Here is a sample of music activities that can be used to promote successful student interaction. Some of these ideas are based on "Top Ten 'Secrets' for Successful Classroom Management" by Dr. Jean Feldman:[12]

1. After a day filled with "teacher-talk," sing directions to the class to catch students' attention.
2. Provide students with opportunities to "get out the wiggles." Every 20 to 30 minutes during seated desk work, have students stand up and. . .

SINGING

MOVING

   - listen to classical music and mirror the teacher's movements.
   - sing a song with motions.
   - play a singing game.
   - dance, march or exercise to upbeat music.

3. Use songs to keep students' interest high during the day as new lessons in different subject areas are introduced. Try the "mystery song" approach to let students guess what subject they will be studying next.

LISTENING

4. Use songs or CDs to signal transitions in the classroom—time to go to specials, time to clean up centers, time to line up for lunch, time to take out math books, and so forth. One teacher used a teacher-made CD of favorite "moving" songs to signal transition times. "On the Road Again" signaled the change from centers to circle time. "Sweet Home Alabama" signaled the time to clean up and get ready to go home at the end of the day, and so forth. Very quickly, the students were singing along enthusiastically with each song!

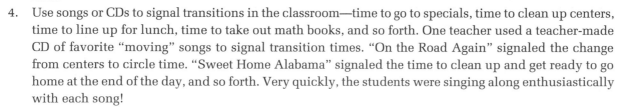

LISTENING

SINGING

5. Use "Piggyback Songs" to review and reinforce social skills such as manners, listening, sharing, and friendship. "Are You Sleeping" is an "echo" song (where singers copy the leader), and is easy to use with students. "Bill Grogan's Goat" (or "My Aunt Came Back" with the same tune) is also an echo song.

6. Memorize several finger plays (Appendix 3). Use these engaging materials to get the attention of primary students.

Thinking It Through

In a small group, discuss and analyze the methods in which your former teachers used music activities to promote successful student interaction and learning.

Suggestions for Further Study

Explore the website for the Center on the Social and Emotional Foundations for Early Learning (CSEFEL) www. vanderbilt.edu/csefel/documents/booklist.pdf. The booklist sections (for students up to age 8) include:

- Being a Friend
- Accepting Different Kinds of Friends
- General Feelings
- Happy Feelings
- Sad Feelings
- Angry or Mad Feelings
- Scared or Worried Feelings
- Caring About Others and Empathy
- Problem Solving
- Self Confidence
- Good Behavior Expectations
- Family Relationships
- Bullying/Teasing
- Grief and Death

Read *Brain-Based Learning: The New Paradigm of Teaching* (2008, 2nd edition) by Eric Jensen. Published by Corwin Press.

Recommended Student Books

Fox, Mem. (2007). *Whoever You Are.* (L. Staub, Illus.). Orlando: Voyager Books.
Fox has created a simple refrain to celebrate human connections.

Katz, Alan and Catrow, David. (1996). *Take Me Out of the Bathtub.* New York: Margaret K. McElderry.
Silly lyrics to familiar tunes (piggyback songs).

Katz, Alan and Catrow, David. (2001). *I'm Still Here in the Bathtub.* New York: Margaret K. McElderry. Silly lyrics to familiar tunes (piggyback songs).

Spinelli, Eileen. (1996). *Someone Loves You, Mr. Hatch.* New York: Simon & Schuster Children's Publishing. Looks at the effect that friendship and love can have.

CHAPTER 2 | **A FRAMEWORK FOR TEACHING AND LEARNING**

Several discoveries in the teaching/learning body of knowledge have affected the authors' teaching positively. These came to be included in our teaching storehouse through years of trial and error in the classroom. The ideas selected to share are to help students avoid the same trials and errors when they become teachers. For those beginning in a teaching career, our desire is to help them achieve success in the elementary classroom.

HOWARD GARDNER

Howard Gardner (b. 1943 in Scranton, Pennsylvania) has been Professor of Education at Harvard since 1986. A student of Jerome Bruner, Gardner assumed co-leadership of Harvard Project Zero from Nelson Goodman in 1971, which has become one of the leading educational research centers in the United States. His *Frames of Mind: The Theory of Multiple Intelligences* (1983) is considered pivotal in modern psychological theory. He has also written *The Unschooled Mind: How Children Think And How Schools Should Teach* (1993), *Intelligence Reframed: Multiple Intelligences for the 21st Century* (2000), *The Disciplined Mind: Beyond Facts and Standardized Tests, the K-12 Education that Every Child Deserves* (2000), and *Multiple Intelligences: New Horizons in Theory and Practice* (2006).

Multiple Intelligences Theory

Until Gardner's work, 'Reading, Writing and 'Rithmatic' has been more than a line in an old song. Most schools' testing of students has been heavily weighted for reading comprehension and mathematical computation.

This is particularly true of standardized tests such as the SAT or ACT. Since the passing of *No Child Left Behind* educational reforms, American education has seen an even greater emphasis upon assessment in math and reading. Society has long looked at the concept of "intelligence" as only involving areas of deductive reasoning or linear thought. Through his writings and research, Gardner has caused a re-evaluation of the way intelligence is viewed, from a single capacity to a set of intelligences that all people possess in varying degrees. He states that the purpose of education is *understanding*, demonstrated by the ability to use learned information in new situations, transferring between disciplines.

In his *Theory of Multiple Intelligences*,[1] Gardner developed a set of criteria, or signs, to define intelligence based upon analyzing the abilities that enable human beings "to resolve genuine problems or difficulties that he or she encounters and, when appropriate, to create an effective product—and must also entail the potential for finding or creating problems—thereby laying the groundwork for the acquisition of new knowledge."

In his original work, Gardner formulated a list of seven areas of intelligence, which he called Multiple Intelligence (MI), while allowing for the possibility of more. The first two we traditionally equate with IQ. The next three are commonly associated with the arts and the final two are referred to as the personal intelligences. Later in his writings, Gardner added an eighth intelligence.

All human beings possess varying abilities in all intelligences. Our uniqueness comes from the way they combine within each of us. In his description of the first seven intelligences, Gardner cites famous people who exemplify his theory, people who expanded their fields into new areas through their work.

The original seven intelligences plus the recent addition are:

- *Linguistic* (word smart): Along with logical–mathematical, this is the most common area associated with traditional notions of IQ (Intelligence Quotient). This entails the ability to understand the use of words to communicate ideas and complex meaning. Individuals are able to express themselves rhetorically or poetically and usually excel in public speaking and/or writing. Examples: T. S. Elliot and Virginia Woolf.
- *Logical–Mathematical* (number smart—linear thinking): In Gardner's words, it entails the ability to detect patterns, reason deductively and think logically. Often involving mathematical operations, this intelligence is most often associated with scientific processes. Example: Albert Einstein.
- *Musical* (sound smart): Musical acuity is associated with people who are able to think and communicate in sound. Beyond the recognition of pitches, tones and rhythm, these people are able to hear and create forms and structures within the sounds that create expression and meaning. Examples: Wolfgang Amadeus Mozart and Igor Stravinsky.
- *Bodily–Kinesthetic* (physical smart): This intelligence encompasses the potential for using one's body to solve various life challenges and express ideas and feelings through gesture. These people are often able to use tools with great precision and timing. Dancers and athletes excel in this area as they use their minds to control bodily movements. Example: Martha Graham.
- *Spatial* (shape or picture smart): Often referred to as visual–spatial, this intelligence involves the ability to perceive, organize, and transform space. Individuals are able to recognize and use the patterns of pictures, colors, and shapes to express thoughts and feelings. Example: Pablo Picasso.
- *Interpersonal* (knowledge of others—people smart): This refers to the ability to understand, perceive, and discriminate between the moods, feelings, and intentions of others. These people are able to work effectively with people and are often seen as charismatic and empathetic. Example: Mahatma Ghandi.
- *Intrapersonal* (knowledge of self—self smart): This intelligence involves the capacity to understand oneself, have deep appreciation for one's own feelings, thoughts, and motivations. These individuals have a high degree of imagination, originality, confidence and independent will. In Gardner's view they have an effective self-model and are able to use it to regulate their lives. Example: Sigmund Freud.
- *Naturalistic* (environmental smart): Persons with abilities in this intelligence are able to recognize, categorize, and draw upon features of nature. They are uniquely aware of their surrounding environments and the effect of themselves and other factors upon it. Gardner does not specifically cite examples but one could look to John James Audubon or Jacques Cousteau in this area.

Gardner suggests that specific activities can use several intelligences: "In dance, for example, bodily kinesthetic intelligence is important, but so is musical intelligence, spatial intelligence and probably other intelligences as well."

Using Multiple Intelligences Theory in the Classroom

The arts educator Elliot W. Eisner recommends that we organize the curriculum "to optimize whatever potential intelligences individuals possess."[2] Arts education is essential if the intelligences of every child are to be developed. In teaching, remembering these areas, and offering learning opportunities in each will help bring success to the learners. One topic, one concept, one skill could be approached from multiple, or all, areas to bring about deeper understanding and mastery.

In her article *Multiple Intelligences: Gardner's Theory*,[3] published in 1996, Amy C. Brualdi[4] states "the teacher can show students how to use their more developed intelligences to assist in the understanding of a subject, which normally employs their weaker intelligences. For example, the teacher can suggest that an especially musically intelligent child learn about the revolutionary war by making up a song about the historical facts."

This is an amazing approach, for example, that calls for concentrating on teaching students with weaker intelligences in Logical–Mathematical or Linguistic by finding creative ways to teach through a child's strengths in spatial, musical or bodily–kinesthetic intelligence rather than forcing students to spend more and more time doing the same old worksheets. Gardner's approach values classes with Music, Art, and PE specialists. These classes can serve to give students self-confidence and more tools to tackle challenges in the classroom.

One skilled educator, Dr. Mary Ellen Titus,[5] who uses Gardner's Multiple Intelligence theory in her teaching, states, "All children are gifted. You just have to discover how."

Small Group Student Activity

"The Animal School" by George Reavis

Discuss "The Animal School" with a small group and relate it to Gardner's Multiple Intelligences theory. Share a summary of your discussion points with the full class.

This fable was written when George Reavis was the Assistant Superintendent of the Cincinnati Public Schools back in the 1940s! This content is in the public domain and free to copy, duplicate, and distribute.

Once upon a time the animals decided they must do something heroic to meet the problems of a "new world," so they organized a school.

They adopted an activity curriculum consisting of running, climbing, swimming, and flying. To make it easier to administer the curriculum, ALL the animals took ALL subjects.

The duck was excellent in swimming—in fact, better than his instructor; but he made only passing grades in flying and was very poor in running. Since he was slow in running, he had to stay after school and also drop swimming in order to practice running. This was kept up until his web feet were badly worn; so then he was only average in swimming. But *average was acceptable in school, so nobody worried about that except the duck.*

The rabbit started at the top of the class in running, but he had a nervous breakdown because of so much make-up work in swimming.

The squirrel was excellent in climbing until he developed frustration in the flying class, where his teacher made him start from the ground up instead of the treetop down. He also developed "Charlie horses" from over-exertion and then got a "C" in climbing and a "D" in running.

The eagle was a problem child and was disciplined severely. In the climbing class he beat all others to the top of the tree, but insisted on using his own way to get there.

At the end of the year an abnormal eel that could swim exceedingly well and also could run, climb, and fly a little had the highest average and was named valedictorian.

The prairie dogs stayed out of school and fought the tax levy because the administration would not add digging and burrowing to the curriculum. They apprenticed their child to a badger and later joined the ground hogs and the gophers in order to start a successful private school.

Learning Modalities: How Do Students Learn?

In contrast to Gardner's eight Intelligences, which he refers to as "tools for learning" or ways to demonstrate intellectual ability, what are the *ways* that students learn? Learning styles or modalities are described as three basic approaches:[6] by listening (aurally); by reading, seeing or watching (visually); or by doing a motion or touching something involved with the learning activity (kinesthetically). These are the styles learners use to process and retain information. Usually one of these modalities will be predominant or preferred in a learner, though they will have some proficiency in all. Individuals who like to read about something to learn it, or need to see something, not just hear it, or prefer watching someone demonstrate "how to" are probably visual learners. Those who enjoy being told about a subject, or receiving verbal instructions rather than written ones, or learning by listening to lectures and discussions are most likely aural learners. Those who enjoy learning by "doing something" through movement, gesture or the use of manipulatives are in all likelihood kinesthetic learners. Many people are exceptional in more than one modality.

Successful teachers, when planning a lesson, include activities in all three learning modalities to ensure the highest learning occurs in the classroom. Examples include:

- *Aural*—Including musical opportunities in a lesson will help learners understand concepts and retain information. They can sing songs that include the information, listen to recordings that set mood or exemplify historical settings or culture, or create musical rhymes to organize the information. Music is the aural art.
- *Visual*—Using visual representation for each lesson will help learners achieve better understanding of the material presented. Writing on the board, including a picture, graph or map and making pictorial representations will resonate with the visual learner.
- *Kinesthetic*—Adding gesture or movement to a learning activity will greatly help the kinesthetic learner. Drawing in the air, tracing patterns, including sign language, and using manipulatives all serve to reinforce desired outcomes and add an enjoyable element to the learning.

JEROME BRUNER

Jerome Bruner (b. October 1, 1915 in New York) is one of the premier psychologists, philosophers and educational researchers of modern times. Bruner's work has been influential in many areas including moving psychology from behavioralism to cognitivism and eventually to constructivist models, and leading in the creation of the "Head Start" early childhood system. His major works are *The Process of Education* (1977) and *Acts of Meaning* (1991).

Cognitive Learning Theory

Jerome Bruner stated,[7] "we begin with the hypothesis that any subject can be taught effectively in some intellectually honest form to any child at any stage of development." This led to his work in the development of the spiral curriculum, where a concept is introduced at one level and revisited at successive levels and ages, each time with deeper understanding and mastery. The emphasis in this theory is that later teaching builds upon earlier experiences to create an even more mature and explicit understanding of the concept.

Another key to Bruner's theories is his emphasis upon the concept of intuitive thinking as opposed to analytical thinking. Where analytic thinking arrives at answers through deductive reasoning using step-by-step processes of scientific inquiry, intuitive reasoning allows the learner to explore a question through discovery, instinct, and personal experience without the need for constrictive process. The student is capable of a degree of familiarity without the initial inclusion of overwhelming vocabulary, facts and details. Bruner states,[8] "it may be of the first importance to establish an intuitive understanding of materials before we expose our students to more traditional and formal methods of deduction and proof."

Bruner highlights three key ways in which children transform experience into knowledge: through action (enactive), through imagery (iconic) and through written forms (symbolic). Much of a child's learning involves the negotiation of these three areas.

- *Enactive* learning—The child learns by doing. Hands-on activities lead the student to intuitive understanding of any concept. The learner is actively involved in the learning process through manipulatives and participation. For example, a child would sing the notes "mi, re, do" on a neutral "loo" syllable, while moving his or her hands in a downward direction, following the movement of the voice.
- *Iconic* learning—Students learn to transform pictures and graphs into representative concepts. A visual icon or illustration provides imagery and metaphor for learning a concept.

  For singing "mi, re, do," the following lines drawn on the board help children learn the concept of higher and lower, and equate singing lower perhaps with walking down stairs.

  —
  　—
  　　—

- *Symbolic* learning—Students are able to transform appropriate symbols, such as notes, into meaning and action. Musically this involves the use of proper notation systems. Further, the student is able to function on an abstract level and draw conclusions regarding meaning and value from the works studied and performed. For example, show "mi, re, do" on the staff with notes as the last segment of the learning activity.

The implications for Bruner's theories are first to let the student explore and discover concepts through their own meaning-making processes. Learning involves mastering each of the increasingly complex modes, enactive to iconic to symbolic. After allowing the child to make their own intuitive connections, the teacher can guide the student to deeper understanding, using strategies that require analysis, specific terminology, and further guided activities as suggested by the spiral curriculum.

Music is unfortunately often taught in the reverse. Students are presented with the actual symbolism first. The staff and note names and rhythmic values and all sorts of information are presented and "drilled" in class before any music-making occurs. Perhaps this reversal in the learning process is partly the reason many people think they are not musical.

ELLIOT EISNER

Elliot Eisner (b. 1933 in Chicago, Illinois) has established himself as one of the foremost leaders of arts education and educational reform. As the Lee Jacks Professor of Art and Education at Stanford University he has published over 300 articles and 15 books. Of most significance to this book's purposes are *The Kind of Schools We Need* (1998) and *The Arts and the Creation of the Mind* (2002). Eisner is one of the leading thinkers and writers in the area of Aesthetic Education and proponents of Discipline Based Arts Education.

The Aesthetic Mode of Knowing

Eisner suggests that each art form has the potential to influence experiences and in doing so alter the way in which we understand our world. He asserts that the written word cannot adequately represent all the ways people understand. Eisner[9] outlines seven modes of knowing: Aesthetic, Scientific, Interpersonal, Intuitive, Narrative/Paradigmatic, Formal, and Spiritual.

In establishing the Aesthetic mode, Eisner suggests that life is primarily qualitative as opposed to the quantitative, fact, and numbers-based way schools approach it. The Aesthetic mode is a process that can be used to create works of science as well as art.

In both cases the creator and/or audience is seeking a "rightness of life" for the problem at hand. He comments,[10] "Scientists, like artists, formulate new and puzzling questions in order to enjoy the experience of creating answers to them."

While inclusion or emphasis on the arts is not necessarily the only way to achieve this goal, infusing the arts into other areas of the curriculum facilitates a clearer path to understanding the world in which we live.

The Aesthetic Mode involves the recognition, organization, and manipulation of the various forms in all human activity. Eisner states:

- All things made, whether in art, science, or in practical life, possess form.
- Form is not only an attribute of or condition of things made; it is a process through which things are made.
- The deeper motives for productive activity in both the arts and the sciences often emanate from the quality of life the process of creation makes possible.

Infusing the arts into our classrooms helps transform the ways in which students think and solve problems. Senses are refined and honed so that the world is experienced in increasingly subtle and complex ways.

17

By promoting and exercising the imagination, students are able to see, hear, touch, taste, and smell that which is not readily accessible. The arts provide new models for making meaning of the world, and they give unique access and understanding into the parts of human experience that are expressive and meaningful but defy verbal description. Eisner[11] summarizes:

1. Humans are sentient creatures born into a qualitative environment in and through which they live.
2. The Sensory system is the primary resource through which the qualitative environment is experienced.
3. As children mature, their ability to experience qualities in the environment becomes increasingly differentiated.
4. Differentiation enables children to form concepts. Concepts are images formed in one or more sensory modalities that serve as proxies (representatives or substitutes) for a class of associated qualities.
5. Concepts and the meanings they acquire can be represented in any material or symbolic system that can be used as a proxy for it.
6. The child's developing ability to differentiate, to form concepts, and to represent those concepts reflects the use and growth of mind.
7. Which aspects of the environment will be attended to, the purposes for which such attention is used, and the material the child employs to represent it influence the kind of cognitive abilities the child is likely to develop.
8. The decision to use a particular form of representation influences not only what can be represented, but also what will be experienced.
9. The arts invite children to pay attention to the environment's expressive features and to the products of their imagination and to craft a material so that it expresses or evokes an emotional or meaningful response to it.
10. A major aim of arts education is to promote the child's ability to develop his or her mind through the experience that the creation or perception of expressive form makes possible.

For Eisner, approaching subjects from an aesthetic basis, where students are allowed to feel, ponder, reflect, and create, leads to greater motivation. People have a basic need to lead a stimulating life. He asserts that knowledge is something that one discovers, not something one makes. Teaching students to recognize and understand the various forms of life that defy language, to break down the various forms of any given object or activity, allows the student to apply personal meaning to that object and retain its essence. Through aesthetic experience we can participate vicariously in situations beyond our reach. Students are motivated to inquire, to ponder, to examine, and to learn.

JEAN PIAGET

Jean Piaget (1896–1980) was a Swiss psychologist who specialized in studies of cognitive development. He served as the Director of the UNESCO International Bureau of Education, Geneva from 1929 to 1967. His research dealt with one basic subject—he studied how knowledge grows. Piaget published more than 50 books and 500 papers in addition to 37 volumes in the series "Etudes d'Epistémologie Génétique" (Studies in Genetic Epistemology). His book, *Science of Education and the Psychology of the Child*,[12] contains excellent information for any elementary teacher regarding the need for more active methods of learning.

Stages of Cognitive Development

The work by Jean Piaget places students in developmental stages or levels, and they learn in relation to certain characteristics within each level according to his research.[13]

Stage	Years	Cognitive Development
Sensorimotor	0–2 years	motor-action learning
Preoperational	3–7 years	intuitive learning
Concrete Operational	8–11 years	logical with concrete experiences
Formal Operations	12–15 years	abstract thinking

The stages of cognitive development identified by Piaget, while associated with characteristic age spans, vary for every individual. In addition, each stage has many detailed structural forms. For example, the concrete operational period has more than 40 distinct areas covering classification and relations, spatial relationships, time, movement, chance, number, conservation, and measurement.

MADELINE HUNTER

Madeline Hunter (1916–1994) was a California educator whose ideas have helped thousands of teachers improve their teaching skills. As principal of University Elementary School, a laboratory School at UCLA, she saw test scores significantly rise through the application of her ideas, results later replicated in inner-city school settings. She put her lesson plan elements together after spending thousands of hours personally observing master teachers in her school. She later served as Professor in Administration and Teacher Education at UCLA. Hunter produced 17 videotape collections, and authored over 300 articles and 12 books including *Teach for Transfer*, and *Mastery Teaching*.

How to Plan a Lesson

Madeline Hunter suggested various elements that might be considered in planning for effective instruction. In practice, others compiled these elements into the "Seven Step Lesson Plan," a template to use with lesson planning and teaching. This model was designed to increase learning for students. Using these steps is a great help for preparing effective lesson plans.

Anticipatory Set or Setting the Stage

Do something to get the student's attention focused on the lesson. This setting the stage for learning should take place as students are coming into class or are moving from one activity to another.

It could be a question posed to the class. Perhaps hold up a paper sack and ask the students what they think is inside. It could be a review of something previously taught that will be continued in today's lesson. Use anything to draw their minds toward the lesson.

Beginning teachers discover that children, like adults, have much to think about. Just because the teacher stands up and starts a lesson, there is no assurance that the children are attending mentally.

State the Objective

Madeline Hunter teaches us that telling the students what they are going to learn increases the learning. "We are going to be learning about. . ." "By the end of today's lesson you will be able to. . ."

Teaching: Teacher Input

This is the point when the teacher gives information to the student that is needed to accomplish the objectives of the lesson. Possibilities might include using the board, a chart, or the overhead. The information perhaps could be given using a video or a map or PowerPoint presentation. Disseminating information to the students is the goal.

Teaching: Modeling

Showing an example of what is an acceptable product or process helps the learning progress. This could be a poem, a rhythmic composition, steps to follow in the group, correct documentation of the group's work, or a skill such as "play the drum like this."

Checking for Understanding

The teacher takes time to check the student's comprehension of the material. One strategy is to pose a question, having children show "thumbs up" if they agree or "thumbs down" if they disagree. Giving four possible answers and asking children to indicate with their fingers (1, 2, 3, or 4) held under their chins which answer is correct can achieve this step. "Are they with you?" is what is being checked. Questions that are designed so that every student is required to answer are the most effective.

Guided Practice

At this stage in the learning, involve the students in the plan. The teacher carefully helps students interact with the lesson material (follow me). Madeline Hunter indicates this point in the lesson to be crucial for future success. Guiding students to a point where they can accurately and successfully accomplish the material in the lesson insures they can proceed successfully. The learners should go through all the steps of the task, or at least enough so the teacher can judge their predicted success. Walking around and looking at answers, listening to groups as they work, or evaluating written material helps the teacher involve the students.

Closure

Closure is a wrap-up of the lesson, a review and evaluation of what has been learned. To "hammer down" the information presented in the lesson by going back to the objective statement brings the lesson to an appropriate conclusion. It helps students process the material as they reflect on the lesson. It gives students a sense of accomplishment, and can be used to provide a final assessment of the material before moving into other activities.

Independent performance

If needed, this is the point where students will be using the skills or information learned without help from the teacher. It can be homework, or something for them to think about on their own. Letting students perform the tasks or sing the song or solve the problem without any help from the teacher is essential for practicing the new skill or process.

Individual Student Activity

Connection Lesson: Teacher Show and Tell[14]

Using Hunter's lesson plan and a piggyback song you find online, connect Music and one of the following subjects: Social Studies, Math, Science, Language Arts, PE, Safety, Health, or Nutrition. Present it to the class. Give everyone a handout of your lesson. (Lead the class in your song; sing "Ready, Sing" on the first pitch of the song). Sample handout included in Appendix 4. (Rubric on teachers' website: www.routledge.com/textbooks/9780415878234)

Connection lessons are examples of students learning *through* music.

GLORIA LADSON-BILLINGS

Gloria J. Ladson-Billings (b. 1947) is a Professor of Education at the University of Wisconsin. She is an American author, pedagogical philosopher, and teacher educator, who speaks to the issues of educational incongruity in teaching African American children in the 21st century. She is the author of *The Dreamkeepers: Successful Teachers of African-American Children* (1994), and a past-president of the American Educational Research Association (AERA). She has also written articles for two books, *The Many Views of Diversity: Understanding Multiple Realities* by Marjorie Hall Haley (George Mason University) and Charles R. Hancock (Ohio State University), and *Improving Schools for African American Students, A Reader for Educational Leaders*, edited by Sheryl J. Denbo and Lynson Moore Beaulieu.

Multicultural Education

Culturally relevant pedagogy is a term created by Gloria Ladson-Billings[15] to describe "a pedagogy that empowers students intellectually, socially, emotionally, and politically by using cultural referents to impart knowledge, skills, and attitudes." Her work is widely recognized in multicultural education, research, and teacher education.

Participating in culturally relevant teaching essentially means that teachers create a strong link between students' out-of-school and school lives, while still meeting the expectations of district and state standards. Written in 2009 in "My Learning Story"[16] on the Rethink Learning Now website, she shared the following experience from her elementary school days:

"My most memorable learning experience came as a result of being a student in Mrs. Benn's fifth grade classroom. Despite being in a de facto segregated school overcrowded with baby boomers, Mrs. Benn

21

was a no nonsense, challenging teacher who wanted students to know that they were capable of learning any and everything because they came from a nation of people who had overcome immeasurable odds. In Mrs. Benn's class we learned to sing in Latin, Italian, French, and German. She took what must have been a rag-tag group of poor and working class African American students all around the city of Philadelphia to sing concerts at nursing homes, community centers, and churches. However, more significant than the singing opportunities was Mrs. Benn's focus on the history of our people. Most of us thought she must have been making things up. How was it possible that a Black man had earned a PhD from Harvard? How could it be that a Black man had performed open-heart surgery? Who on earth would believe in a Black explorer? Mrs. Benn assured us that these were aspects of our history that we needed to know. They were powerful reminders of who we were called to be."

Teachers using culturally relevant teaching discover, create, and use the experiences of the students as relevant background for their lessons and methodology. Gloria Ladson-Billings' work in culturally relevant pedagogy is extremely helpful in crafting a multicultural approach to teaching. She is making a major contribution to the field of multicultural education.

Valuing and working with diversity in learners is becoming more and more important. According to the U.S. Department of Education, National Center for Education Statistics (2004):

The number of children ages 5–17 who spoke a language other than English at home more than doubled between 1979 and 2004. Between 1979 and 2004, the number of school-age children who spoke a language other than English at home increased from 3.8 million to 9.9 million, or from 9 to 19 percent of all children in this age group.

The percentage of racial/ethnic minority students enrolled in U.S. public schools dramatically increased between 1972 and 2004. Further, 43 percent of public school students were considered to be part of a racial or ethnic minority group in 2004, an increase from 22 percent in 1972.

Action Research

By incorporating these learning and teaching theories into planning and instruction, teaching will be better received by the students and learning will be improved. We often teach as we were taught, even if it was not the most effective procedure. Teachers aware of learning theories, and willing to use the findings, break the outmoded patterns of teaching.

The strategies recommended in the following chapters often incorporate the theories and ideas discussed in this chapter. Teachers in the field can conduct their own research, often labeled *Action Research*, by exploring what works best for instructing their own students.

An elementary school teacher could group his or her students randomly and try teaching the same material to each grouping of children, but by using a different approach or method with each group. By evaluating the results, the teacher can decide what seems to produce the best results for the students in his or her own classroom. With so much emphasis in education on assessment, gathering data, and using the information to constantly improve instruction, this plan could be very helpful.

Individual teachers, as well as the authorities quoted in this chapter, are professionals involved in the learning process with students. By examining the methods used to instruct within one's own classroom, a teacher becomes a collaborator of those knowledgeable individuals involved in educational research. Hopefully, this book will empower teachers to explore the treasures awaiting those who use music and the arts as an integral part of the curriculum.

District Elementary Arts Philosophy

Another very important part of a "Framework for Teaching and Learning" is a quality district philosophy that clearly states the goals and expectations for the elementary arts programs in a school district and in each school. One of the most important features in this philosophy should be the clearly stated important relationship between arts specialist teachers and elementary classroom teachers. Here is a sample District Elementary Music Philosophy that, with implementation that meets the MENC Opportunity-to-Learn Standards,[17] would lead toward "a complete education" for all students. For example, as stated in these standards, the efforts of music specialists should be "complemented by classroom teachers, who have the unique opportunity to make music a part of the daily life of the students and to integrate music into the total curriculum."

Sample Philosophy

This district's elementary music program strives for excellence in teaching and learning in and through music; learning in and through the arts is fundamental to a complete education for all students. Students receive an essential music education taught by music specialists with scope and sequence curriculum in every school. Students extend their music learning through the work of their classroom teachers who integrate and infuse music in their classrooms. Music and cultural community organizations, exhibits, and live performances all contribute to expanding every student's knowledge and appreciation of music, and capacity for creative musical endeavor.

Working together, the specialists and the classroom teachers, with additional community resources, will be able to provide the "complete education" that we value for students, one with a multi-faceted music curriculum. This is the ideal learning environment for students that the authors hope to see in school districts across the country.

Thinking It Through

1. Could technology be used to facilitate learning in each of the Multiple Intelligences?
    In a small group, pick two of the intelligences and discuss specific teaching/learning activities and equipment/software technology tools that would support those classroom activities. For instance, some items that would be useful to enhance learning in the Musical Intelligence would be:

    *   Video and audio recorders—to digitize singing, musical instrument performance
    *   Music clips—to add to reports

2. List careers related to each of Gardner's eight intelligences that would be suitable for those with special strengths in that intelligence. For example, poets and writers could be listed for Interpersonal Intelligence, salespeople for Intrapersonal Intelligence, and surgeons for Bodily–Kinesthetic Intelligence.

Suggestions for Further Study

For some insights into the way the Multiple Intelligences theory has evolved, read Howard Gardner's article written in 2003 and titled "Multiple Intelligences after Twenty Years" (http://pzweb.harvard.edu/PIs/HG_MI_after_20_years.pdf).

Read articles and books by Thomas Armstrong that describe Gardner's work as a framework for educational practice:

"Multiple Intelligences in the Classroom." Alexandria, VA: Association for Supervision and Curriculum Development, 1994.

"Multiple Intelligences: Seven Ways to Approach Curriculum," *Educational Leadership*, November 1994.

Multiple Intelligences in the Classroom. Alexandria, VA: Association for Supervision and Curriculum Development, 2nd edition, 2000.

Read more about Elliot Eisner's ten lessons on why the arts are important to the wider curriculum: http://artseducation.suite101.com/article.cfm/elliot_eisner_s_10_lessons#ixzz0LRIRkzbs.

Read other excellent publications on subjects covered in this chapter:

Arts with the Brain in Mind (2001) by Eric Jensen. Published by Alexandria, VA: Association for Supervision and Curriculum Development.

Teaching with the Brain in Mind (2005) by Eric Jensen. Published by Alexandria, VA: Association for Supervision and Curriculum Development, revised 2nd edition.

Multiple Intelligences: Best Ideas from Research and Practice (2003) by Kornhaber, Fierros, and Veenema. Published by Allyn & Bacon.

Culture of Education (1996) by Jerome Bruner. Published by Harvard University Press.

CHAPTER 3 | INSIDE THE MUSIC: THE BASIC ELEMENTS OF MUSIC

When baking cornbread, the cook starts with the ingredients—cornmeal, flour, sugar, eggs, milk, salt, and baking powder. With music, we also start with the ingredients, only in music we call these basic "ingredients" elements. The elements in music are those basic parts, rather like raw ingredients for cooking, that when mixed together create different types or styles of music.

When tapping a foot to the music, or "keeping time" with the car radio by tapping fingers on the steering wheel, the person is reacting to the element *rhythm*.

When humming a tune, one is remembering the element *melody*, or *pitch* as it is sometimes labeled. (Pitch is an easier term to use with some modern music that has no singable tune, but does have pitch.)

Friends at a picnic singing "Row, Row, Row Your Boat" around the campfire are singing a round, creating *harmony*. The sound from a string quartet or four-part choir also is harmony. Two or more different tones sounding at the same time creates harmony.

Form is a very interesting musical element, and often one that is unknown to the casual listener. Music is composed with a structure, or form, providing strength and meaning to what we hear. The form helps our ear enjoy the music, much as the form of a building helps give strength to the structure and beauty to the design. Several forms will be discussed including ABA, AB, ABACA(DA) or rondo, and theme and variations.

The other basic element is *expressive qualities.* This element involves several different components:

- The sound sources, what is making the sound in music, are called *tone color*, or *timbre*. When listening to a piano solo, the tone color is piano, or keyboard instrument. When listening to a jazz combo, the tone color is usually trumpet, keyboard, string bass, saxophone, clarinet and percussion. A recording of a female folk singer accompanying herself on a guitar has the tone color of female voice and guitar.
- The louds and softs (quiet) of music are called *dynamics*. These variances of loudness give interest and variety to the music. It helps make the music more enjoyable and creates tension and release within the music.
- The *tempo* or speed of the music is also an important expressive quality.
- Expressive qualities such as texture, style and articulation can also be included in this list.

All of these aspects of the sounds we know as music combine to create special aural experiences for the listener.

Music

Sounds and silence moving through time.

Sounds organized into patterns.

Elements of Music

- *Rhythm*
- *Melody (pitch)*
- *Harmony*
- *Form*
- *Expressive qualities.*

Under each of the elements, rhythm, melody, harmony, form, and expressive qualities (tone color, dynamics, tempo, texture, articulation and style), the basics can be further delineated into components of each element.

In seeking ways to simplify the study of music, the elements can be put into rather simple divisions that can be described by contrasting terms.

Steady beat and no beat—(rhythm)
Long and short—(rhythm)
High and low—(melody and harmony)
Skip, step, and same—(melody and harmony)
Same and different—(form)
Loud and soft—(dynamics)
Fast and slow—(tempo)
Thick and thin—(texture)
Classical, popular, and traditional—(style)

In recalling Bruner's Spiral Curriculum[1], a teacher can start with these basic designations of music, and then begin to deepen a child's understanding by adding complexity to the learning. Thus, high in music might in successive lessons become "higher" by including sounds that are closer together, yet still higher or lower. The same delineations apply to each category. Fast spirals into faster, slow into slower music, loud into louder and so forth as the teacher helps students learn more and more about the art of music.

Dr. Sue Snyder[2] suggests that any of these contrasts can be used to "spice up" classroom content:

For example: When a rule must be remembered, choose a musical concept such as high/low, and have the students say the phrase high, low, in the middle, higher, lower, half high and the other half low, half low and the other half high, mixing up the highs and lows, all at one level. By the time they have done all these repetitions, they will have orally rehearsed the phrase so many times it will most likely be remembered. This works even better when movement is added for kinesthetic reinforcement.

By thinking in these terms, rather than using the complex vocabulary, both the musical novice and the young child can intuitively analyze music with confidence. Playing games with listening by using two bells, one high in pitch and one low, is a start to musical learning. When the students hear the high sound, they stand tall with arms stretched overhead, and when they hear the low pitch they crouch down close to the floor with hands tucked around their knees. The teacher is helping them learn to be aware of sounds and listen more carefully, and the activity is fun at the same time! For all the students know, the teacher is just playing a game with the class. Little do they know that all sorts of learning opportunities are beginning for these fortunate students.

LISTENING

MOVING

The following activities will help a classroom teacher get started with the exciting prospect of including music instruction in the curriculum. The challenge is to observe the learning that takes place for the students. Using music in the elementary curriculum is just like adding spices to cooking—it enhances the experience, and helps students retain the memories.

Student Project (partner)

Textbook Survey[3]

With a partner, complete the Music Textbook Survey by examining a teacher edition of a current elementary music textbook to see how music elements are taught, plus the other information requested. (The Music Textbook Survey is available on the teachers' website: www.routledge.com/textbooks/9780415878234)

Teaching Rhythm

Rhythm has two aspects: beat (pulse) and pattern (rhythm of the words).

An activity involving the nursery rhyme "One, Two, Tie My Shoe" is helpful in learning more about the elements.[4]

One, two, tie my shoe,
Three, four, shut the door,
Five, six, pick up sticks,
Seven, eight, lay them straight,
Nine, ten, a big fat hen.

Follow these instructions.

Step one. Say the nursery rhyme "One, Two, Tie My Shoe." Pat hands on knees while saying this rhyme. Patting rhythmically in a steady repeating pattern is performing the steady beat. This first step might be the only step done with preschool or kindergarten students. Having them take turns tapping the steady beat on a drum as they chant the nursery rhyme also works well. The students could make the beat faster or slower, louder or softer, as they practice this step in the lesson.

Steady Beat or Pulse

The heartbeat of the music.

Say the rhyme again, putting a mark on the board or a large chart for every steady beat.

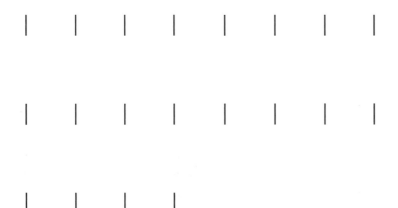

Count the number of steady beats on the board. Have the students discover how many beats are in the rhyme. The number is 20, but don't just tell them. Make the students "figure it out." It's part of the fun of the game.

At the end of the line of beats, draw a double bar that indicates "the end" in music. ‖

Step two. Now say the poem, accenting the following words (older students may go into this activity the same day, but younger ones may need to do it the next day)—some of the beats have been accented:

One, two, tie my shoe. **Three** four, shut the door,
Five, six, pick up sticks. **Seven**, eight, lay them straight.
Nine, ten, a big fat hen.

Accent

A beat that is accentuated or given emphasis. Often creates sets of beats, usually in sets of 2, 3, or 4, in children's music.

Go to the line of drawn beats, say the rhyme again with the group, and mark which beats are accented.

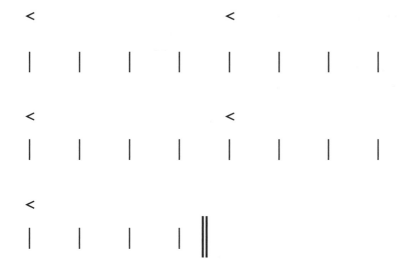

Step three. Now draw a straight line before each accented beat. These straight lines are called barlines, and the music has been divided, or measured, into groups of four. These groupings are called *measures* in music.

Of course, when students are learning music in this manner, they are also exploring mathematical concepts as well. These measures of music are actually sets of beats.

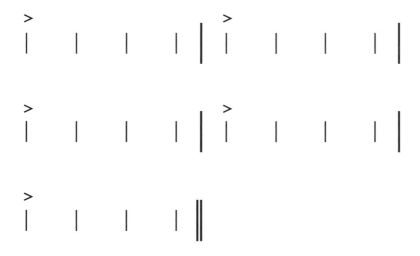

Barline

A line drawn before the accented beat to group the steady beats into sets.

It measures the music.

Measures

The sets of beats created by the bar lines are called measures.

Step four. Next let the hands "speak the words." The teacher can ask the students, "Did you know that my hands can talk?" Clap the rhythm of the words to "One, Two, Tie My Shoe." This is introducing the students to *rhythm patterns* (or *rhythm of the words*). Sounds can be longer or shorter.

Below each steady beat on the chart or chalkboard, decide with the students if the word spoken on that beat has one sound or two sounds. Using elementary music terms, a shorthand version can be used to indicate this. One version is used in the example below.

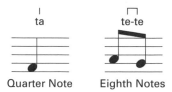

The teacher guides the students into making a decision on the beat, or its division, by having the students pat ONE steady beat on their knees while the teacher claps the words. So, the first beat will have the word "One" clapped. Ask the students if this is a single sound (*ta*) or two sounds (*te-te*). They will decide it is a single sound. Below the notated beat, draw a straight line, or a *ta*, using a different colored marker. This represents the stem of a quarter note in musical notation. The *te-te* symbols represent the stems of eighth notes.

The chart should now look as shown below.

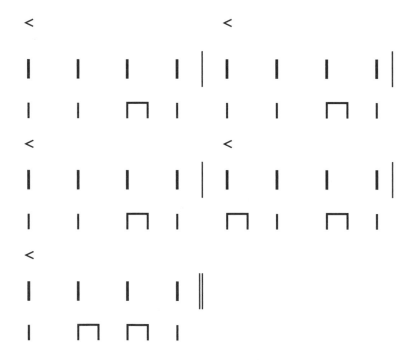

Step five. At this time, the students can clap the rhythm patterns, play them on percussion instruments, or say different words for *ta* and *te-te*. For example, "Maine" could be substituted for the *ta* notes and "Kan-sas" for the *te-te* notes. Or students could say "pear" for the single sound notes and "ap-ple" for the two sounds of the *te-te* notes. Flower names (rose, jas-mine), car names, and cereal names are only a few categories that will work well. They could select instruments with different pitches, and play the *ta* words with a higher pitch, and the *te-te* words with a lower pitch.

30

Teaching Melody

Step six. The next step in our nursery rhyme activity is to introduce the element of *melody*. The rhyme can be sung using only two tones, *high* and *low*.

- Sing the rhyme using *high* and *low* while singing. Add in movement—students can stand and squat, or use their arms to show the high and low sounds.
- Go back to the chart and decide whether each tone is either a *high* or a *low*.
- Draw two lines as a staff below the chart as shown. After singing and drawing each pitch, the chart should look as shown below.

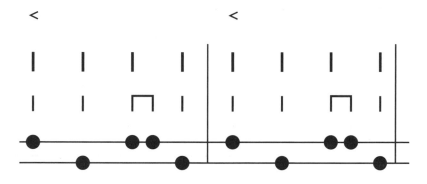

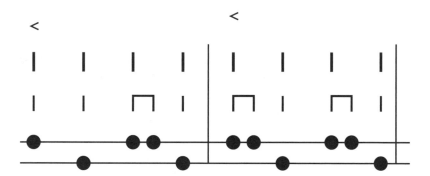

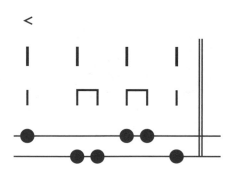

- Extend the stems on the second row down to the right side of the note heads, and musical notation has been created.

PLAYING

Students can perform the melody with the proper rhythm on two keys of the piano, G and E above middle C, or using these two bells from a resonator bell set (borrow one from the music teacher). Have one student put their right-hand index finger on G, and their left-hand index finger on E. Then that student can play with mallets as another student points to the music on the board.

Another way to perform the notes is for all the students to play them on G and E on the recorder. The sense of accomplishment is incredibly rewarding for students when they discover they can "read" music and perform it.

A Word to the Wise

An elementary teacher can do the "One, Two, Tie My Shoe" activity with their own classroom by pacing it according to the interest, ability, and attention span of the students. A first-grade child might only be able to say the rhyme and pat their knees the first day. Then, space the rest of the activity, perhaps over a six-week period. The idea is to introduce the elements in a meaningful way. By sixth grade, students would be able to do much of the activity in one or two days. The entire process can be repeated using another rhyme, verse or poem.

PLAYING

Full Class or Individual Student Activity

Begin the Recorder Unit

The goal is to perform B–A–G songs as a minimum requirement. Options for going further are given. Have students complete pre-test over music symbols (on teachers' website: www.routledge.com/textbooks/9780415878234) at the beginning of the recorder unit.

Rhythm

LISTENING

Full Class Student Activity

Listen to the Candyall Beat track from *Pulse: A Stomp Odyssey Soundtrack Album*. Clap the steady beat along with the musicians from Brazil who perform this percussion piece used during Carnival. Listen to the complex rhythm patterns that are used.

Note and Rest Symbols, Names and Relationships

Try singing each note on a neutral syllable and pointing to each number on a number line. For example, when singing a whole note in common time (⁴⁄₄), when the sound begins, point to zero and then with each beat point to 1, 2, 3 and stop the sound when you reach 4. This provides a visualization of how the sound lasts for four beats of duration. Likewise, the half note sounds for two beats, and so forth. A *rest* signifies a period of silence in music.

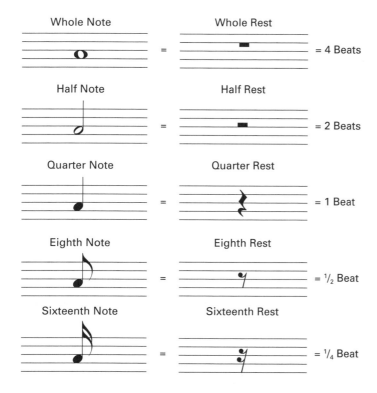

A dot following a note or rest increases its duration by half the original value. For instance, in common time where a quarter note receives one beat, the dotted quarter note would get one and a half beats.

Time Signatures

The music generally used with children has an underlying pulse or beat. Time signatures are used to indicate the underlying pattern of beats to the performer. The top number indicates how many beats are in a measure. The bottom number indicates the type of note that gets one beat.

²⁄₄   Two quarter notes in a measure is called "two-four" time—it is in duple meter (sets of two beats).

³⁄₄   Three quarter notes in a measure is called "three-four" time—it is in triple meter (sets of three beats).

⁴⁄₄   Four quarter notes in a measure is called "four-four" or "common" time—it is in quadruple meter (sets of four beats).

⁶⁄₈   Six eighth notes in a measure is called "six-eight" time—it is in (compound) duple meter, and is performed with two beats in a measure.

Practice reading rhythms and time signatures:

- Read "Oh! Susannah" and "America" with rhythm syllables (*ta, te-te*). Discuss the time signatures and meters. Sing the songs while patting the steady beat.
- Read the "Bate, Bate" chant with rhythm syllables (*ta, te-te*). Discuss the time signature and meter. Perform the chant as a round for an extra challenge. Also, try adding an *ostinato*—a short phrase that is persistently repeated. The repeating idea may be a rhythmic pattern, part of a tune, or a complete melody. In this case, let partners create their own eight-beat rhythm pattern to perform with body percussion as "Bate, Bate" is chanted.

SINGING

Songbook Selections

Get America Singing. . .Again!

Full Class Student Activity

Listen to the Grain Song track from *Pulse: A Stomp Odyssey Soundtrack Album*. Identify the meter or sets of beats used in this song from South Africa.

Melody

Up, Down or Stay the Same

In even the most difficult music ever written, the pitches in a melody can only move up, down, or stay the same.

Step and Skip

Melodies move up and down by step or by skip.

Skips can be large or small.

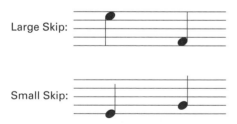

Staff

Melodies are written on a "staff." Notes on the five lines and four spaces are shown on page 36. The lines and spaces are read from the bottom up. In the treble clef, the lines are E–G–B–D–F, and the spaces are F–A–C–E.

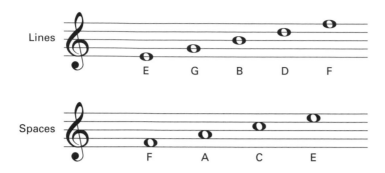

SINGING

Sing the melodies to these songs and look for steps, skips, and staying the same in the melodies.

Listening Activities: Melody

Listen to the wonderful melodies composed by Wolfgang Amadeus Mozart for the first movement of his famous *Eine Kleine Nachtmusik* (*A Little Night Music*). Listen to how the melodies move up, move down, or stay the same in the two themes.

LISTENING

Read about the composer and the composition, and then listen to 1st Movement, *Eine Kleine Nachtmusik* by Mozart while following the Listening Map.

The Composer

Wolfgang Amadeus Mozart (1756–1791) was born in Salzburg, Austria. He was considered a child genius. As a toddler he quickly learned to play keyboard instruments and the violin. At 12, he was already composing symphonies, operas and sonatas. He toured all across Europe, performing for royalty. Because of his constant travels, Mozart eventually learned to speak 15 different languages.

Mozart wrote over 600 compositions in his short lifetime. As he was writing a Requiem Mass in 1791, he felt ill. He felt as if he was writing his own requiem, or funeral music. On December 5, 1791, he died. Many people consider Mozart the greatest composer who ever lived.

The Composition

Eine Kleine Nachtmusik, a light orchestral composition, was written to be played at a garden party or any such event where background music was needed to filter out the small talk that was going on. Mozart composed this piece in 1787, and it is possible that it is the most popular of all of Mozart's works.

Listening Selection

LISTENING

P & I	1st Movement, *Eine Kleine Nachtmusik* by Mozart	CD Track 5
Listening Map		Appendix, p. 260

(For more information on melody and scales, see Appendix 5.)

Harmony

Rounds

Rounds sung or played create harmony. Try singing familiar songs such as "Row, Row, Row, Your Boat," and the following songs as two- or three-part rounds.

Songbook Selections

SINGING

Get America Singing. . .Again!

P & I	"Frère Jacques" French Round	16
I	"Music Alone Shall Live" Traditional round	30
I	"Dona Nobis Pacem" Traditional canon	30

Chords

Two or more tones sounding together create harmony. Chords create one type of harmony. Chords can be played on the guitar or the piano to accompany many children's songs and can also be sung. Try singing the chords written for harmony parts in these songs.

LISTENING

Form

Music is created with sections that sometimes repeat and sometimes alternate with different sections. These sections create interest for our ears as we listen. To teach someone to recognize form, they must first be able to recognize *Same* and *Different*.

To assess student understanding of this concept, the teacher can play a game with the children. Play a short melody on a recorder. Then, play a melody again. Have the children stand if the two melodies are different, and stay seated if the melodies are the same. Or be pretend robots. Give the directions: for *Same*, "move your legs like a robot," and for *Different*, "move your arms like a robot." Or, have children hold up a square shape for same, and a circle shape for different.

After learning to hear and see that a melody or phrase is either repeated *Same* or not *Different*, students are ready to learn some musical forms.

The sections are often labeled with letter names, and sometimes in students' books, with geometric shapes.

A   B   A

□ ○ □

ABA Form

ABA is a very common form in music. The same section is heard at the beginning and at the end, with a contrasting section in the middle. It can be introduced by listening for the form of "Twinkle, Twinkle Little Star," which is in ABA form. Students relate to this form as "hamburger form."

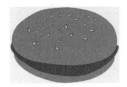

Bun-Meat-Bun

38

Another example of ABA is an Oreo cookie, with the cookie part on each side and the cream filling on the inside. One fun activity for all grade levels is to play an ABA piece (the "March" from the *Nutcracker Suite* works well) and challenge the students to eat the cookie as they listen to the music: only eating the A part, or cookie on one side, when they hear the A section; eating the cream filling when listening to the B section; and finishing the last A cookie piece when hearing the last A section. This activity serves as an evaluation also. By observing them eating the cookie, the teacher can see how well the students understand ABA form.

LISTENING

Listening Activities: ABA Form

Read about the composer and the composition, and then listen to "Russian Dance" (*Nutcracker*) by Tchaikovsky while following the Listening Map.

LISTENING

The Composer

Russian composer Tchaikovsky (1840–1893) had a career that began slowly, but eventually made him world famous. Born into a middle-class family, he studied music early, but got his degree in law. He took a job at the Ministry of Justice, but his heart yearned for music and composing. Finally, he was allowed to study at the prestigious St. Petersburg Conservatory of Music. At the age of 26, his first symphony was performed with great success and he gradually gained a reputation as a composer. Eventually he wrote ballets, symphonies, and operas that are still performed today.

The Composition

The *Nutcracker* ballet is based on the story "The Nutcracker and the King of Mice" written by Hoffman, and revised by Dumas. The basic plot is the story of a young girl who dreams of a Nutcracker Prince. The "Chinese Dance" occurs in the second Act when the Prince has taken Clara, the young girl, to the Kingdom of Sweets. The Sugar Plum Fairy entertains them with a celebration of dances, one of which is the "Russian Dance" or "Trepak."

Demonstrate ABA form

Each person takes two plates. Try out some ways to make movements with the two plates, and share these ideas with one another. While listening to the first A section of "Russian Dance," feel the meter in sets of two, and then move the plates to match the music for the first eight beats (first phrase). Change the movement for the next eight beats (second phrase). Continue exploring ways to move the plates during the whole selection. One way to become creative is go beyond all the known ideas.

MOVING

Before the whole piece is heard again, get into pairs. Plan who will be the *mirroring* leader for the A sections. The other person will lead during the B section. The follower moves to reflect the leader as if he/she were looking in a mirror. Start with just mirroring the paper plate movements, but eventually mirror whole body movement. Be careful to always be able to look at your partner (no turning around). Use creative ideas that match the music.

This paper plate activity is excellent for many reasons. When used in the elementary classroom, it helps shy kids successfully begin creating movements to music if they have something in their hands.

Scarves or strips of construction paper can be used in place of the paper plates. Giving the opportunity to every child to be "the leader" adds another layer of importance to this type of partner activity.

LISTENING

Listening Selection

P & I   "Russian Dance" (*Nutcracker*) by Tchaikovsky   CD Track 7
Listening Map   Appendix, p. 262

Partner Student Activity

P & I   Demonstrate understanding of ABA form with paper plate mirroring.

Rondo Form

Another musical form is the rondo, where the A section is repeated after each differing section. ABACA or ABACADA form is a rondo. This form can be referred to as a "club sandwich" to help students understand rondo form.

> bread (A),
> > bacon, lettuce, and tomato filling (B),
> > > bread (A),
> > > > ham slices (C),
> > > > > ending with bread (A).

Students can design their own club sandwiches to create a sandwich rondo. Select sounds or instruments to represent each part, and play the Sandwich Rondo.

A   Students tapping on the desk with a pencil eraser, or using home-made rhythm sticks (create two sticks for each student using newspaper, magazines, or paper, markers, and tape) to play the rhythm of the words "Club Sandwich" four times for the A section.
B   Students clapping could perform the rhythm of "bacon, lettuce, and tomato filling" two times for the B section.
C   Students tapping their feet on the floor could perform the rhythm of "slices of ham" four times for the C section.

Perform this musical sandwich with the ABACA rondo form.
    For practice in independent learning, divide the students into small groups, and have each group design a musical sandwich. Perform each composition in class, having the "listening" groups evaluate the

40

success of the "sandwich." Are the sections easily understood? Can others hear the rondo form? *Sam's Sandwich* by David Pelham (see "Recommended Student Reading" at the end of the chapter) is a clever book to read during this activity.

Listening Activities: Rondo Form

Read about the composer and the composition, and then listen to "Viennese Musical Clock" (*Háry János Suite*) by Kodály while following the Listening Map. Raise a hand when each new section begins.

The Composer

Zoltan Kodály (1882–1967) was born in what is now Slovakia. He died in Budapest, Hungary after a long and very productive life. His compositions are part of early 20th century styles of the Contemporary period.

In 1900, Kodály began to study music at the Franz Liszt Academy of Music in Budapest, Hungary. Because Kodály's father worked with the Hungarian Railway System, he was easily able to travel around and learn about the music of his country. He began to collect traditional Hungarian folk music, which he often used in his compositions. Kodály lived most of his life in Budapest, even during the difficult war times. He composed music for orchestra, chamber ensembles, and voice, but the suite from his folk opera *Háry János* is the best known and most widely performed of all of his compositions.

In addition to being a popular and respected composer, Kodály developed the widely acclaimed "Kodály concept" of teaching music. It is used in Hungary, in many schools in America, and around the world today.

The Composition

"Viennese Musical Clock" (Besci harangjatek) is from Kodály's folk opera *Háry János*, which premiered in 1926. This particular selection is a musical description of the scene where János, the hero of the story, visits the Imperial Palace in Vienna. The famous musical clock in front of the palace amazes him. Each time it strikes the hour, it plays a tune while mechanical figures come out and move around a circular track. This selection is an example of rondo form: ABACADA, with an introduction (a beginning section) and coda (an ending section).

Form four movement groups—label each one as one of the sections (A, B, C, D). Each group is made up of partners who plan their own routines of steady beat moves (find meter first). Hand clap and hand jive moves can be used. Listen to "Viennese Musical Clock" again with partners moving within their groups during the correct section. (The A section group will perform each time their section is repeated.) Everyone taps an imaginary wristwatch to the beat during the Introduction and Coda.

MOVING

Listening Selection

LISTENING

| I | "Viennese Musical Clock" (*Háry János Suite*) by Kodály | CD Track 15 |
| Listening Map | | Appendix, p. 264 |

Partner Student Activity

| I | Demonstrate understanding of rondo form with creative movement. |

Theme and Variations Form

Theme and variation is another very interesting form to teach students. This form allows the composer to take one theme or melody and change it somehow for each variation. The form is written: A (or Theme) A1 A2 A3 A4 A5, etc.

Clever Ways to Enhance Lessons using Theme and Variations

- Discuss the potato as theme A. What ways can we change or vary the potato? Baked, mashed, au gratin, fried, scalloped, etc.
- Use the original Coke can for A, then find all kinds of different Cokes to represent theme and variation. Use diet Coke for A1, caffeine-free Coke for A2, cherry Coke for A3, diet caffeine-free Coke for A4, etc. Play a theme and variation composition, for example, *Variations on "Ah, vous dirai-je, Maman"* by Mozart. Display the Coke cans at the appropriate time.
- Use potato chips packages and all the varieties—plain, sour cream, barbeque, dill pickle, ranch.
- Different types of pastas are another way to illustrate theme and variations. Or, use soups to illustrate different varieties—chicken noodle, tomato, potato, vegetable, or any other example from our world of merchandise and marketing that fits the "variation" model.

Listening Activities: Theme and Variation Form

Sing "Simple Gifts" and become familiar with its melody. Read about the composer and the composition, and then listen to "Variations on Simple Gifts" (*Appalachian Spring*) by Copland while following the Listening Map. Raise a hand when a new variation begins. Listen closely to hear the "Simple Gifts" song melody each time it occurs. Discuss the basic music elements that were changed in each variation, including the featured instrument(s) that perform the theme. (Theme played on the clarinet, Var. 1—oboe and bassoon, Var. 2—strings, plus the theme is augmented or stretched, Var. 3—trumpet, plus changes in tempo and dynamics, Var. 4—clarinet and bassoon, Var. 5—full orchestra.)

The Composer

Aaron Copland (1900–1990) was an important American composer. He composed ballet and orchestral music as well as choral music and movie scores. Copland was the first classical music composer to win a Kennedy Center Award. His compositions are wonderful examples of the Contemporary period of music history.

Copland's parents came to the United States from Russia and settled in New York City, where he was born and raised. His family lived above their store in Brooklyn. He studied composition in France with the famous teacher Nadia Boulanger. She inspired him to use American folk music material in his compositions. His music often included jazz, ragtime and cowboy songs. His popular music for the ballet *Appalachian Spring* uses American folk songs, including "Variations on Simple Gifts."

The Composition

Copland chose the melody of "Simple Gifts," a traditional Shaker hymn, to be the theme of his theme and variations piece, a part of the ballet *Appalachian Spring*. This same melody was heard during Barack Obama's 2009 Presidential Inauguration Ceremony in "Air and Simple Gifts" by John Williams.

Appalachian Spring premiered in 1944, and featured the celebrated dancer Martha Graham. Copland was awarded the 1945 Pulitzer Prize for Music for this composition.

Copland described this section of the ballet, written to describe the lives of pioneer farmers from the 1800s, as:

> Scenes of daily activity for the Bride and her Farmer husband. There are five variations on a Shaker theme. The theme, sung by a solo clarinet, was taken from a collection of Shaker melodies compiled by Edward D. Andrews, and published under the title 'The Gift to Be Simple.' The melody most borrowed and used almost literally is called 'Simple Gifts.'[5]

Songbook Selection

Get America Singing. . .Again!

| I | "Simple Gifts" Traditional Shaker hymn | 39 |

LISTENING

Listening Selection

| I | "Variations on Simple Gifts" (*Appalachian Spring*) by Copland | CD Track 16 |
Listening Map   Appendix, p. 265

SINGING

Individual Student Activity

Demonstrate understanding of form by describing the ways a known melody is changed in a theme and variations selection.

Verse/Chorus Song Form

One of the most commonly used forms in children's songs is verse/chorus. Observe this song form while singing the following selections.

SINGING

Songbook Selections

Get America Singing. . .Again!

P & I	"Home on the Range" Traditional cowboy song	23

Appendix

I	"Chíu, Chíu, Chíu" Uruguayan folk song	199

Expressive Qualities

Instrumental Tone Colors

Full Class Student Activity

Watch *Young Person's Guide to the Orchestra* (a DVD from Phoenix Learning Group).

Tone color is the sound source in music, and is sometimes called *timbre* (tam-ber). An interesting aspect of instrumental tone color includes categorizing instruments into groupings labeled as "families." Orchestral instruments are grouped into "families" according to commonalties of the instruments. The four families of instruments are string, brass, woodwind, and percussion. String instruments all have strings that are plucked or bowed. Brass instruments have mouthpieces to blow through and are made of metal or brass. Woodwind instruments use a person's air or wind to create the sound, and were once all made of wood. Most have single or double reed mouthpieces. Percussion instruments are struck to create a sound.

44

String Family Instruments

- Violin
- Viola
- Cello
- Bass
- Harp

Brass Family Instruments

- Trumpet
- French Horn
- Trombone
- Tuba
- Baritone/Euphonium

Woodwind Family Instruments

These are further divided into single- and double-reed instruments. The mouthpieces of single-reed instruments have only one thin piece of bamboo or reed. The double-reed mouthpieces have a folded-over piece of very thin reed or bamboo, thus the term double-reed.

- Flute
- Piccolo

(*Single Reed)*
- Clarinet
- Bass Clarinet

(*Double-Reed)*
- Oboe
- English Horn
- Bassoon
- Contra Bassoon

Percussion Family Instruments

- Xylophone
- Marimba
- Tambourine
- Maracas
- Bass Drum
- Timpani (or Kettle Drums)
- Chimes
- Snare Drums
- Cymbal
- Bells
- Gong
- Triangle

Piano is included in the percussion family because internal hammers hit the strings.

Classroom percussion instruments can be divided into four families of unpitched instruments:

* Woods
* Metals
* Drums
* Scrapers/Shakers

LISTENING

Full Class Student Activity

Listen to the American Indian Dance Theatre track from *Pulse: A Stomp Odyssey Soundtrack Album*. Identify the classifications of the percussion instruments used in this music.

Listening Activities: Instrumental Tone Colors— Symphony Orchestra

All four families of instruments are used in the modern symphony orchestra. Read about the composer and the music and then listen carefully to "Malagueña" (*Andalucia Suite Espagnole*) by Lecuona, performed by an orchestra.

The Composer

Ernesto Lecuona (1896–1963) was a Contemporary Cuban-American composer. A child prodigy, he gave public piano concerts at age 5, and was composing by the age of 11. Lecuona was an amazingly prolific composer, writing over 400 songs, 170 piano pieces, 37 orchestral works, 11 film scores, numerous ballets, and an opera. He added Latin and Afro-Cuban elements to his music. Beginning in 1931, Lecuona began writing film scores, turning out three that year alone for MGM. Living primarily in Cuba, he also had homes in New York City and Florida.

The Composition

"Malagueña," from *Andalucia Suite Espagnole*, became an instant hit when it was written in 1927. It is probably the composer's most famous piece, whether in its original form as a piano solo, its song version, or in its countless other instrumental arrangements.

LISTENING

Listening Selection

I   "Malagueña" (*Andalucia Suite Espagnole*) by Lecuona   CD Track 22

Listening Activities: Instrumental Tone Colors—Concert Band

Listen to *Early Light* by Carolyn Bremer, performed by a concert band. Three families of instruments—the brass, woodwind, and percussion—are used in marching and concert bands (also called wind ensembles). The brass family is expanded by the additions of the cornet, baritone and bass trombone. The woodwind family is expanded by the additions of three types of saxophone—alto, tenor, and baritone. The percussion family can be expanded by the addition of ethnic percussion instruments (cabasa, agogo bells, squeeze drums, log drums, thumb piano, bongo drums, etc.).

Read about the composer and the composition, then listen for the brief snippets of melodies from the "Star Spangled Banner" that occur throughout the piece. After listening to *Early Light*, compare and contrast the sound of the concert band to the sound of the symphony orchestra.

The Composer

Carolyn Bremer (b. 1957) is a Contemporary American composer. She studied at the Eastman School of Music, and received a Ph.D. in composition from the University of California, Santa Barbara. She was Chair of Composition at the University of Oklahoma from 1991 to 2000 where she held the O'Brien Presidential Professorship. Currently, she is Professor and Area Director of Composition and Theory, and Associate Department Chair of the Bob Cole Conservatory of Music at California State University Long Beach.[6]

The Composition

Early Light is a mainstay in the concert band repertoire, receiving hundreds of performances each year. It was premiered in July 1995. The melody is made up of new material plus many snippets taken from the "Star Spangled Banner." Carolyn Bremer, a passionate baseball fan since childhood, drew on her feelings of happy anticipation at hearing the national anthem played before ball games. The slapstick instrument heard near the end echoes the crack of the bat hitting a long home run.[7]

Listening Selection

LISTENING

I   *Early Light* (for band) by Carolyn Bremer   CD Track 21

(For more information on classifying instruments, see Appendix 5.)

Vocal Tone Colors

Vocal tone colors come from the sound source of the human voice. These sounds are often labeled by qualities of male and female singers. These qualities include the range of pitches that can be sung easily as well as the color of the voice. Some of the common voice labels are:

Female Voices	*Male Voices*
Soprano	Tenor
Alto	Bass

Listening Activities: Vocal Tone Colors

Listen to a choral selection. Read about the composer and the composition, then listen to the "Hallelujah Chorus" while following the Listening Map, Appendix 7, p. 261. Note the four sections of the choir—soprano, alto, tenor and bass. Listen carefully to the tone color of each section as they enter separately, then the tone color that results from all the sections singing together.

The Composer

George Frideric Handel (1685–1759) was born in Germany, but is buried in England's Westminster Abbey with other national heroes. He was a German-English composer in the Baroque period of music history.

Handel was a child prodigy. He began composing operas at a young age, and by his twenties he was the highest paid composer on earth with people fighting for seats whenever he performed. Handel worked for a royal employer for several years in Germany as court composer. Through an unusual set of circumstances, his ex-boss became George I of Great Britain. Handel, who was already in England, began working again for the new king in London, and lived there from 1712 until his death. He wrote operas, oratorios, orchestral and choral works, and pieces for organ. His great love was opera, but we know him best for his 1741 oratorio *Messiah*.

The Composition

An oratorio is a large vocal and instrumental work that tells a story, often religious. It is like an opera without scenery, costumes, or acting. Handel's large oratorio *Messiah* was composed in just 24 days for orchestra, chorus, and soloists. Handel always worked quickly, but this was very fast even for him. It is said that he did not leave his room for days at a time and had his meals brought to him on a tray. Handel had been going through a difficult time as a composer, and *Messiah* restored his fame and reputation.

Today *Messiah* is performed around the world. It is sung in churches as well as in concert halls, especially the very popular "Hallelujah Chorus" from this oratorio. There is a story that during one of its first performances in London, King George II began the tradition of standing during the performance of the "Hallelujah Chorus." This tradition is still followed today.

Listening Selection

I   "Hallelujah Chorus" (*Messiah*) by Handel   CD Track 3   **LISTENING**

Full Class Student Activity

Listen to the Moremogolo Tswana Traditional Dancers track from *Pulse: A Stomp Odyssey Soundtrack Album*. The music of the Tswana Dance performed by this singing group from South Africa has many similarities to the "Hallelujah Chorus." Compare and contrast the music of both groups.

Teaching Dynamics

Dynamics are the musical louds and softs included in the performing of music. Using different dynamic levels gives the music variety and keeps the listener interested in the music.

Many musical terms, including dynamic markings, used worldwide are written in the Italian language. Because the early Catholic Church, headquartered in Vatican City in Rome, had composers writing music and musicians performing music who spoke Italian, the musical terms were written in the common language for communication. These early church musicians also were the ones copying or notating the music for worship services, again most being Italian speakers, so terminology continued to be in Italian. The music would find its way into other countries, and the people would learn to interpret the directions for making music. The Italian terminology was the accepted practice, and continues even today. If these early composers and musicians wanted a composition performed quietly or softly, they would write the Italian word *piano* which means soft. For loud, they would use the Italian word *forte* meaning loud. As a result, the early piano was called a pianoforte because it could play both loud and soft. Through the years, the name was shortened, and we now know the instrument as the piano.

Through the ages, the Italian terms have become, through common usage, employed universally to indicate dynamic markings, tempo markings, and other musical directions. The terms are often designated by only the initial.

Common Dynamic Markings

p	*piano*	soft	*f*	*forte*	loud
pp	*pianissimo*	very soft	*ff*	*fortissimo*	very loud
mp	*mezzo piano*	moderately soft	*mf*	*mezzo forte*	moderately loud
cres.	*crescendo*	gradually getting louder	*decres.*	*decrescendo*	gradually getting softer

---

Teaching Tip

The term "soft" as applied to sound is an abstraction for most students. They are never told to be "soft" by their parents or teacher. They are told to be "quiet." Soft to students denotes feeling or texture; "the teddy bear feels soft." "The towel I dry off with after a bath is soft." Teaching them to associate the term soft with quiet music is no easy step, especially for young students. It is sometimes more successful to use the terms "loud/quiet" to start, and then change "quiet" to "soft" as they begin to understand the concept.

Teaching Tempo

The speed of the beat is labeled the tempo. Beyond the basic fast, slow, faster, slower, etc., there are Italian terms that have been assigned to specific beat speeds. A metronome is used to measure the number of beats per minute (bpm).

Common Tempo Markings

Presto	very fast	(168–200 bpm)
Vivace	lively and fast	(140 bpm)
Allegro	fast and bright or "march tempo"	(120–168 bpm)
Moderato	moderately	(108–120 bpm)
Andante	at a walking pace	(76–108 bpm)
Adagio	slow and stately (literally, "at ease")	(66–76 bpm)
Largo	very slow	(40–60 bpm)

Experience singing two wonderful folk songs, "A la rueda rueda" and "This Little Light of Mine," at different tempos and with different dynamic levels.

SINGING

Texture, Style, and Articulation

Texture in music refers to the thick or thin sounds of the music achieved through the sounds produced by the various instruments or voices, the number of instruments or voices, performing at one time, and by the dynamic qualities of the sounds. How many layers of sound are present?

Music styles include the broad categories of classical music, traditional music, and popular music. Examples from the hundreds of more specific styles are blues, country, electronic, folk, heavy metal, hip hop, jazz, reggae, and rock.

Full Class Student Activity

Listen to The Jersey Surf Drum & Bugle Corps and The Jackie Robinson Steppers track from *Pulse: A Stomp Odyssey Soundtrack Album*. Identify the two different marching band percussion styles performed (traditional corps style and "Drumline" style with highly syncopated, foot-stomping, body-moving rhythms), and indicate when each one is heard. *The New York Times* called marching bands "a particular form of American folk art, in which music and bodies work in tandem to create spectacles of design, movement and sound that rival the precision dancing of the Rockettes."[8]

Articulation (tonguing or bowing) in music can produce sounds that are very smooth and connected (*legato*). It can also produce sounds that are short and detached (*staccato*). Some musical sounds or pitches can also be accented (<).

Thinking It Through

Test yourself! Do you understand how sounds are organized in a musical composition? Can you name good musical examples for each element? Do you know what each term means?

Rhythm has a steady beat (however, some music has no beat). It is made of sounds and silences of different durations. Rhythm has tempo and meter.

Melody is made up of a series of pitches. It can move upward, downward or by staying the same. It moves by small or large skips or steps.

Harmony is created with two or more sounds occurring together. It can be made with melody plus accompaniment, by singing a round, or in a number of other ways.

Form. Music ideas can be the same or different. Repeated musical ideas unify compositions and contrasting ideas provide variety. Common musical forms include ABA, rondo, and theme and variations.

Tone color varies with the type and size of the material producing the sound (the larger—the lower). It varies with different types of instruments and with different types of voices.

Dynamics (volume) may be soft or loud (*piano* or *forte*). They may be changing, growing gradually louder (*crescendo*) or softer (*decrescendo*).

Tempo (speed) can be fast or slow. It may be changing, growing faster or slower.

Texture in music may be thick or thin based on how many layers of sound are heard.

Style. Music can be in many different styles. Types of styles include jazz, country, rock, classical and so on.

Articulation. Music can be made of sounds that are very smooth and connected (*legato*). It can be made of sounds that are short and detached (*staccato*). Some musical sounds or pitches can be accented (<).

Suggestions for Further Study

Instruments fascinate children. Explore several websites that have pictures of different types of musical instruments.

www.music-with-ease.com
http://classroomclipart.com
http://cybersleuth-kids.com/sleuth/Art_Music_Cultures/Music/Instruments/index.htm
www.oddmusic.com
www.usd.edu/smm
www.freefoto.com

Recommended Student Books

Barnes, Peter W. & Barnes, Carol Shaw. (2005). *Maestro Mouse and the Mystery of the Missing Baton.* Alexandria, VA: VSP Books.
Takes children on a tour through the orchestra and around the Kennedy Center for the Performing Arts in search of a lost baton.

Lithgow, John. (2003). *The Remarkable Farkle McBride.* (C.F. Payne, Illus.). New York: Simon & Schuster Books for Young Readers.
Introduction to sections of the orchestra through a young boy trying to find "the perfect instrument."

Meyrick, Kathryn. (2006). *The Musical Life of Gustav Mole.* New York: Child's Play International.
Gustav is a mole who was born into a musical family. He shares his experiences with individual instruments, and performing groups such as the orchestra, jazz band, and the opera. CD included.

Pelham, David. (1991). *Sam's Sandwich.* New York: Dutton Children's Books.
Fold-out flap book with the look of a real sandwich and easy-to-say, rolling rhymes.

Schulman, Janet. (2004). *Sergei Prokofiev's Peter and the Wolf.* (P. Malone, Illus.). New York: Knopf Books for Young Readers.
Excellent way to introduce children to classical music and the instruments of the orchestra. CD included.

Tripp, Paul. (2006). *Tubby the Tuba.* (H. Cole, Illus.). New York: Dutton Juvenile.
The orchestra's tuba gets tired of repeating "oompah" and learns a melody from a bullfrog. CD included.

Turner, Ann. (1997), *Shaker Hearts.* New York: HarperCollins.
Information concerning the Shaker movement in America.

SECTION II | *SOMOS MÚSICOS*: DOING WHAT MUSICIANS DO

Tantalizing Tidbit of Research

Cognitive neuroscientists at seven major universities have found strong links between arts education and cognitive development (e.g. thinking, problem solving, concept understanding, information processing and overall intelligence). Children motivated in the arts develop attention skills and memory retrieval that also apply to other subject areas.

Learning, Arts, and the Brain (2008)[1]

Even the finest musician is involved in only three main activities in music:

- Listening
- Performing
- Creating

In the elementary classroom, the teacher and students can be musicians, too—*somos músicos* ("we are musicians"). It is important to have a room set up to be "music friendly." A CD player with good speakers, or a computer with good speakers is a must so you can easily have music playing in your classroom at many different times of the day. Collect or purchase a basic rhythm instrument set so students can enjoy playing often. Find a good corner of the classroom to put a "listening center" with a CD player or cassette player with headphones. Add music-related books, a class-compiled songbook of favorite songs, a selection of music choices, and use this space as a bonus choice when work has been finished. Hang pictures of famous musicians with brief bios added around this area.

The following three chapters will guide teachers and their students into activities as listeners, as performers and as creators.

CHAPTER 4 | **LISTENING**

How We Listen to Music

Listening is something all of us do, everyday, all day long. But how do we listen to music? Composer Aaron Copland, in his book *What to Listen for in Music*[4] explains that we listen to music on three separate planes:

1. The Sensuous Plane

    As we listen on the "sensuous plane," we listen for the sheer pleasure of the musical sound itself. Attention is devoted to where the sound is coming from, how the sound quality would be described, and how loud or soft it is.

2. The Expressive Plane

Listening on the "expressive plane" helps us discover what feelings and emotions the piece is communicating. What is the meaning behind the music?

3. The Musical Plane

When listening to music on the "musical plane," we focus on its musical elements—the melody, form, rhythm, harmony, and expressive qualities heard in the music.

People are now spending time listening to music at a level unsurpassed within history. Ride any public transit, look around and observe everyone tuned into music devices. Most of the time, these people are listening on the "sensuous" or the "expressive" planes. While it is fun to listen and concentrate on each of the three listening planes, it is the "musical plane" that students need to be helped to understand. This chapter will assist by giving practical ideas for how to "tune up" students' "musical plane" listening ears. This type of listening leads to a deeply satisfying aesthetic experience. A related outcome of this type of listening experience is learning how music reveals something about the place, time, and people who created it.

Learning to perform the skill of listening well alleviates many problems for the student and for the teacher. Music, the art form that requires listening, is a perfect conveyance for helping students develop into excellent listeners who have "attention and focus" for all kinds of listening tasks. Children enjoy listening to music. To them it is fun, and excellent teachers know that learning should be enjoyable.

The aural art, music, cultivates the skill of perceptive, involved listening. Teaching children to be active listeners, a gift to be enjoyed for the rest of their lives, is also a classroom activity that all teachers, regardless of talents or skills, can do. Furthermore, it is also a skill intertwined with many of the additional teaching suggestions in this book.

Tantalizing Tidbit of Research

The entire brain is engaged when a person listens to music.

Zatorre and Peretz (2001)[5]

LISTENING

How to Teach Students to Listen

Experiences in Sound-Collecting Walks

The beginning of listening instruction is helping students attend critically to what they are hearing. In our noisy world, this task may be more difficult than first thought. We are bombarded by sounds: on "hold" on the phone, at the grocery store, in the elevator, in the doctor's office. Some children have to be reminded to take time to listen because they have practiced years of "tuning out" sounds.

Sound-Collecting Walks[6] provide a primary class activity devoted to listening. It entails digitally recording sounds as the class or a smaller group walks along listening for sounds in their world.

The walks can be taken outside, recording nature sounds, or throughout the school building locating sounds in the school environment. Sounds can be collected on the playground, in the cafeteria, or just about anywhere!

These *Sound-Collecting Walks* can be part of a field trip or a special class outing. Once the recording is made, classify the sounds in various ways—long/short sounds, loud/soft sounds, high/low sounds, nature-made/man-made sounds, fast/slow sounds, inside sounds/outside sounds. Having the children recognize the opposite nature of some sounds, such as fast as opposed to slow, creates opportunities to begin critical thinking skills. The more refined aspect of listening begins to develop as well. The sound may represent something that is "relatively" fast, but not "extremely" fast. Students should also identify the sound sources.

Students can find or draw pictures to illustrate the sounds. Classroom books can be produced to accompany the recording. Large picture books made by the children displayed on a table in the classroom become inviting places to quietly listen and reflect.

Sharing sound recordings with other classes is very entertaining. When no visual image or picture accompanies a sound, deciding what is creating the sound can be quite challenging. A kettle can sound like a jet plane! The challenge of identifying sounds on Mrs. Smith's class recording is great fun for the children.

Older students can be assigned to groups, each of which goes on a different *Sound-Collecting Walk.* These recordings can be shared and discussed, and can become the basis of a creative writing assignment or an art experience.

Sound collecting activities can also occur in the classroom. For example, it is fascinating for children to listen to the sounds made by different shoes. Sit in a circle, let one child be "it" and walk around the outside of the circle while the students quietly say the "New Shoes" poem by Frida Wolfe, listening to the sounds of the shoes. A different child can walk on each verse. Leather soles will make different sounds from rubber-soled shoes; sandals will produce a unique sound, as will flip-flops.

MOVING

LISTENING

New Shoes, New Shoes,
Red and pink and blue shoes,
Tell me, what would you choose,
If they'd let us buy?

Buckle shoes, bow shoes,
Pretty pointy-toe shoes,
Strappy, cappy low shoes;
Let's have some to try.

Bright shoes, white shoes,
Dandy-dance-by-night shoes,
Perhaps-a-little-tight shoes,
Like some? So would I.

BUT
Flat shoes, fat shoes,
Stump-along-like-that shoes,
Wipe-them-on-the-mat shoes,
That's the sort they'll buy.

Experiences in Listening to Live Music Performances

Many school districts offer concert series during the year for students. These sometimes are made available through an area symphony orchestra or through a local college or university. Local high schools have opportunities for elementary students to attend their performances. Some parent/teacher groups raise money to bring music events to their schools.

Wise classroom teachers take advantage of all these concerts for their students. The most successful ones include student preparation prior to the event. If the school has a music teacher, this person should be able to help the students learn about the composers and compositions. In addition, the classroom teacher can check out library books on music, composers, concerts, and orchestral instruments to display in the room. Finding links into classroom curriculum is an excellent way to give students more connections to the music. Playing the musical selections they will hear at the concert during seatwork or reading time or other quiet class times will help students prepare for the concert. Students need to be informed audience members; understanding how to attend a concert, how to listen, and how to respond to a music performance.

One approach to listening to beautiful music is the concert hall, where expected behavior may be unfamiliar. Fortunately, classroom teachers can readily teach the necessary information to students at a young age so they can enjoy concerts for the rest of their lives.

A general rule of thumb to discuss is the link between *location* and *proper behavior*. The behavior that is expected from the audience in a gymnasium for a rock concert is quite different from the behavior expected of that same group of people seated in a performing arts center concert hall to hear a symphony orchestra perform. And that behavior is different than the expectations for an audience at an outdoor concert by that same symphony orchestra!

Here are some common questions about attendance in a concert hall musical performance, countered by the expected behaviors. Many of these behaviors can also be useful for student performances in the classroom.

QUESTIONS	BEHAVIORS
When should we clap?	In an orchestra performance, applause is first given to the Concert Master/Mistress, the first chair violinist, who comes out on stage to help the orchestra tune. Applause is always given for the arrival of the conductor on stage.
	Applause is expected at the end of compositions. If unsure, watch the conductor. When the conductor lowers his or her hands down to the side, it is proper to applaud.
	Symphonies and Concertos have more than one movement. They are to be performed without applause between movements.
	In the case of an opera or musical theater setting, applause is given as the conductor walks into the pit area in front of the stage.
	In voice recitals, the music is often presented in sections, usually grouped according to language. Clap at the end of these sections.
	In jazz concerts, applause is often given after improvised solo performances, even though the music continues.
	The best rule of thumb—watch those seated close by!

How should I prepare Children should hear the music often before the concert as part of
students for the concert? classroom activities. Share information about the composer, and
background on each piece. The musical elements of each selection should
be clearly explored.

A discussion of the best ways to show respect for the performers should
be held.

Respect for the performers can be based upon having a discussion with students about how the musicians are thinking, using both sides of their brains as they perform.

With the left brain, they are dealing with four big issues, all at the same time:

- First—they are reading a foreign language (music notation), a code that takes highly developed language skills to read.
- Second—they are doing math computations (dividing) the whole time. The duration of notes is all fractional—halves, quarters, eighths, sixteenths.
- Third—the musicians have to be thinking about the technical aspects of their instruments. What fingers must be put down, how to blow and hold their mouths to get the best sound, how to pluck the strings or hold the bow, how to play in tune with the full group, and so forth.
- Fourth—they have to think about if they are playing in the right style. Is each note loud enough, soft enough, long enough, short enough, connected enough?

Amazingly, with all this going on, they are also using the right brain to communicate the feelings, the emotions, the meaning behind the music that the composer has created. Together, all this results in a remarkable performance for those who are listening, the audience.

Listening attentively to music can become a great joy. Why do people drive long distances or go to great lengths just to get to a concert? One reason might be that they have experienced the special mind and body "salve" that live music experiences afford. After the concert, ask the students what other reasons they would have for attending more live music performances.

Experiences in Listening Using the "Rule of Three"

Music education research provides us a clue for teaching listening successfully. Through research studies we know that repeated listening to a composition produces a more valuable musical experience for the listener. Repetition allows the music to become familiar for the listener who then is more inclined to "like" it. The music becomes a friend or something well known that is pleasurable.

In applying that research, called the "Rule of Three"[7] to classroom instruction, teaching three planned listening experiences at three different times of the year for each musical composition selected becomes the goal. This suggestion, though different from earlier educational practices, is in agreement with James Eison who advocates that less material be taught more effectively. "Teach less better!"[8]

Often in school, large amounts of information are covered, but not taught well or effectively, with no emphasis on whether the student has learned it or not. College survey courses devote a semester to this type of instruction. The format includes the teacher disseminating much information to grade-oriented students, who then find themselves memorizing the material for a test. After taking the test, and often scoring very well, the students then promptly allow their minds to forget the material because it was not taught or learned effectively.

In much the same way, music teachers were once taught to select for each grade level a large number of musical compositions that would be listened to once during the year. The "Rule of Three" recommends teaching a fewer number of compositions, but presenting them at three different times in three different lessons.

Suggestions for using the "Rule of Three" will be given with the recommended listening lessons in this chapter.

Experiences in Listening Starting with Creating

The authors have found that creating a sound story or composition is an ideal introduction to meaningful listening lessons. Once the children have told a story in sound, they listen with heightened interest and attentiveness to another composer using similar approaches to composing. Programmatic music—music composed to tell a story—is especially effective with this teaching strategy. Children actively listen to Smetana's *The Moldau (Vltava)* or Dukas' *Sorcerer's Apprentice* after they function as composers themselves. Listening lessons hold new meaning because the children can relate to the music as both listeners and composers.

LISTENING

Listening Activities: *The Moldau (Vltava)* by Smetana

Read about the composer and the composition, and then listen to the music while following the sentence strips (see student activity) as the story is heard in the music.

The Composer

Czech composer Bedrich Smetana (1824–1884) was a child prodigy. He became a very famous composer known best for writing nationalistic music. In his operas and symphonic poems, he drew on legends, history, characters, landscape, and ideas of his native land.

The Composition

The music of *The Moldau (Vltava) from Ma vlast* tells the story of a river, beginning with the tiny tributaries and streams coming together into a mighty moving river. The listener can hear the river deepen as the cellos and other low strings begin to play. The story the music tells without words is of a boat floating on the river Moldau, moving past a forest, with passengers observing a group of hunters, and next a wedding party in a Czech village with much celebration and dancing. The music continues the story with the sun setting, and the boat anchoring for the night. The moonlight on the water creates images of nymphs dancing. At the dawning of the new day, the boat continues down the river where a series of dangerous rapids must be crossed. The boat is able to continue on safely through the rapids, arriving in the city of Prague where church bells in the steeples ring out a welcome.

Full Class Student Activity

CREATING

The children can create a composition designed to tell this story in sound.

- They first select sounds to make the water music, beginning very quietly at first to represent the tributaries. Tone bells played up and down in a glissando work nicely. Start softly on only one instrument, gradually adding more sounds until the river sound is formed.
- Go through the story with the children choosing different sounds to tell the events.
- With no words, tell the story only in sounds.
- Use sentence strips to write each event in the story. Place the strips in a pocket sentence strip holder.
- As a child points to the sentence strips in the correct order, the other children play the sounds that tell the story.
- When playing the sound composition in this manner, they are following a conductor, just as the orchestra does.
- After they complete their sound story, tell the children that music composed to tell a story is called program music. Someone else has also composed a musical story about this theme, *The Moldau (Vltava)*, a wonderful example of program music composed by Smetana.

Listening Selection

LISTENING

I   *The Moldau (Vltava) from Ma vlast* (excerpt)   CD Track 13

Further Listening Activities using the "Rule of Three"

By following the "Rule of Three" for listening, myriad possibilities exist. Some weeks later, children could listen a second time to *The Moldau (Vltava)* as they draw their favorite scene, which will later become part of a mural for the classroom. A third listening experience could be in relationship to a study of waterways or rivers of the world. A study of the Czech Republic would be a perfect time to listen again. Transportation study could motivate another listening to this composition about river travel. Creative writing is always a possibility for the classroom teacher in conjunction with programmatic music. What were the people on the boat doing? Where was their home? Who were the hunters in the forest? Who was being married in the village? What did the boat travelers eat? Why were they going to Prague? All these questions can stimulate creative writing experiences for the children.

Listening Activities: *Variations on "Ah, vous dirai-je, Maman"* by Mozart (Twinkle, Twinkle Little Star)

Read about the composer and the composition, and then listen to *Variations on "Ah, vous dirai-je, Maman"* and complete the student activity.

The Composer

Austrian composer Wolfgang Amadeus Mozart (1756–1791) was a child prodigy who came from a very musical family. His father was a composer, and his sister was also very talented. He began composing music at the age of 4. He toured Europe as a virtuoso performer during his childhood and teenage years. During Mozart's short lifetime he composed over 600 compositions. He died when he was only 35 years old.

The Composition

Variations on "Ah, vous dirai-je, Maman" was written by Mozart when he was 26 years old. It is believed that he heard the original French melody in the 1770s during his travels in France. It is a solo piano piece with 13 sections—the first section is called the theme, and the other 12 sections are variations of the theme. Mozart was incredibly gifted at "improvising" or creating variations on melodies on the spot. Each of the variations in this piece is very interesting, and it sounds as if Mozart was enjoying himself when he wrote it.

CREATING

Full Class Student Activity

A marvelous, successful classroom composition activity can be planned using the children's song, "Twinkle, Twinkle Little Star."

- Start with a picture of a star on a poster or sketched on the board. Ask children to name things that come to mind when they see this picture. List the words or phrases on the board or overhead as the children state their ideas. Words might include "galaxy," "well done" as in gold star, "sheriff's badge," "movie star," or "Christmas tree."
- Now have the children name songs that have "star" in them. Suggestions probably will include "Star Spangled Banner," "Star Light, Star Bright," and of course "Twinkle, Twinkle Little Star."
- Have everyone sing the "Twinkle" tune or "theme" together. Write the word "theme" on the board with the term "melody."
- Explain to the children that they are going to create a theme and variations composition on the Twinkle theme. Let small groups explore ways to change or vary the theme. Usually they will explore singing it faster or slower, or changing the rhythm, or letting two people sing at the same time with a body percussion accompaniment idea. Move from group to group, helping them alter and elaborate on their ideas, making it better. Finally, have everyone sing the theme together, followed by each group's variation.
- In conclusion, let the children listen to Mozart's piano piece, *Variations on "Ah, vous dirai-je, Maman"* which is a Theme and Variations composition on the tune we recognize as "Twinkle, Twinkle Little Star."

Again, the children will listen with great interest to "another composer's work" as it relates to what they have composed. (This plan incorporates the Creative Thinking ideas of E. Paul Torrance, see Chapter 6, page 99.)

Further Listening Activities using the "Rule of Three"

When adhering to the "Rule of Three", two additional activities should be planned for listening to Mozart's *Variations on "Ah, vous dirai-je, Maman."* The students could design listening maps, either in small groups or individually, to use with the composition. They could research facts about Mozart and present a play about his life and work. A timeline showing the age in which Mozart lived could be created, listing scientific discoveries, historical information, and world events that occurred during his life.

Creating writing and art projects could also be used for extended listening opportunities. The children could write a pretend letter from Mozart to his mother while he was on tour. What was it like to be a child prodigy? How did it make him feel to perform before royalty when he was only six years old? What was travel throughout Europe in a stagecoach like for a young boy? Scenes from Mozart's life and times could become artworks to decorate the classroom. What were the clothes like? Compare today's clothes with those worn by Mozart. How would he like to wear jeans?

Experiences in Listening Using Children's Books

There are many books that have been written to tell the story of *Nutcracker*, the famous ballet. One example, *The Nutcracker* by Susan Jeffers, includes beautiful illustrations. If the students read this book in class, listening to selections of Tchaikovsky's music will enrich the reading experience. Children could read the story and learn about the composer before listening to the music.

Listening Activities: Children's Books

Review the information about the composer and the composition in Chapter 3, and then listen to "Chinese Dance" from *Nutcracker* by Tchaikovsky. What is the form of the piece?

Further Listening Activities using the "Rule of Three"

The "Rule of Three" could be followed by having the students hear the music once more while watching a video clip of this part of the ballet. Again, art and creative writing are always possibilities for the classroom teacher. A study of the composer, who had an unusual life, will be interesting for the students. One interesting fact: he thought his head was going to blow off his body, so he conducted orchestras performing his music with one hand as he held onto his head with the other hand.

Another excellent example of program music, Prokofiev's *Peter and the Wolf*, has been designed and illustrated as a book by Warren Chappell.[9] The pictures, with musical themes included, make the story come alive for students. Supplying the visual to accompany the aural experience provides a more successful listening event for many children. A second listening activity could involve puppets made from small brown paper sacks or from drawings by the children attached to craft sticks. The puppets can be used to tell the story as the music is heard. A third activity could focus on identifying the solo instruments featured in the music—flute, violins, clarinet, oboe, bassoon, and French horns. Students could be given small flash cards with these instrument pictures, and be told to hold up the picture of the instrument as it is heard in the music.

Other music selections that connect to the world of children's literature are:

Level	Composition	Composer
P & I	*Beauty and the Beast*	Tchaikovsky
I	*Billy the Kid*	Copland
I	*Cinderella Suite*	Prokofiev
I	*Hansel and Gretel*	Humperdinck
P	*Mother Goose Suite*	Ravel
P	*Once Upon a Time Suite*	Donaldson
P & I	*Peer Gynt Suite No. 1*	Grieg
P	*Peter and the Wolf*	Prokofiev
P	*Sleeping Beauty Waltz*	Tchaikovsky
I	*Symphonie Fantastique*	Berlioz
I	*The Sorcerer's Apprentice*	Dukas
P	*Three Bears*	Coates
I	*Till Eulenspiegel's Merry Pranks*	R. Strauss

Experiences in Discovering the Art of Music

Good art has three qualities:

* Unity
* Variety
* Balance

Listening to a wide range of music helps students discover these qualities in compositions. Throughout the year, students can apply these standards to music and art. Their art criticism skills will be honed, and they will know why they like or dislike a certain piece of music. It is beneficial to have the ability to discuss both verbally and in writing the qualities of music and art. Words represent and pinpoint knowledge. Additionally, because they are using higher level thinking skills of compare and contrast, these exercises are good for their brains—much like aerobic exercise is good for the body.

The "Hallelujah Chorus" from Handel's *Messiah* is an excellent example of unity, variety, and balance in music. This classic work from the Baroque period of music history (see page 48) is part of the oratorio *Messiah*. An oratorio is a large work for orchestra, chorus, and soloists, usually on a religious theme.

- In the beginning of the chorus, the voices are singing in four-part harmony. Handel then has the voices singing in unison (all the same melody line), interestingly as the contour of the melody suggests a large "M." Then, he has the voices return to their four-part singing. This planned part of the composition creates variety, unity and balance for the listener. Even when we are not cognizant of this feature, our ears are pleased with the sounds.

- Continuing with the composition, we find a section starting with the text "The kingdom of this world is become" which is very smooth in sound, creating great variety from the more jagged feeling of the music heard previously.

- The fugal or "follow the leader" section begins with the words "and he shall reign" starting with the basses, followed by the tenors, then altos and last by the sopranos. Again, this section provides variety within the composition, yet is balanced by the similar lengths of the music sung by each voice part.

When asked if this composition may be included in the curriculum of a public school in the United States, some elementary education majors often answer "no." This misguided interpretation of following the First Constitutional Amendment within the public schools is unfortunately quite common. However, teaching a classic work of art as a music education experience is completely within the law.

As read previously in this discussion of the "Hallelujah Chorus," the composition was discussed musically as to the inclusion of the qualities of unity, variety, and balance. The selection could also have been taught emphasizing musical elements such as vocal tone color (see Chapter 3) or melodic treatment, or through a study of instrumentation, or by examples of repetition/contrast or from a variety of other musical features. The "Hallelujah Chorus" was chosen as an example of a great work of art, not as a religious or doctrinal lesson, and is therefore a legal as well as an educationally sound inclusion for a listening activity.

Listen to the "Hallelujah Chorus" by Handel to hear the specific examples of unity, variety, and balance when they occur in the music.

Listening Selection		
I	"Hallelujah Chorus" (*Messiah*) by Handel	CD Track 3

LISTENING

Experiences in Listening to Several Versions of the Same Musical Composition

Comparing two or more versions of the same piece of music can be a very captivating listening lesson for the elementary-age student. By having students listen to one selection and then to a second version and comparing and contrasting the two, higher level thinking skills are required. A form to use with listening to two versions of the same song is in Appendix 5 (Compare/Contrast Music Sheet).

Listening Activities: "The Star Spangled Banner" by Francis Scott Key

Many versions of the National Anthem are available, and provide a perfect segue into a patriotic music unit or a study of early American history. Listening to a version played by a wind ensemble, vocal versions sung by Sandi Patty or Marvin Gaye or José Feliciano, and the electric guitar version played by Jimi Hendricks at Woodstock produce very different feelings in the listener. A blank chart listing "Same—Different" for each of the versions can be given to students, to be completed either individually or in small groups. Discussing points of the performances that are the same and what makes them different as well as *why* they are different is an analysis skill requiring students to mentally compare and contrast what they heard. Questions of which version was the favorite and why involves evaluation, another higher-level thinking skill.

Songbook Selection

Get America Singing. . .Again!

| I | "The Star Spangled Banner" by Francis Scott Key | 44 |

Listening Activities: "Flight of the Bumblebee" by Nikolai Rimsky-Korsakov

"Flight of the Bumblebee" is available in several versions. The original version is from *The Tale of Tsar Saltan* and features the flute. Many versions exist with trumpet solos. Yo-Yo Ma and Bobby McFerrin, on their CD *Hush*,[10] have a recording of "Flight of the Bumblebee" which is performed by voice and cello. All these selections can be contrasted or two versions can be selected for comparison, helping elementary children improve their listening perception.

An interesting story about the bumblebee, which according to the size of the body and the smallness of the wings should not be able to fly, has reached "urban legend" status. Mathematicians and scientists have conducted numerous experiments and aerodynamic studies about this insect. Using a search engine on the internet produces numerous "hits" with material about the topic. If it were a fixed wing airplane, it would not fly. The bee can fly only because of the speed of its wing movements. This story has spawned many lessons about trying hard, working to achieve, and such.

Read about the composer and the composition, and then listen to "Flight of the Bumblebee" (*The Tale of Tsar Saltan*) by Rimsky-Korsakov.

The Composer

Russian composer Nikolai Rimsky-Korsakov (1844–1908) had no formal musical training when he decided to start composing, so he taught himself orchestration—the skill of arranging music for orchestral instruments. He eventually became so good at orchestrating, he wrote a book on it that is still in use today. He became a professor of composition at the highly respected St. Petersburg Conservatory of Music, where he taught students such as Prokofiev and Stravinsky, who later became famous composers.

The Composition

"Flight of the Bumblebee" was written as part of an opera, *The Tale of Tsar Saltan.* The opera was based on the fairy-tale poem of the same name written by Pushkin, a famous Russian poet. Magic spells and exciting events were occurring when this selection is performed in the opera.

Listening Selection		
P & I	"Flight of the Bumblebee" (*The Tale of Tsar Sultan*) by Rimsky-Korsakov	CD Track 11

LISTENING

Listening Activities: "Danny Boy" Traditional Irish Folk Song

LISTENING

The Irish folk song "Danny Boy" provides many examples for listening to a variety of versions. The lovely melody of this song is an ancient Irish tune often called "Londonderry Air." Percy Grainger's *Lincolnshire Posey* for concert band uses the folk tune as a theme, and many contemporary groups including the Chieftains have recorded it. Also, many vocalists through the years have sung "Danny Boy," including opera, latino, and country singers. In 2008, The Ten Tenors (from Australia) recorded it on their album *Nostalgica*. Ray Price, a country and western artist, performed "Danny Boy" with strings and created quite a furor among country and western audiences who felt he had left his roots by adding orchestral strings to a country music recording. Another very interesting performance is by Ruben Blades (Rubén Blades Bellido de Luna) from Panama. A beautiful version of "Danny Boy" is on his 2002 *Mundo* album.

Enjoy singing and listening to this very popular song.

Songbook Selection		
Get America Singing. . .Again!		**SINGING**
I	"Danny Boy" (Londonderry Air) Irish folk song	12

Listening Through the Historical Periods to Western Art Music

MOVING

LISTENING

Student Project (small group)

With two partners, design a movement activity to reflect the form, rhythm, and expressive elements of an assigned listening selection (marked with an asterisk* below). Prepare a handout with information on the composer, and a way to incorporate the music into another subject area. Specify the instruments heard and the meter. Give specific movement directions, written to match the form. Make a presentation to the class, explaining your handout and teaching the movement activity. Use paper plates, scarves, or props, if desired. Make copies of your handout for each class member.

Baroque (1600–1750)

Events during this period include:

- Jamestown, Virginia founded
- Henry Hudson explored the Hudson River
- Telescope invented by Galileo
- Rembrandt van Rujn painted *Night Watch*
- Sir Isaac Newton's *Mathematical Principles* published
- Harvard College founded in Massachusetts
- Reign of Louis XIV, King of France

Famous authors during this period include:

- John Milton
- Molière
- René Descartes
- Ben Jonson

Music included on the CD:

• *Rondeau, Overture (*Suite*) No. 2 by Bach	Track 1
• 1st Movement "Spring" (*The Four Seasons*) by Vivaldi	Track 2
• "Hallelujah Chorus" (*Messiah*) by Handel	Track 3
• *Hornpipe (*Water Music*) by Handel	Track 4

Classical (1750–1820)

Events during this period include:

- Herculaneum and Pompeii rediscovered
- George Washington elected first president
- Reign of Catherine the Great, Empress of Russia, Louis XVI reigns in France
- Thomas Jefferson elected third president
- French Revolution
- Louisiana Purchase

Famous authors during this period include:

- Benjamin Franklin
- Jonathan Swift
- Voltaire
- Wolfgang von Goethe
- Jane Austen

Music included on the CD:

- 1st Movement (*Eine Kleine Nachtmusik*) (excerpt) by Mozart   Track 5
- *Variations on "Ah, vous dirai-je, Maman"* by Mozart   Track 6

Romantic (1820–1900)

Events during this period include:

- Telephone, phonograph, electric light bulb and motion picture camera invented by Edison
- American Civil War
- Morse invented telegraph
- Victoria was Queen of England
- The Alaska Purchase

Famous authors during this period include:

- Ralph Aldo Emerson
- Elizabeth Barrett Browning
- Charles Dickens
- Leo Tolstoy
- Mark Twain

Music included on the CD:

- "Russian Dance" (*Nutcracker*) by Tchaikovsky   Track 7
- *"Chinese Dance" (*Nutcracker*) by Tchaikovsky   Track 8
- *"Elephant" (*Carnival of the Animals*) by Saint-Saëns   Track 9
- "Swan" (*Carnival of the Animals*) by Saint-Saëns   Track 10
- *"Flight of the Bumblebee" (*The Tale of Tsar Saltan*) by Rimsky-Korsakov   Track 11
- *"Wild Horseman" by Schumann   Track 12
- "The Moldau" (Vltava) (excerpt) by Smetana   Track 13

Contemporary (1900 to present)

Events during this period include:

- Wright Brothers' flight
- Model-T Ford introduced
- World Wars I and II
- Great Depression
- U.S. astronaut John Glenn orbited the earth
- U.S. astronauts landed on the moon
- Fall of the Berlin Wall
- Bombing of the World Trade Center, NYC
- Wars in Iraq and Afghanistan

Famous authors during this period include:

- Robert Frost
- Ernest Hemingway
- Virginia Woolf
- Maya Angelou
- James Michener
- J.K. Rowling

Music included on the CD:

- *Gymnopedie* No. 1 by Satie   Track 14
- "Viennese Musical Clock" (*Háry János Suite*) by Kodaly   Track 15
- "Variations on Simple Gifts" (*Appalachian Spring*) by Copland   Track 16
- 3rd Movement Symphony No. 1 ("Afro-American") by Still   Track 17
- *The Stars and Stripes Forever* by Sousa   Track 18
- Mars (*The Planets*) by Holst   Track 19
- *What a Wonderful World* by Bob Thiele and George David Weiss   Track 20
- *Early Light* (for band) by Carolyn Bremer   Track 21
- Malagueña (*Andalucia Suite Espagnole*) by Lecuona   Track 22

Thinking It Through

In small groups, discuss the following quotes from William H. Yoh, Jr. and Daniel A. Carp:

> "Music acts as a blueprint, testimonial, and archive to the people and the events of the Antiquity, Middle Ages, Renaissance, Baroque, Classical, Romantic, and Contemporary Eras. As listeners, we are able to experience a piece of history through a performance of a musical selection."
>
> William H. Yoh, Jr.[11]

> "Music is one way for young people to connect with themselves, but it is also a bridge for connecting with others. Through music, we can introduce children to the richness and diversity of the human family and to the myriad rhythms of life."
>
> Daniel A. Carp, Eastman Kodak Company Chairman and CEO[12]

Share experiences where you have learned about a historical period or event, or about another culture through the study of a musical selection.

Suggestions for Further Study

The Music Educators National Conference website, www.menc.org, is a good resource for strategies for dealing with the issue of the use of religious music in schools. Here is the position statement from that website:

> It is the position of MENC: The National Association for Music Education that the study and performance of religious music within an educational context is a vital and appropriate part of a comprehensive music education. The omission of sacred music from the school curriculum would result in an incomplete educational experience.

Here is a brief look at the legal history of sacred music in the public schools:

> The first court case dealing specifically with music, *Florey v. Sioux Falls School District 49-5,* (1980) was appealed to the 8th U.S. Circuit Court of Appeals. The court's ruling upheld the Sioux Falls school policy, which allowed the teaching of religious songs for educational purposes.
>
> More recent cases include *Bauchman v. West High School* (1995—dismissed); *Brandon v. the Board of Education of the Guilderland Central School District* (1980, 1981), and *Widmar v. Vincent* (1981).

Teachers who choose to include religious music in their curriculums must educate themselves on the legal and school policy issues, particularly teachers of young students.

Recommended Student Books

Hughes, Langston. (2003). *Works for Children and Young Adults: Poetry, Fiction, and Other Writing.* (D. Johnson, ed.). Columbia, MO: University of Missouri Press.

Excellent stories, poems and short books written by a famous African American author. Includes *The First Book of Rhythms*, and *The First Book of Jazz*.

Krull, Kathleen. (2002). *Lives of the Musicians*. (K. Hewitt, Illus.). New York: Sandpiper.
Short biographies of several composers such as Beethoven, Mozart, Joplin, and Gilbert & Sullivan.

Showers, Paul. (1993). *The Listening Walk*. (Aliki, Illus.). New York: HarperCollins.
Great as a story about sound and as a jumping-off point for taking your own walks.

CHAPTER 5 | PERFORMING

Why We Should Involve Our Students in Musical Performing Activities

Music study develops skills that are necessary in the workplace. It focuses on "doing," as opposed to observing, and teaches students how to perform, literally, anywhere in the world. Employers are looking for multi-dimensional workers with the sort of flexible and supple intellects that music education helps to create as described earlier. In the music classroom, students can also learn to communicate and cooperate better with one another.

Music study enhances teamwork skills and discipline. In order for an orchestra (or a rock band or a drum line) to sound good, all players must work together harmoniously toward a single goal, the performance, and must commit to learning music, attending rehearsals, and practicing.

Music performance teaches young people to conquer fear and to take risks. A little anxiety is a good thing, and something that will occur often in life. Dealing with it early and often makes it less of a problem later. Risk-taking is essential if children are to fully develop their potential.

Benefits of Music Education[1]

One of the most important components in teaching music to students is to help them become performers of music. When thinking of the word "perform," most Americans probably think of professional musicians who make their livelihood by singing or playing instruments on a stage for large audiences, and by producing CDs of their music to sell. Actually, families singing together at home or in the car, young children humming while they play, messing around with a guitar in a bedroom, and singing in the shower are all musical performance activities. Performing music doesn't have to be on a stage in a concert setting. In many cultures, singing, dancing, and playing instruments are a part of everyday life and people embrace the opportunity to participate.

Performing can be a natural activity in the classroom, with little polishing needed. Students will be very willing to perform for their teacher and for each other. Musical activities are natural for children and they need opportunities and encouragement, especially from the classroom teacher, to further develop these skills. Classroom teachers do not need extensive training in order to sing and make music with their students. Singing, playing, and moving are musical performance activities that fit into the classroom setting.

Singing

Why We Should Involve Our Students in Singing

"I don't sing because I'm happy; I'm happy because I sing."

William James, American psychologist and philosopher [2]

"O, she will sing the savageness out of a bear!"

William Shakespeare, English poet and playwright [3]

"Music and singing are a fun and effective way to help young children learn. Music supports self-expression, cooperative play, creativity, emotional well being, and development of social, cognitive, communication, and motor skills."

Shelly Ringgenberg, author of Music as a Teaching Tool: Creating Story Songs [4]

Anyone Can Learn to Sing

The fortunate person is one who enjoys singing. Many people go through life thinking they are incapable of singing in tune. Research is full of studies showing that anyone, if they have no vocal damage or disabling hearing condition, can learn to match pitch and sing.

"Well, they haven't heard me," is an almost audible response to these research findings because many people feel they cannot sing. If a person is able to yell at someone and their voice has some natural up and down movement, and their hearing is normal, they can learn to sing.

Of course, it is easier to teach singing to a young child who has not experienced negative statements from teachers, family, or peers criticizing their singing voice. But remember the research, *anyone can learn to sing*. If someone wants to sing, they can learn. Deciding to do it is the first step. Singing in the shower, singing to the radio, singing at church are all good activities in developing a singing voice.

Helping students find and use their singing voice is something the classroom teacher can do. The students are relaxed with their teacher, they trust that this person is not going to do something embarrassing to them, and singing together builds community. Plus, when they grow up, the students will be able to sing the "Star Spangled Banner" at ballgames without feeling embarrassed and, in addition, the principal will be thrilled and the music teacher will be grateful. What a gift to give.

Matching Pitch

Helping students match pitch can be achieved through these primary classroom activities:

*   For anyone unaccustomed to singing, the best way to become comfortable is to sing simple sol–mi (the fifth and third note of the major scale) songs. "Rain, Rain, Go Away" is probably the most common song that can be sung with two pitches.
*   Call roll by singing. Teacher sings the child's name on the pitches sol–mi. The child sings the response, "I'm here" using the same pitches. As the students get better at matching pitch, try changing the pitch

levels. Move the sol–mi higher or lower to see if the child can match the pitch. A teacher who consistently uses this activity through the school year will have students matching pitch by the end of the year.

Always encourage the children honestly. "You're getting better," or "You are going to learn this" are statements that help students feel they can do it!

"Natural Chant of Childhood"

Primary students taunting on the playground are singing sounds called the "Natural Chant of Childhood." "You can't catch me," or "Nanny Nanny Boo Boo" are sung on this series of pitches. Listening to students at recess time will almost always result in hearing some child or group of students singing these pitches. No one teaches them either, yet every generation of students will know this little tune.

The tones are actually:

sol   sol   mi   la   sol   mi

Using these tones that are naturally easy for most students to sing will help with tone matching. Playing singing games using the "Natural Chant of Childhood" is good practice for singing. Below are a few suggestions for you to try.

SINGING

Song for Lining Up

Sing for students to line up. "Let's Line Up for Lunchtime" can be sung to the "Natural Chant of Childhood." The song might go something like this:

> Let's line up for lunchtime,
> Let's line up right now.
> What a great group of students,
> Lining up for chow!

Make up the words on the spot, the sillier the better, and the students will be laughing and singing, just for the fun of it! They don't know that they are also learning to match pitch.

Songs for Specific Times

Making little songs for recess, for library, for almost anything the students are to do is good.

Sing when it is time to pick up before the end of the day. Everyone will feel much better doing it this way rather than the teacher nagging students to gather up their belongings and put away their books. As teacher begins to sing, students can join in with a light, lovely singing voice as they line up to leave the room.

Song for a Ball Game

A fun primary singing game using a basketball or other large ball can be sung with a simple "Natural Chant of Childhood" melody. Arrange the children in a circle and invite one child to start bouncing the ball on the beat. Ask the whole group to sing the song "Bounce High, Bounce Low, Bounce the Ball to Jericho." The child bouncing the ball then sings "Bounce the Ball to [Ben]" (singing the name of the child who receives the ball).

All	"Bounce High, Bounce Low,
	Bounce the ball to Jericho
	Bounce High, Bounce Low,"
Student	"Bounce the ball to [a child's name]."

The receiving child chooses another child, and bounces the ball to the new player. Again, the whole group sings until the line where the "bouncer" sings alone. After each child has bounced the ball, they sit down, but continue to sing with the group. The children sit down and keep singing after having their turn so that the class can easily see who is left to call on. This game is fun, helps children learn the names of their classmates, and gives practice in "singing alone and with others," which is the first standard in the National Standards of Music.

Song for a Guessing Game

Another excellent primary singing game using the "Natural Chant of Childhood" involves a guessing game that enhances students' thinking skills by having them focus on a lesser-used sense—that of touch. Have a bag of small, inexpensive surprises—plastic dinosaur, rubber rabbit, leather ball, "diamond" ring, rubber snake, plastic doll's table, etc. Ask a child to reach into the bag, describe what they are touching and then try to name it. This game can also be played using large plastic letters and numbers. Write on the board the items, letters, or numbers that have been identified. Then play the singing game, using the "Natural Chant" melody:

SINGING

Teacher:	"Who has the ring?"
All:	"Who has the ring?"
Student:	"I have the ring."
All:	"[Beth] has the ring."

Repeat until all students have had a turn. Anything using music adds to the day. Music is a part of all of us—like breathing! Using singing games to review material or to introduce a new topic works well.

Helping the Child Who Is Not Yet Matching Pitch

If a child cannot match pitch at all, and seems to "growl" the sounds on a low pitch, they perhaps haven't discovered how it feels to move the voice. Playing games that require making sounds can be the magic combination for certain students.

SINGING

- Asking children to make the sound of a siren, starting with a low sound, going higher, then back to a low sound can accustom a child to moving the voice.
- Invite all the students to do the "game" together because the emerging singer doesn't need to feel singled out. Plus the other students will want to do the game.
- Start with their bodies in a kneeling position close to the ground, hands on the floor. As they make the sound of the siren, and the sound goes up, the students stand up and stretch their arms high.
- Return to the low position as the pretend siren comes back down.

Points to Remember

- If a child can "holler" to a friend on the playground and it sounds normal, the child is not a monotone.
- Keep telling children they can learn.
- Boys match pitch later than girls.[5] Even as late as fourth grade, some boys are just beginning to match pitch.

The mind is a powerful tool, and believing is a very important part of learning. Teachers are sometimes like doctors who need to convince their patients that a cure is possible. Believing that one will get well is important to medical cures, and the same is true in learning. Help children "believe" they can learn by saying, "You're going to get it." This is a true statement, because the research has proven that people can learn to sing on pitch.

Singing Together

It is not difficult to get a room of students of all ages to begin singing together. With a clear tone sing "Ready sing" on the first pitch of the song and in the tempo selected. It really works! Use as light and pleasant a sound as possible. After getting the students started, avoid singing too much with them. If you always sing with the class, the students will become dependent upon you. Singing independence is the objective for your students. In addition, quality recordings should be used every day to present your students with good models of children singing.

Use the Rote Method for teaching simple songs (see page 6). If the song is in verse/chorus form, teach the chorus first, then sing the verses yourself while the students join in with the chorus. Teach the words and melody of the verses the next day.

Often teachers place the pitch too low for children, whose vocal cords are shorter and therefore produce higher pitches. Children should also sing in a range where they will find and use their lighter singing voices, rather than their heavier speaking voices. Giving students experience in using their "singing" voices as compared to their "speaking" voices is helpful in establishing the difference. So raise the pitch to an appropriate level for children. Loud "shout-singing" is never an appropriate sound for children.

What is an appropriate pitch level? As described by Patricia Hackett and Carolyn Lindeman in *The Musical Classroom*,[6] here are general developmental characteristics of students' singing voices:

- K–first grade
  Students' voices are light and small; singing range is generally limited to five to six pitches; in-tune singing is a challenge; singing with a pleasant light tone and many opportunities to sing individually and with others should be encouraged.
- Second to third grade
  Students' singing ranges increase from five to ten pitches and in-tune singing with a clear, open, and unforced quality should be encouraged; with more control of their singing voices, singing becomes more accurate and expressive as they sing alone and with others.
- Fourth to fifth grade
  Students' singing ranges are larger than an octave and may have as much as 12 or more pitches; vocal cords and lungs are more developed so better control of voices and breathing results; boys' voices are more resonant and girls' are clear and light.

Selecting Appropriate Songs

Many book sources are available for songs appropriate for the elementary student. Some collections, available in bookstores or online, are noteworthy:

- Ruth Crawford Seeger (2002) *American Folksongs For Children*, published by Music Sales America
- John Feierabend (2003) *The Book of Children's Song Tales*, published by Gia Publications
- Katalin Komlos and Peter Erdei (2004) *150 American Folk Songs: To Sing, Read and Play*, published by Boosey and Hawkes
- Eleanor Locke (2004) *Sail Away: 155 American Folk Songs to Sing, Read and Play*, published by Boosey and Hawkes
- Patricia Shehan Campbell (2007) *Tunes and Grooves for Music Education*, published by Prentice Hall

Professional recordings for singing along can be remarkable assets to the classroom teacher. (Warning: some recordings are pitched too low for the students. The best way to ensure that the recording is a good model is to choose recordings that feature children singing.) Some of the Disney Sing-Along CDs and DVDs are fun to use with elementary students, as well as *Singing with TREBLEMAKERS, Songs for Young Singers,*[7] *Singing with TREBLEMAKERS, Our Favorite Folk* Songs, and *Wee Sing Songbooks* and *CD Sets*.

Recordings for the classroom music series from Macmillan and Silver Burdett are available. Asking the music teacher to make a copy of the students' favorite songs will be especially popular. The students will be thrilled because they are getting to sing their favorite songs outside of music class, and the music teacher will be thrilled that a classroom teacher is singing with their students. Repeating the songs many times is an excellent idea, especially with younger students, as it helps them gain confidence in their singing voices.

Create in-class performance opportunities for the students. Applause and compliments should end each performance. Many students need to learn how to accept applause and compliments graciously.

Song Maps

There are many ways to present songs to students. Using song maps is one of the best. Visual learners will benefit the most from this approach.

Individual Student Activity

Song Maps

Follow the two basic types of song maps:

1. Point on the beat around the pictures of the song map with key word or phrase pictures.
2. Tap on the beat on each picture on the steady beat song map.

SINGING

Song Maps

Appendix

Songbook Selections

Get America Singing. . .Again!

Once students learn a song, many different activities can be used to enjoy it again and again. Here are a few examples that can be used with K–sixth graders:

- Everyone sings the song together, quietly keeping a steady beat.
- Sing the song softly; sing it loudly.
- Sing the verses loudly, and the chorus softly, or the reverse.
- One group sings while the other group hums or whistles.
- One group sings while the other claps hands or pats thighs on a steady beat.
- One group plays rhythm sticks on the rhythm of the words while the other sings.

- The students add various kinds of rhythm instruments such as triangles, rhythm sticks, sand blocks, tone blocks or tambourines on the beat while singing the song.
- Move while singing the song. Use a slow tempo, then a fast tempo.
- Bounce large balls on the beat while singing the song.
- Listen to various singers' renditions of the song.
- Have students make up their own words to the melody.

Playing

Why We Should Involve Our Students in Playing

"Setting my mind on a musical instrument was like falling in love. All the world seemed bright and changed."

William Christopher Handy, American musician known as the "Father of the Blues"[8]

Putting an instrument in a child's hand can be all the motivation needed to get even the shyest child involved. Drums, triangles, woodblocks, tone blocks—all the instruments from our memories of elementary school will work. Also, "found sounds" can be instruments. Tapping the side of a desk with a pencil or shaking a potato chip can with a few pebbles, rice or beans inside also produces instrumental sounds.

Instrument playing is a huge treat for students. Save playing instruments as reward activities, or only use them on Fabulous Friday afternoons.

One warning! *Do not* let this be the scenario in the classroom:

A box is sitting on the floor filled with random instruments which appear to have been haphazardly thrown in. It is music time, and students come to the box and grab one instrument to "play" while teacher puts on a musical tape or CD. They end up "beating the tar out" of the instruments with this wild sound erupting from the room. They usually are "playing" their instruments whether the music is playing or not. It is difficult to get them to put the instruments back in the box. Discipline is on the verge of dissipating into chaos.

Such bedlam is not music, but it is a scene often found when visiting classrooms, especially with very young students.

Teachers need to direct the playing of instruments through games and activities that will increase students' motor skills and reading skills, and that will also help them learn to play more musically. The teacher needs to set specific rules for playing. For example:

- Instruments stay in laps until directed to play.
- Instruments are played to make "music", not noise.
- Some instruments use a mallet, some are played with the hand—always play them correctly.

Approaches for Playing

Create Rhythmic Charts

Using Rhythmic Charts helps primary students learn to read music, and also to read words. The students can clap or play a percussion instrument on the rhythms. By reading the charts, which can be performed successfully by most students, they also learn left to right directionality. As students read one line, at the end they return to the beginning of the next line, thus they are practicing an important component of learning to read.

The charts should start with pictures, which are read left to right. This would be called a steady beat chart. Gradually the symbol | (ta) is added to the words. Eventually, the beat is divided and the symbol ⊓ (te-te) is learned. These symbols will become the quarter note and the eighth note in actual musical notation. This is an excellent activity to reinforce learning about syllabication. It also reinforces the concepts of steady beat and rhythm.

Teachers can design original charts. Usually, charts are in three lines, with four beats per line. Putting these pictures on large charts allows the students to come up and point to the pictures as the other students say it. Be sure they keep a steady beat while they read. Teacher can say, "One, Two, Ready, Go," with a steady beat and then have the students join in. An example of a teacher-made chart would be:

PLAYING

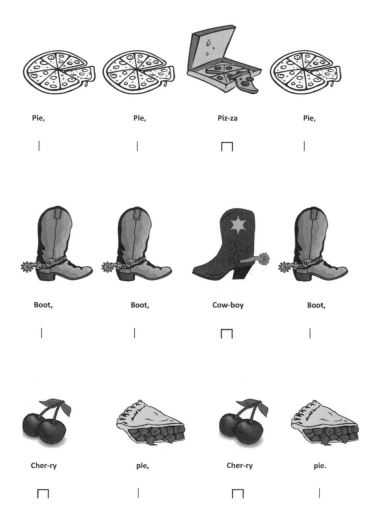

Pie,	Pie,	Piz-za	Pie,
Boot,	Boot,	Cow-boy	Boot,
Cher-ry	pie,	Cher-ry	pie.

The next step would be to pick instruments to play on the words, rather than say the words. Students are reading and performing from a score when they do this activity.

PLAYING

Perform Chants and Nursery Rhymes

> Horse and a Flea and three blind mice,
> Sat on a curbstone shooting dice,
> Horse he turned and sat on the flea,
> "Oops" said the flea, "There's a horse on me!"

As a group, say the poem rhythmically. Then the poem can be performed using body percussion that will be transferred to instrument sounds. Students again are performing from a score. This activity can be modified to be challenging for K–sixth graders.

- Ask the students to select one or two words in each line and draw a circle around them.
- They then say the poem, snapping their fingers on the circled words.
- Do the same with one or two different words, this time drawing squares around the words.
- They say the poem, snapping fingers on circled words and clapping on squared words.
- Students pick a phrase to underline.
- They say the poem, snapping fingers, clapping, and adding pats on the knees on the underlined parts.
- Now they "say" the poem using only the body percussion. For success, everyone should "mouth" the words, but not say them out loud. By only doing the body percussion sounds on the appropriate words, a sound composition is created.
- Next ask the students to select instruments to substitute for the body percussion sounds. A hand drum could play the squared words, a triangle the circled words, temple blocks the underlined parts, or whatever the students want to select. (Borrow instruments from the music room, make instruments, or use found sounds from the room or home.)
- Say the poem as a group, adding the instruments on the appropriate words. Then play the "composition," mouthing the words, having only the instruments make the sounds.

CREATING

- Create an ABA composition (see page 38), instrument sounds only on A, and body percussion sounds only on B. Any combination of sounds can be created. Students arranged in groups can decide what ABA form they choose to perform.
- Add an ostinato—an underlying repeating accompaniment that plays throughout the composition—to make the creative experience more musical and cohesive.
- Insert an introduction and a coda to enhance the musical experience. One idea might be to take a small musical idea, change it very slightly, and include it at the beginning and end of the piece.
- On a different day, divide the class into three groups. Have Group 1 say the poem while Group 2 taps the steady beat and Group 3 claps the circled words. Substitute instruments for taps and claps.
- After any poem or song is learned, play the steady beat on drums, and the rhythm of the words on sticks.

PLAYING

Create and Perform a Rhythmic Composition

Organize instruments into the following categories of sounds:

Click	tone blocks, rhythm sticks
Jingle	sleigh bells, tambourines

Rattle	maracas
Scrape	guirro
Ring	finger cymbals, triangle
Membranic	drums

After categorizing the sounds, create a rhythmic composition with the class, using the ta | and te-te ∏ from the charts or the rhythm of the words from the chants. Designate which sounds will play the different rhythms. This activity can be adapted for all grade levels.

PLAYING

Pictures or color-coding (rattles are red, clicks are green, etc.) can indicate which instrument plays where. Students draw or highlight the rhythms with different colored markers, which direct students holding certain instruments when to play. It is like reading a code, and the mind becomes actively involved in this performance game. Use the rhythmic patterns to teach categories (fill in names of foods, fruits, cars, pet names, etc.). Students can see how words are divided into syllables as well as having good brainstorming practice.

Listening Activities: Perform Using a "Play Along" Map

LISTENING

"Play Along" listening maps are a wonderful way to involve intermediate students in performance. This experience allows the child to "become" part of the orchestra or band performing. It takes careful listening and accurate rhythm reading skills.

PLAYING

Read about the composer and the composition, and then listen to "The Stars and Stripes Forever" by Sousa while following the Listening Map. On a second listening, add different types of classroom rhythm instruments (woods, metals, etc.) or found sounds in a "play-along" experience while following the Listening Map.

The Composer

Sousa's father was a trombonist in the U.S. Marine Band, and he saw very early on that his son was very talented. He enlisted the 13-year-old John Philip in the Marine Band as an apprentice. In his late twenties, John became the conductor of the U.S. Marine Band, where he had learned so much in his teens. The Marine Band became one of the finest military bands in the world during the 12 years Sousa led it. Many of his marches were composed during this time. After leaving the Marine Corps, he formed his own band, which performed concerts around the world. Large audiences came to see "The March King" and his band. He always wore white gloves to conduct.

The Composition

"The Stars and Stripes Forever" is the best known and most often performed Sousa march. It is so popular in the United States that it is often included in the list of American national music selections and is called our official National March.

Listening Selection

I   March "The Stars and Stripes Forever" by Sousa   CD Track 18
Listening Map   Appendix, p. 267

PLAYING

Perform Layered Rhythms

This activity can be used with intermediate students.

Have a line of 12 beats

1 2 3 4 5 6 7 8 9 10 11 12

Make up patterns using the 12 beat line.

1 - - 4 - - 7 - - 10 - -

Students clap only on the numbers left in the pattern. Create a group of these lines and read straight through them.

- 2 3 - 5 6 - 8 9 - 11 12

1 2 - - 5 6 - - 9 10 - -

1 - 3 - 5 - 7 - 9 - 11 -

1 2 3 - 5 6 7 - 9 10 11 -

- 2 - 4 5 - 7 - 9 10 - 12

Assign different instruments (or body percussion and found sounds) for each line. Have a drum keep the steady beat. Layer the different instruments in, playing repeatedly the same line (as an *ostinato*). Get all the instruments playing the different patterns at the same time and it will sound much like African drumming patterns. This creates a fascinating *carpet of sound*, and can be a delightful accompaniment to the reading of African poems.

Perform Using a Grid

PLAYING

Students in 2nd grade and above levels are directed to place two beats in each box on the grid. All the boxes must be different. Use quarter notes (ta), eighth notes (te-te), half notes (ta-ah), half, quarter and eighth rests. Once the boxes are filled, read the grid from left to right. Then read it "bingo style," diagonally, and in reverse. Play instruments, assigning one instrument to each line.

CREATING

Full Class Student Activity

LISTENING

Listen to the Les Percussions de Guinée track from *Pulse: A Stomp Odyssey Soundtrack Album*. Discuss how the sound of this drum ensemble from the Republic of Guinea in West Africa compares to the class performance of Layered Rhythms.

Moving

Why We Should Involve Our Students in Moving

"When the music changes, so does the dance"

African proverb[9]

"Give me the beat, boys, and free my soul. I wanna get lost in your rock and roll."

Mentor Williams, composer of "Drift Away"[10]

Moving to music is a natural expression for students. In one activity with a group of third graders, the students were moving only certain body parts while listening to a very rhythmic selection. "Move only your hands," directed the teacher, while she encouraged the students to think of different ways to move their hands to the music.

The activity continued as the teacher would direct, "Move your hips" or knees or elbows or ears—the more outrageous, the better because it forced the students to think creatively. As the activity was going along, with the teacher continuing to suggest different body parts to move, one little girl named Mary Louise urgently requested in a loud voice, "Let my feet go, let my feet go!"

It was not normal behavior for Mary Louise to shout out in class, as she was a rather quiet, reserved child. This delightful activity was so all-encompassing to her body, mind, and spirit that she felt compelled to shout out her desire to "let go!"

87

The teacher does not have to be Fred Astaire or wear a leotard and tights with ballet slippers to include movement in the classroom. Using these "tried and true" games will work. Applying the label "game" is sometimes more successful for some students than the term "dance." Some teachers try games where the students do not hold hands with one another for beginning experiences, and that also proves to be successful.

MOVING

To Drum Sounds

1. Take a drum (borrow it from the music teacher or make one out of a coffee can) and play a steady beat. Have the primary students walk to the beat. Try to match the natural heartbeat speed of the students with the steady beat.

This is a locomotor movement. Locomotor movements include walking, skipping, running, trotting, tiptoeing, and gliding: any movement that goes somewhere. Think of a train locomotive moving down the track.

---

2. For this game, play two drums of differing sizes, one with a higher pitch. Tap a steady beat on the lower drum and ask the students to walk with bent knees. Tap a steady beat on the higher pitched drum, and ask the students to tiptoe to the beat. Alternate the sounds so the students must respond with their body as to what they are hearing.

   Low Low Low Low
   High High High High

   Mix up the patterns such as:

   High Low Low Low
   High Low High Low

3. If there is a drum with a metal part attaching the drumhead to the wooden body of the drum, play a steady beat on the drumhead and then tap the metal part in a steady beat, alternating wood and metal sounds. The students walk forward to the drumhead sound, and backward to the metal sound. They can also decide on different ways to walk to the metal sound—sideways, in a circle, with a partner, or whatever they decide can work.

> ## Teaching Tip
>
> These are wonderful activities for fillers in between lessons. When changing from math to reading time during the day, do one of these movement games. The change-of-pace activity brings a refreshing atmosphere to the classroom. The result for learning is rather amazing as well. The word "Recreation" can be read as "Re-Creation." Using movement games as "filler" activities helps the students re-create their attitudes and motivation for learning.

Also, this practice of using "filler" games keeps the amount of on-task time in the classroom especially high. Some classrooms are filled with dead time—when the students are sharpening pencils, getting out books, or lining up at the door to go outside. Making transitions into learning experiences by using movement games keeps the motivation elevated and maintains order in the classroom.

Other Sounds for Movement

MOVING

Not all movement has to be done with a drum. A variety of games that include movement can be used, some of which require very little space in the classroom.

Find a metal sound such as a cymbal or triangle or lid to a pot that when hit keeps on sounding. Have the primary students stand and "plant their feet" like trees with roots. Play the metal sound, and the students are directed to keep moving as long as the sound is heard. They can use arms, bend at the waist, twist the body, but the key to this movement game is to keep the feet from moving yet somehow keep the body moving as long as the sound is heard.

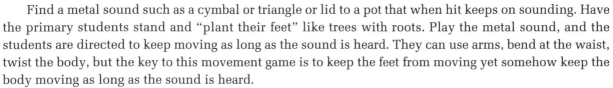

This movement is called a non-locomotor movement. Bending, swaying, twisting, reaching, and stretching are all examples. Non-locomotor movements do not move the body from one spot to another.

Teaching Tip

With movement activities, students may have to be taught to respond without "going wild." Often, they have been so rigid in school that any freedom is taken to the extremes. Learning self-discipline is an important life skill, and these games can promote students becoming self-disciplined learners.

Students enjoy these movement games, so setting the rules and keeping them will help maintain order in class. Having students "find their own space," not touching anyone, will offer a good start. Children who break the rules must sit down. No one wants to "sit" while the others are having fun.

Movement Games

MOVING

Mirroring

Mirroring is fun for students (see page 39). Students face a partner and decide which of the two will be the leader. When teacher plays the cymbal, the leader of the pair moves while the sound is heard, and the partner follows the leader, as in a mirror. After a few times moving to the sound, switch leaders. The rule is that they have to remain in their small spaces, as though facing a mirror that remains stationary. (Even turning around does not work.) Change this activity to have students use the "mirroring game" as they listen and move to music. Hit a drum when the leader should switch.

Walking the beat

Walking the beat of a poem is great fun for primary students. Tap a steady beat on an instrument such as a woodblock. After the students become good at walking the beat, have them "freeze" when the sound stops. Read the poem and tap the beat, stopping at unusual spots. The students must stop when the sound stops. Shel Silverstein's book *Where the Sidewalk Ends* (1974, HarperCollins) is a treasure-chest of poems.

Teddy Bear, Teddy Bear

MOVING

Old favorites such as "Teddy Bear, Teddy Bear" and other jump-rope songs and chants are good resources for primary movement games.

> Teddy bear, teddy bear, turn around,
> Teddy bear, teddy bear, touch the ground.
> Teddy bear, teddy bear, hands up high,
> Teddy bear, teddy bear, reach the sky.

Songbook Selection

Appendix

P	"Teddy Bear, Teddy Bear" Traditional	190

I Had a Loose Tooth

MOVING

Another popular game for primary students goes with the poem "I Had a Loose Tooth" (attributed to several different authors). Students love this game because they relate to losing teeth. Say the poem while having the students walk to a steady beat. A drumbeat can be added to reinforce the steady beat, but it isn't a requirement. Make sure the students walk in random paths around the room, not in a big circle like a mixing bowl.

> I had a loose tooth, a wiggly, jiggly loose tooth.
> I had a loose tooth, hanging by a thread.
> So I pulled my loose tooth, this wiggly, jiggly loose tooth.
> And put it 'neath the pillow when I went up to bed.
> The fairies took my loose tooth, my wiggly, jiggly loose tooth.
> So now I have a nickel and a hole in my head.

After the students are very comfortable walking to the steady beat of the poem, raise the difficulty level. Every time "loose tooth" is said in the poem, the students must turn and walk in a different direction. Practice this several times, watching for the students to become more proficient at listening and changing movements at the correct point in the poem.

Next add in another requirement to the game. In addition to turning on "loose tooth," have the students make their body wiggle and jiggle on the words "wiggly, jiggly." Again, practice this part of the game, observing the students walk a steady beat, turn, and go in a different direction on "loose tooth" and wiggle and jiggle at the appropriate time. This doesn't seem particularly difficult, but moving, listening, and doing all the different parts of the game requires concentration, decision-making and self-discipline.

Finally, on "hole in my head," add the last movement requirement. When the students hear the words "hole in my head," have them tap hand on their heads rhythmically to the words.

This poem is a reinforcement for discovering rhyming words and repeating words, and it is simply a charming activity for having a great time in class!

Folk Dances

Folk dances are a wonderful way to bring culturally relevant experiences into the classroom. Find and teach folk dances from America, other countries, and other cultures. Appropriate folk dances can be found for K–sixth grade students.

Full Class Student Activity

Add a grapevine dance to Israeli folksong "Havah Nagilah."

Directions: Step right—step behind right foot with left foot. Step-hop on right foot while swinging left foot in front of the right foot. Step-hop left, and swing right foot in front of the left foot. Begin pattern again. This is a six-beat pattern for music that is in sets of four.

MOVING

Songbook Selection

Get America Singing. . .Again!

I   "Havah Nagilah" Israeli folk song   21

SINGING

An excellent resource to use with folk dancing is the New England Dancing Masters series.[11] These are wonderful books with CDs of folk and other types of dances. The "Chimes of Dunkirk" and "Listen to the Mockingbird" include early American, some Canadian, and some English dances. There is an excellent library of YouTube online dances to go with these books.

More Folk Dance Music for Kids and Teachers by Sanna Longden has a variety of enjoyable ethnic dances for all levels of learners of folk dances.[12]

Tantalizing Tidbit of Research

Phyllis Weikart, an expert on movement and learning, believes that movement is important in language development with students. Her research[13] indicated a link between a child's ability to clap a steady beat and success in language learning. Here are interesting findings from her study done in the late 1990s:

Students who were competent with steady beat, in comparison with those who were not, tended to perform better in reading comprehension and math; and they had clearer enunciation and speech flow, better attending abilities, higher levels of coordination.

Weikart (2002)[14]

Learning to Move to the Beat

MOVING

Through her research and publications, Phyllis Weikart[15] has designed steps to use in helping students learn to move successfully. She recommends incorporating these strategies with teaching students movement:

- Say and do the movement.
- Whisper and do the movement.
- Think and do the movement.

Thus, if students were being taught the step–step–bend–bend movement pattern, they would be instructed to do the movements as they say the words aloud. Then the students would progress to doing the step–step–bend–bend movement pattern and whispering the words. Finally, they would "think" the words as they do the movement.

Additionally, Phyllis Weikart's research suggests that both hands patting the knees at the same time in a steady beat is less difficult and therefore more successful than alternating hands on the knees. Thus, early experiences with steady beat should include activities in which the students pat their knees with both hands. As they become more proficient, begin with the alternating hands activity. Students will be keeping the beat as they pat right hand on right knee, left hand on left knee, keeping the pattern "right–left–right–left."

Marching can be a difficult movement for some students. Sometimes going through hand movement games prepares the child for greater success with the large motor skills required in marching. Such an idea will be reversed planning for many teachers.

Often, even with very young students, a typical classroom scenario includes the teacher playing a music CD and directing the students to "march around the room to the music." By using the Weikart research, the students should be taught to keep a steady beat by patting hands on knees before they are instructed to use the legs with marching. Then, when they do start to learn to march, having the child say and do, whisper and do, then think and do sets the stage for more successful movement experiences.

It is interesting that what is very simple for some students, such as marching to a steady beat, presents a struggle for others. By teaching the "right" research-driven method, a child can be successful in learning to move, and can be spared the frustration often resulting from "not knowing how" to move to the music.

Thinking It Through

Elementary classroom educators work closely with parents, interacting with them often throughout the school year. Communicating effectively with parents is critical in soliciting their support of their child's learning. In a small group, pick singing, playing or moving and draft a parent letter describing a few specific classroom activities and giving the importance of these music activities you are using in your classrooms.

Suggestions for Further Study

Read two articles on singing with children:

"A Responsibility to Young Voices" (1986) by Peggy Bennett. Published in the *Music Educators Journal*, 73.
"The Benefits of Vocal Exploration" (1993) by Madeline S. Bridges. Published in *General Music Today*, 6.

Examine *Tunes and Grooves for Music Education* (2007) by Patricia Sheehan Campbell, published by Prentice Hall to find interesting information and wonderful songs from around the world including Africa, Asia, and the Americas.

Read *Movement in Steady Beat* (2002, 2nd edition) by Phyllis Weikart, published by High Court Press. Also, find a favorite movement activity to use with students in *85 Engaging Movement Activities, Learning on the Move, K-6 Series* (2002) by Phyllis Weikart, published by Delmar Cengage Learning.

Recommended Student Books

Auch, Mary Jane. (1997). *Bantam of the Opera.* New York: Holiday House.
Luigi the Rooster gets his chance to sing Rigoletto when the star tenor and understudy both come down with the chickenpox.

Bynum, Eboni and Jackson, Roland. (2004). *Jamari's Drum.* (B. W. Diakite, Illus.). Toronto: Groundwood Books.
An African boy saves his village by playing the djembe.

Carlson, Nancy. (2006). *Harriet's Recital.* Minneapolis: Carolrhoda Books.
About a dog that didn't want to dance in her recital but then ended up loving the experience.

Reich, Susanna. (1999). *Clara Schumann: Piano Virtuoso.* New York: Clarion Books.
A biography of the child prodigy.

Ryan, Pam Munoz. (2002). *When Marion Sang.* (B. Selznick, Illus.). New York: Scholastic.
Tells the poignant story of Marian Anderson.

CHAPTER 6 | CREATING

What is Creativity?

According to Robert Harris in his book *Creative Problem Solving: A Step-by-Step Approach*,[4] creativity involves three components:

- An Ability. A simple definition is that creativity is the ability to imagine or invent something new.
- An Attitude. Creativity is also an attitude—the ability to accept change and newness, a willingness to play with ideas and possibilities, a flexibility of outlook, the habit of enjoying the good, while looking for ways to improve it.
- A Process. Creative people work hard and continually to improve ideas and solutions, by making gradual alterations and refinements to their works.

Everyone has substantial creative ability, especially children. Often all that's needed to be creative is to take the time for it.

The Creative Experience

Creating New Words to Familiar Songs (Piggyback Songs)

Using TV theme songs, create new words to the tunes. These new "theme songs" will be used to gather students for different activities during the day. For example, the *Bat Man* theme could have the words:

CREATING

SINGING

> Math Time!
> Time to get our books and pencils; don't forget the paper either,
> Math Time!
> We are learning long division; we are getting good at reason,
> Math Time!

Students can sing the words as they get their books out and find the page in the book. By using music to "set the stage" for learning, the atmosphere in the classroom will be more inviting for engagement in math activities. Eric Jensen[5] states "Music in the curriculum, both as a subject of study and as accompaniment to the learning process, may be a valuable tool for the integration of thinking across both hemispheres of the brain." What a wonderful combination! Learning and Music!

Partner Student Activity

Write Your Own Piggyback Song[6]

With a partner, write your own piggyback song on a given subject. Choose a familiar song or TV theme song. Brainstorm all the words/ideas for your assigned topic. Arrange these words to fit the rhythm of the tune you picked—counting out and matching the number of syllables in each line works best. Try to "make sense" with the words you picked. Mark the spots where rhyming words occur and match your verses to this pattern. Sing it! (Examples of subjects are given on teachers' website: www.routledge.com/textbooks/9780415878234)

Elementary students are naturally creative. They look at their world without limitations. A child thinks "what if" or "why not" rather than "you can't do that." As a result, guiding students into creative activities and encouraging creative expression should be natural, normal, and vital components of the elementary curriculum. Such creative experiences can lead students into problem-solving approaches to thinking, establishing patterns of cognition that will prove beneficial to them throughout their lives.

Many adults believe that they are not creative. They will adamantly declare that they possess not even a hint of creativity in their whole beings. Often an adult will jokingly describe the lack of creative ability with statements such as "I can't even draw stick figures." Some think to be creative means taking a photograph chosen to hang in a gallery, or performing on a stage in front of a large audience, or making a hot-selling DVD, or painting the Sistine Chapel ceiling, or composing the Ninth Symphony, which is all true. However, creative thinking is also choosing a blouse to wear with a skirt different from the one usually picked, or deciding on additional ingredients to add to a recipe for using ground meat. It means looking at issues in different ways. Creative thinking means coming up with several different solutions to a problem.

Creating Visual Guides To Music

To help students understand new songs more easily and to incorporate other learning modalities, a visual guide—a song map—can be created. These maps help students sing with heightened awareness, thus understanding more about what they hear in the music. Review the song maps (used in Chapter 5) in the Appendices.

Student Project (partner)

Create a Song Map

With a partner, create your own song map. Choose a song from the songbook. Create one of the following:

- A steady beat tapping map
- A key word or phrase map

Use the examples in the book as models.

Simple Student Activities Requiring Creative Responses

In primary classes, these can be done in cooperative learning groups or individually.

- Explore three ways to play an instrument.
- Think of three ways to clap hands.
- Find three different sound sources in our classroom that can be played.
- Walk to the door a different way.
- Find three ways to make a circle with your body.
- Make the first letter of your name with your body.

Creating with Body Percussion

Full Class Student Activity

Listen to the Rooftop track from *Pulse: A Stomp Odyssey Soundtrack Album*. Identify the different body percussion sounds that are used by the group Stomp in this performance.

Using levels of body percussion sounds for composition and accompaniment patterns can be another creative venture for students. Make a four-line staff, where the top line is to be the "snap" sound, the second line the "clap" sound, and so forth. Notate the sound patterns by placing Xs on the lines, using the plan of four sounds in a grouping, or measure.

CREATING

PLAYING

Snap __x_____	x__x_____		
Clap _____x_____		x____x___x_	
Pat _____x_____	x___x_____		
Stamp _____x_		x_____	

The students can create many different patterns and perform them. They can sing a song while performing the patterns as they sing, which is quite demanding, rather like mental aerobics! They can number the different patterns, and then perform number "143," which is really groups 1 and 4 and 3 played as a set.

Telling the students "There are 28 [the number of students in the class] students in our class, and there can be 28 different compositions [or answers or examples], all correct" is an interesting thought for them. All of us can be right, and all different.

Some writers on creativity believe that everyone is capable of being creative, although some individuals have had "blocks" placed on their thinking. Incidences in life happen that leave individuals feeling that they are not creative. When a teacher says not to color the chicken blue, the child's creative decision-making is being blocked. Even though students are genuinely very creative, life experiences and statements from others tend to crush the creative spirit. Picasso said, "It took me four years to paint like Raphael, but a lifetime to paint like a child."

The Future

Daniel Pink, in his best-selling book *A Whole New Mind: Why Right-Brainers Will Rule the Future*[7] states that "The future belongs to a very different kind of person with a very different kind of mind. The era of 'left-brain' dominance, and the Information Age that it engendered, are giving way to a new world in which 'right-brain' qualities—inventiveness, empathy, meaning—predominate." Our world now demands creative thinking in the work place. Mr. Pink continues in his book to call for enhanced use of instruction in music and art in schools in order to expand students' right-brain abilities.

An interesting note on creative thinking and college preparedness involves Robert J. Sternberg, an American psychologist and psychometrician and the Dean of Arts and Sciences at Tufts University. He developed a test for high school students to be used with the SAT called the Rainbow Project Assessment.[8] The Rainbow Project Assessment was developed in collaboration with the College Board and gives scores for analytical, practical, and creative thinking. It has been found to double accurate prediction of freshman-year performance, and also very substantially reduce differences in scores between ethnic groups.

For our students to be able to contribute positively as adults, creative thinking is a necessity. In addition to workplace demands, few aspects of life are "black and white" or have "one right answer." Consider these questions:

- Should I buy a house, or rent one, or move into an apartment?
- Should I buy a new car, or a used one, or lease a car?
- Should I sell the car and use mass transit?

- Should I replace the electric heater with gas?
- Should I refinance now or wait?

All of these questions have many possible answers, all of which might be correct at a given time.

The ability to solve problems and think with a "what if" slant to mental reasoning is a valuable and sought-after skill, and a required ability for living successfully in the world of the 21st century.

No longer can a child memorize enough facts to succeed in life. This child must be able to think creatively. Cancer cures will come from someone thinking creatively. Researchers must learn to examine situations from many different vantage points. The elementary teacher is teaching tomorrow's adults, the keepers of the flame, the voters who will decide on issues that will influence our world. These leaders of tomorrow must be provided with tools to help them grow up and successfully take their place in society. They need to be given innumerable opportunities during their elementary schooling to think in creative ways.

Tantalizing Tidbit of Research

Research conducted between 1987 and 1998 on young people participating in the arts for at least three hours on three days of each week throughout at least one full year demonstrated the following. They were:

- four times more likely to have been recognized for academic achievement;
- being elected to class office within their schools more than three times as often;
- four times more likely to participate in a math and science fair;
- three times more likely to win an award for school attendance;
- four times more likely to win an award for writing an essay or poem.

Dr. Shirley Brice Heath, Stanford University, for Carnegie
Foundation for The Advancement of Teaching[9]

The Creative Process

Process in Preference to Product

The following activities are designed to spur creative thinking skills in elementary students. One important key for teaching creative activities is to remember this:

PROCESS is more important than PRODUCT.

The teacher should be more concerned that the students have many opportunities to think and act creatively,[10] rather than being overly concerned with the resulting poem or painting or word choice. Often the product is not particularly memorable, and will probably not "live through the test of time." The more important aspect is that the child had the experience of being involved in the creative process.

Torrance Levels of Creative Thinking

E. Paul Torrance,[11] an early researcher in gifted education and creative thinking, developed a list of levels to move through in encouraging creative thinking.

1. *Fluent*   Letting the ideas flow
     The first, or lowest, level of creative thinking

2. *Flexible*   Changing ideas, bending ideas
     The second level of creative thinking

3. *Original*   Creating new ideas
     The third level of creative thinking

4. *Elaborative*   Refining the ideas
     Trying different approaches
     The fourth level of creative thinking

5. *Evaluative*   Asking "what is correct" and "what could be improved"
     Evaluating the work
     The fifth and highest level of creative thinking

Teaching Tip

In using these Torrance steps or levels with children, start with *words*, a secure area.

Sample Class Composition

One topic to which students will readily respond is breakfast cereals.

CREATING

1. Have the students name different breakfast cereals, writing the brand names and noting them with "ta" and "te-te" on the board. (*Fluent*) The list will be long and varied because elementary students know many different brand names, thanks to the cereal aisle at the grocery store and Saturday morning cartoons.

    One way for all the students to participate is to go down the line, or around the circle, having each child name a cereal. If choosing this plan, institute the "PASS" rule. If a child cannot think of a cereal to name, they say "Pass" and the game moves to the next child. This frees the students to think without pressure. The teacher should not comment on any student's contributions during this part of the activity. By saying, "Oh, what an interesting comment" to one child, the response from all the others tends to be, "I can't think of anything that good!" or "John is her favorite. Wonder why she likes him best?" Of course, these thoughts squeeze out the creative thinking, where the emphasis of the activity is really intended. By commenting on one child, the free flow of ideas has been limited for most of the others.

2. Next, have the students arrange the words from the list into a rhyme or chant. In changing the ideas from a list of words on the board into a poem, a higher level of creativity is reached. (*Flexible*)

Have the students turn the words into rhythms. "Grape-Nuts" becomes two eighth notes followed by a quarter rest, or a quarter rest followed by two eighth notes. In general, words with two syllables become eighth notes; words with one syllable become quarter notes.

3. Have the students clap the rhythm patterns, or clap the first line, snap the second line, pat the third, and stamp the fourth line. (Choosing the word "stamp" rather than "stomp" will produce a better sound from the class.) The list of words now is evolving into a rhythmic sound composition. It is no longer a list or words or a chant. It is a sound composition. (*Original*)

4. Have the students transform the sound composition into an ABA or a rondo form (see page 38). This could be done by the full class or by small groups.

    • One could use body percussion for A and the words for B.
    • Add an introduction and a coda. Use dynamics at some point in the composition.
    • Try different ideas, deciding which ones seem to work best. (*Elaborative*)

5. Record the sound composition. Listen to it as a group. Have the students decide what is good about it and how it could be improved. (*Evaluative*)

    • Asking questions such as "What sounded especially good?" helps students point out the best parts.
    • Asking, "How could we improve?" or "Where are our weaker parts?" still is phrased positively, but focuses on areas for improvement.

Teaching Tip

It is very important to help children discover the positive. They tend to focus only on the problem spots, rather than recognize that many good points were achieved.

Compositional Formula

One way to have students be successful in a creative assignment is to use a compositional formula. While there are many formulas that could be used, here is one idea of how this might be done. It will establish some requirements, set some limits, and will function as a tool for stimulating the creative experience.

• Use a form (ABA, theme and variations, rondo—see Chapter 3)
• Include dynamics in the composition
• Have an introduction
• End with a coda
• Add an ostinato

Although *the process is much more important than the product*, having the addition of an ostinato tends to hold the piece together.

To review, an ostinato is an underlying repeating rhythmic pattern. A boogie-woogie bass is a type of ostinato. A handclap pattern performed by several students can serve as an ostinato. Repeating phrases of sounds or words can be an ostinato. In a "cereal" composition, the words *snap, crackle, pop* followed by a finger snap can be performed over and over by a group of students as the rest of the composition is performed, somewhat "on top" of the ostinato, by the remainder of the students. This ostinato should be softer dynamically than the composition.

An introduction is something that goes before. It could be the ostinato performed a designated number of times before the composition starts. It could be four students tapping a drum eight beats, or a musical phrase sung or hummed. Whatever the composer decides is correct.

A coda is an ending. The word literally means "tail" in Italian. Again, the ostinato could be repeated several times, gradually getting softer (decrescendo). Or a loud hit on a drum could end the piece. Tell the students, "Remember, you are the composer. Whatever you choose is correct. How should we finish it?"

Sample Formula Composition

Introduction: States in the U. S. States in the U. S. (repeat 2×)

Ostinato: Continue repeating the Introduction (*piano*)

A Section: Al -a -ba-ma, New Jer-sey, Co-lo-ra-do, Maine;

Speak softly

Tex-as, Ok-la-ho-ma, Ar-kan-sas, Kan-sas.

B Section: U-ni-ted States of A – mer – i – ca!

(repeat 2× with a crescendo)

A Section: Repeat A section, *forte*

Coda: All shout, at the direction of the conductor, "America!"

Using Technology to Create Musically

Educating 21st-century children involves stepping up the use of technology to teach them. We don't know what the future looks like, but we do know it will be technology rich.

Adding Accompaniments to Poetry

CREATING

Using GarageBand, a program installed on Macintosh computers, students can record and mix their own songs. By using the built-in microphone on most computers, a teacher can have students read poems of their choice or ones they have written into the GarageBand program. Then using the loops of musical sounds performed on many different instruments that are included in the program, students can create musical accompaniments for the poems to enhance the poetry performances. The experience of choosing which musical loops to include involves every aspect of creative thinking.

Furthermore, voices or instruments (guitar, recorder, etc.) can be recorded using either the built-in microphone or, for better quality, a professional microphone plugged into a USB or Firewire audio interface (http://m-audio.com). A USB (piano) keyboard controller or the musical typing function in the program can also be used to create original melodies and accompaniment.

Adding Soundtracks to Movies

CREATING

GarageBand can also be useful in adding soundtracks to student- or teacher-produced movies. John Maklary, experienced Tech Coordinator at K-8 school in Houston, Texas, designed a project where still pictures from the internet were put into a PowerPoint program. These pictures can have titles and script added as needed for clarification. Then the PowerPoint can be moved into the iMovie program. This movie can then be moved into GarageBand, or vice versa, and loops of sound or recorded instruments can be added as a soundtrack. The experience of choosing which musical loops to include in order to enhance the story-telling aspects of the movie involves every aspect of creative thinking.

PC users can also take advantage of music creation possibilities. These applications are examples of software that will do much of what GarageBand does for Mac users.

Pro Tools M-Powered 8	www.m-audio.com/index.php?do=products.main&ID=9651226c4dacf85d4d6a5377d29c4eb5
MixCraft	www.acoustica.com/mixcraft/index.htm
Sony Acid Music Studio	www.sonycreativesoftware.com/musicstudio

Student Compositions

CREATING

An easy-to-use program that allows individuals or small groups of students to create musical compositions is included as part of the Music Ace Deluxe[12] software package. The creative Music Doodle Pad allows students to easily compose and hear their own musical creations using a variety of instrumental sounds. Students can also listen to and modify popular music selections from the Jukebox section of the Music Doodle Pad. The rest of the program covers all the basics of music theory, rhythm, pitch, note reading, and listening. This computer software would be excellent to use in a center for students to explore creating their own music.

Creating Music is a free children's online creative music environment. It's a place for kids to compose music, play with musical performance, music games, and music puzzles. Discover fun and easy ways to make music (www.creatingmusic.com)!

Thinking It Through

In a small group, discuss ways in which you think that business and everyday life might soon be dominated by right-brain thinkers. Explore ideas on expanding your right brain.

Brainstorm with your group on how a YouTube video could be effectively used in a lesson for elementary students.

Suggestions for Further Study

Learn more about ideas presented in this chapter by reading these important authors:

A Whole New Mind: Why Right-Brainers Will Rule the Future (2006) by Daniel H. Pink, published by Riverhead Trade.

Brain-Based Learning: The New Paradigm of Teaching (2008, 2nd edition) by Eric Jensen, published by Corwin Press.

Why And How To Teach Music Composition (2003) by Maud Hickey and Bennett Reimer, published by Rowman and Littlefield.

Explore online music resources:

- Ning.com
- Noteflight
- Tuneblocks
- Drumsteps

Recommended Student Books

Falconer, Ian. (2006). *Olivia Forms a Band.* New York: Atheneum Books for Young Readers.
A piglet and her mother get creative on the day of a fireworks show.

Henry, Sandi. (1999). *Kids Art Works!: Creating With Color, Design, Texture & More.* (N. Martin-Jourdenais, Illus.). Charlotte, VT: Williamson Publishing.
Intermediate students will enjoy making simple creative projects to display. Information about famous artists also included.

Legge, Anne. (2008). *Veggie Friends and Fruits Too: A Children's Cookbook on Creating Healthy Snacks.* Booksurge.
Encouraging children's creativity by working with fruits and vegetables to create healthy snacks.

SECTION III | INTEGRATING MUSIC INTO THE CURRICULUM

Integrating music into the curriculum allows teachers to address the specific elements and concepts inherent in each subject area while facilitating student learning through larger concepts. According to Dr. Sue Snyder, and linking back to the Multiple Intelligences theory of Howard Gardner (see Chapter 2), true integration occurs most successfully in an integrated unit of study with a broad theme or concept that crosses disciplines "so each content area or intelligence can explore the theme in a meaningful way. The integrity of each intelligence or discipline is maintained."[1]

The activities in the following chapters use different integration approaches. For example, music is used to assist memory (e.g., piggyback songs, Chapter 7) as well as being used as one lens through which to explore a topic (e.g, Impressionism, Chapter 11). These approaches make the point that music is important as a form of knowledge in its own right, but can also be used to enhance learning in other subjects.

Facts seem to be learned and retained amazingly well using rhythmic speech and song. The *School House Rock* television series demonstrated this, and so does the long-running educational television icon *Sesame Street*. Many people learned their alphabet to the tune of "Twinkle, Twinkle Little Star."

As a side benefit of using music activities in instruction, engaging the children with music transforms learning from a "task to be done" into something memorable and fun. Through lessons incorporating music, students learn to acquire knowledge that becomes more relevant and significant to them individually.

Music has the component of "fun." We "play" an instrument to make it sound. Children learn better when they are comfortable and enjoying themselves. A favorite saying is "Jump for Joy, Dance and Sing, Music is a Wonderful Thing!"

When the wise teacher draws on music to help teach other subjects, newness weaves into the material to be learned. Music eases into the mind, helping bring freshness and originality to a learning task, and the brain makes connections in new ways.

Music rejuvenates the learning experience; it adds "umph" to the lesson; it supercharges the learning! Music is a key to opening doors to successfully reach children. Read the next chapters to learn how to teach classroom subjects more effectively!

Elementary teachers use integrated curriculum, whole language, and interdisciplinary learning in their classes. But often these approaches to learning are not extended to the arts. Including music activities in every subject that is taught? Certainly, but with a warning label attached! *Be sure to fasten a seat beat as the learning takes off."*

Tantalizing Tidbits of Research

Recent studies show that students who study the arts are more successful on standardized tests such as the SAT. Students who take four years of art and music classes while in high school score 85 points better on their SATs than students who took only one-half year or less (scores of 1,063 vs. 978, respectively). These scores reflect the Critical Reading and Mathematics portions of the SAT only. In the new Writing section of the test, students with four years of art and music classes averaged 523 on the Writing portion of the test—52 points higher than students with one-half year or less of art/music classes (471).

The College Board (2008) College-Bound Seniors: Total Group Profile Report[2]

There is now a strong body of evidence based on meta-analyses of a broad range of studies, which establishes positive significant associations between music and:

- spatial-temporal reasoning (Hetland 2000)
- achievement in math (Vaughn 2000)
- achievement in reading (Butzlaff 2000)
- the reinforcement of social-emotional or behavioral objectives (Standley 1996).

Critical Links: Learning in the Arts and Student Academic and Social Development (2002)[3]

If the arts help define our path to the future, they need to become curriculum partners with other subject disciplines in ways that will allow them to contribute their own distinctive richness and complexity to the learning process as a whole.

Burton, Horowitz, and Abeles (1999)[4]

A collection of research finds that learning in the arts may be uniquely able to boost learning and achievement for young children, students from economically disadvantaged circumstances, and students needing remedial instruction.

Critical Links: Learning in the Arts and Student Academic and Social Development (2002)

Use the following chapters to assist in writing the Integrated Unit described below as a final project. Ideas for integrated activities are given for each subject area. Use these ideas as a springboard to create new teaching materials.

Small Group Student Activity

Integrated Unit[5]

In a group of three, write an Integrated Unit and present it to the class: five days with three lessons per day (Music, Language Arts, Other) developed around one theme. Each lesson will have a music component.

Sample lessons included in Appendices. (Rubric on teachers' website: www.routledge.com/textbooks/9780415878234)

In an Integrated Unit, a broad theme or concept is chosen which cuts across disciplines, so each content area can explore the theme in a meaningful way.

CHAPTER 7 | USING MUSIC TO ENHANCE LEARNING IN LANGUAGE ARTS

Why We Should Involve Our Students in Musical Language Arts Activities

"Music and language share many attributes. Both are primarily auditory-based forms of communication."

Daniel J. Levitin and Anna K. Tirovolas, McGill University[1]

"Early musical training helps develop brain areas involved in language and reasoning. It is thought that brain development continues for many years after birth. Recent studies have clearly indicated that musical training physically develops the part of the left side of the brain known to be involved with processing language, and can actually wire the brain's circuits in specific ways."

Benefits of Music Education[2]

"The limits of my language mean the limits of my world."

Ludwig Wittgenstein, Austrian-British philosopher[3]

"Music is the universal language of humankind."

Henry Wadsworth Longfellow, American educator and poet[4]

Creating Activities

Creating with Music and Children's Literature

The incredible range of literature available to use with children is a rich storehouse for the elementary classroom teacher. Beautifully illustrated books on every conceivable topic line the shelves of most elementary school libraries. These books can become the catalysts that open pathways to a great variety of learning experiences for the elementary child.

Exciting opportunities await the teacher who begins a lesson with a child's book. Part of the fun of using children's literature in the elementary class is watching how the learning evolves and grows. A lesson on social studies may expand into a creativity lesson. Another lesson geared to teaching multicultural awareness may develop into a session on musical compositions. A song added to a book read for sheer pleasure may awaken a link to reading that lasts a lifetime.

Students can practice using the musical elements of dynamics and tempo, as well as different vocal registers, when retelling favorite fairy tales. For example, in *The Three Little Pigs*, using high, medium, and low registers for the voices of the different pigs and the Wolf can develop flexibility in the students' voices. Saying one pig's lines quickly and softly and the Wolf's lines slowly and loudly contributes to an understanding of tempo and dynamics. Try this approach with other favorite stories, poems, chants, and finger plays.

Musical instruments can also be effective tools for emphasizing the actions of characters in children's stories. Children enjoy using sticks, drums, maracas, and other rhythm instruments to imitate story characters running, marching, climbing, walking, and falling. Using melody instruments such as a small bell set or recorder to sound one or more tones or play a run up or down at important moments in the story can enhance the reading of any story or poem.

A recent study[5] was conducted in London which found that children with dyslexia and other reading delays often had difficulty perceiving rhythm in words and sounds. The suggested music activities in this chapter can help strengthen a child's ability to hear rhythm patterns in written and spoken text. It's a fun and engaging way to teach, it addresses the needs of kinesthetic learners, and it promotes interest in reading.

Tantalizing Tidbit of Research

Correlations exist between music training and both reading acquisition and sequence learning. One of the central predictors of early literacy, phonological awareness, is correlated with both music training and the development of a specific brain pathway.

Learning, Arts, and the Brain (2008)[6]

Creating Musical Links to Reading

Music helps build the very basic foundation for learning to read. Children throughout the years have learned the alphabet by singing "The Alphabet Song" to the tune of "Twinkle Twinkle Little Star." Often they think "LMNO" or "LMNOP" is one word because they sing the song that way. By slowing down the singing and by having a child point to the alphabet as they sing, this misconception will be clarified, as the children realize that L is a separate letter, M is a separate letter, and so forth.

By displaying the words to songs sung in class on a chart or on sentence strips in a holder, children are encouraged to read as they sing. We know from the brain research noted above and other studies that music helps children learn. Music helps their brains make connections, it is affective learning that helps them like to learn, and it helps them hear the rhythm of speech. Reading music (simple rhythms, etc.) reinforces many of the concepts necessary for the fluid reading of language. The concepts of left to right, moving to the next row, and especially "reading forward" (keeping the eyes moving ahead in order to perform rhythmically as a group) are great reinforcements of reading skills for the young child.

It also helps them learn to sequence, to learn rhyming words, to understand syllabication, and to learn phonemic awareness. Words are made aurally, and a key to learning to read is to become aware of the sounds associated with reading.

Why would anyone try to teach reading without using music?

Catalysts to Creativity

Grade Levels	K–4th
Language Arts Objective[1]	**3.** Students apply a wide range of strategies to comprehend, interpret, evaluate, and appreciate texts.
Music Objective[2]	**3. Content Standard: Improvising melodies, variations, and accompaniments** d. Students improvise short songs and instrumental pieces, using a variety of sound sources, including traditional sounds, nontraditional sounds available in the classroom, body sounds, and sounds produced by electronic means

1 IRA/NCTE Standards for the English Language Arts
2 NATIONAL MUSIC STANDARDS, MENC

The objectives found in the boxes throughout the following chapters are taken from nationally accepted standards in each subject, and are examples of how the activities given are fulfilling objectives in the various subject areas. These objectives provide a dual focus for these lessons, one concept for each subject.

The sounds suggested in children's books can come alive with music instruction. Sounds can accompany the story, turn into music, and even become compositions themselves as the children develop musically. For example, *Brown Bear, Brown Bear, What Do You See?* and *Polar Bear, Polar Bear, What Do You Hear?* both by Bill Martin, Jr., are excellent books for having young children add sounds associated with words in the text. These books clearly use repetition and contrast to enable children to choose appropriate sounds. The children see the picture of an animal such as a lion and add a body percussion or instrumental sound, creating a sound composition as they go through the book. As extensions of this lesson, the class can research information about bears such as their habitats and different types of bears as well as bears represented in art. A trip to the zoo with pictures drawn by the children of the animals could become the class's own book about *Animal, Animal, What Do You Hear?* or *Where Do You Live?* or *What Do You Eat?*

CREATING

LISTENING

Teaching Tip

The words to *Brown Bear, Brown Bear* can be sung to the tune of "Twinkle, Twinkle Little Star."

109

PLAYING

After reading a book such as *Where the Wild Things Are* by Maurice Sendak, ask the children to think of places in the story for adding sounds. This story of Max, an adventurous boy sent to his room by his mother, suggests interesting sounds. After sharing the children's ideas, read the book again with class members making the sounds in appropriate places. Next suggest that the body percussion sounds can transfer to percussion instruments and have the children select instruments to make the sounds. The tone block or sticks may become the sound of Max running, while the wind chime may represent the sound of the ocean.

The instrument selection process should be a learning experience. Rather than selecting the instrument that makes the sound most like the character or event in the story, children tend to pick their favorite instruments. Using this criterion, a child might pick cymbals to make the sound of a snowflake. Guiding the students in selecting appropriate instruments is a music lesson in itself, often one that requires persuasive teaching.

After choosing instruments, read the story again, this time with the children adding the instrument sounds. Finally, tell the story using only sounds. Tape the sound story and listen to the composition as a class. Ask questions such as "What did you feel was effective about this composition?" and "If you could do this again, would you do anything differently and why?" The evaluation process is a valuable part of this learning experience, requiring the children to use higher level thinking skills.

Creating Sound Compositions

Creating sound compositions is another use of children's books. These compositions can range from the very simple, as in *Brown Bear, Brown Bear, What Do You See?*, to more extended compositions. *The Jolly Postman*, by Janet and Allan Ahlberg, can lead to a delightful rondo.

CREATING

Rondo, a type of ABACA form. The returning A section occurs three or four times.

The book is written as a series of letters delivered by the postman to famous storybook characters. One class using the rondo approach had the postman as the A section. The postman's section had a recurring ostinato pattern that reminded the listener of a rickety bicycle wheel. The contrasting sections forming the rondo included the letter to the wicked witch as the B section, the letter from Jack to the giant as the C section, and Cinderella's letter as the D section.

The witch's letter was portrayed with cackling sounds made by a combination of metal and wooden percussion instruments. The giant's letter was composed of heavy walking sounds, as if made by the ponderous foot of the big fellow. Cinderella's letter had a magical, twinkly quality created by using metal percussion sounds. The resulting rondo told the story, but in a different way.

Creating Musical Poetry

Poems can be presented as choral readings by the full class to practice using the musical elements of tempo, dynamics, high and low vocal registers, and thick versus thin textures. Choose a poem that relates to a theme or subject being taught. Teach the poem by phrase, using the echo method. Use a variety of dynamic levels such as soft (*piano*), loud (*forte*), and gradually louder (*crescendo*). Help the students try out different vocal registers for different parts of the poem. Find the best steady beat tempo for the poem. Is there a section where the tempo should change? To explore thick versus thin texture, ask if there is a section or line of the poem that would be more dramatic if one voice spoke the line, then a few more joined in repeating it until the full class was involved.

Add instruments or body percussion to the choral reading. Ideas to explore could include playing on every noun, playing on every verb, and playing different sounds for different punctuation marks. Or try replacing certain words with sounds that reflect that word or character.

Creating Enhanced Reading Activities

Rhythm in Language: "Swamp Beat" lesson

Grade Levels	K–4th
Language Arts Objective[1]	**9.** Students develop an understanding of and respect for diversity in language use, patterns, and dialects across cultures, ethnic groups, geographic regions, and social roles.
Music Objective[2]	**4. Content Standard:** Composing and arranging music within specified guidelines.
	Achievement Standard:
	Students a. create and arrange music to accompany readings or dramatizations

1 IRA/NCTE Standards for the English Language Arts
2 NATIONAL MUSIC STANDARDS, MENC

Children's books facilitate powerful learning and stimulate creative thinking skills. In language, rhythm is a cadence produced by a pattern of stressed and unstressed syllables. Rhythm occurs in all forms of literature, but is particularly important in poetry and verse. The following "Swamp Beat" lesson could supplement a beginning poetry curriculum, but works well with any kind of reading instruction.

The "Swamp Beat" lesson is based on *Bedtime at the Swamp*, a picture book by Kristyn Crow (2008) which is full of rhythmic wording. The Refrain, "Splish-Splash, Rumba-Rumba, Bim-Bam, BOOM!" repeats often in the book. Try the following steps to create a rhythm-based lesson.

PLAYING

Step one. Read the book to the class, having them echo the Refrain. Read it a second time, and ask the students to clap a steady beat throughout.

> **Bedtime at the Swamp**
> (Steady beat is underlined in the first stanza.)
> I was sittin' by a swamp just hummin' a tune
> With the fireflies dancin' 'neath the fat gold moon
> When off in the distance was a splashin' sound
> So I stood on my tippy-toes and looked around.
>   (Used by permission of the author)

Step two. Arrange the children in small groups with four children in each group.

CREATING

Teaching Tip

The teacher can randomly assign children into groups by counting off "One, two, three, four. . ." but a more effective grouping is to arrange the children according to their strengths. In each group, for example, include a child that is a leader, one that is more shy, one that is a helper, and one that will be able to write. Children in this type of grouping, often called a cooperative learning group, are more likely to function well together.

Step three. Write the words "Splish-Splash, Rumba-Rumba, Bim-Bam, BOOM!" on the board or on a sentence strip. Have each group decide on body percussion sounds for each set of words in the "Splish-Splash" section, starting with body motions "looking like the 'Splish-Splash' phrase sounds." Each child should be responsible for one set of words in the performance (splish-splash, or boom). Give them three minutes to complete the task. Then share each group's results with the whole class, not taking more than five minutes. Read the book again, guiding the children first in keeping a steady beat to the book's text, and then breaking into "parts" in their groups for the refrain.

Step four. Groups transfer their created body percussion sounds to instruments.

- Each member of the group will participate.
- Group must use at least one wooden sound and one metal sound.
- Sounds selected by the group must include a crescendo.

LISTENING

Step five. Groups share their decisions with the whole class. This sound collection can become the A section of a rondo.

Step six. Select words to be the B, C, and D sections.

- "I was sittin' by a swamp" verse could be the B section, with other verses chosen as C and D.
- The words for each section could simply be read, always returning to the A section with groups playing their instruments.
- Then, have different children select instruments to make sounds for each section.
- The final result will be a sound composition in rondo form, performed by the class. For example:

  A. Splish-Splash . . .
  B. Sittin' by a swamp . . .
  A. *Repeat* Splish-Splash . . .
  C. Then out crept a shadow . . .
  A. *Repeat* Splish-Splash . . .
  D. Well, Ma looked us over . . .
  A. *Repeat* Splish-Splash . . .

The whole story of *Bedtime in the Swamp* can be told in sounds with no words. After the groups or individuals have decided on sounds and/or instruments for the sections, go through the book showing the pictures, having the groups perform their sounds with no words at the appropriate pictures. This telling of the story in sound is a forerunner to programmatic music, music intended to tell a story (see
LISTENING page 63.)

112

Step seven. Practice reading skills as follows:

- Using sentence strips, write the words and phrases used for the composition.
- Arrange them in order in a holder, having the children follow the words as the "Swamp Beat Rondo" is performed.
- Invite the children to decide on other arrangements for the rondo and perform them.
- At another time, place the sentence strips out of order in the holder and ask the children to arrange them in the correct sequence.
- Extend the learning by having children clap the steady beat contrasted with the rhythm of the words in other rhythmic poetry examples. Words from folk songs can be used such as "Old Dan Tucker," "I Went to the Animal Fair," and so forth.

Some brain research[7] indicates that such creative experiences utilize the brain in more "complete" thinking operations. Although the healthy brain never functions totally on one side or the other, the left hemisphere is brought into play with the sequencing, ordering, and reading, as the right hemisphere is used with the creative decisions. The emotions, housed in the cortex, are involved because it is fun to do this activity, and the area of the brain involved with emotions is also tied to motivation and memory, leading to learning success.

Creating Enrichment Activities

Enrichment activities with reading offer enjoyment for the whole class as they explore many opportunities to read. The children will develop even more ideas. Movement could be added, words could be expanded into rhyming phrases; anything they want to create is possible. As the class becomes more comfortable with creating, the children will take this type of lesson to unknown destinations through their imaginative word play.

Activities with literature provide perfect enrichment events. The classroom teacher can use longer periods of time engaging the children in creative experiences, resulting in reading enrichment and in musical compositions. Video and audio taping the class at work with these types of creative problem-solving lessons embed evaluation and assessment in the process. Invite the parents to listen to the *Bedtime in the Swamp* composition during Back to School Night. Explain to the parents how the children used creative problem solving to reach their decisions, how every child was involved, and how reading was emphasized along with the creative process.

Creatively Bringing A Book To Life

Another exciting way to enhance reading is by adding the elements of theater and music to a children's book. Experience this concept by using the script of the story of "The Little Red House with No Doors and No Windows and a Star Inside" (Appendix 3). It features narrators who move the story along, plus several characters. Have volunteers act out the story with simple costumes and props. Sing several familiar apple songs at the end of the play.

Divide the class into groups. Each group chooses a children's book to present with puppets or act in simple costumes. Each group also needs to select a song to add to their presentation—at the beginning, middle or end. It can be a familiar children's song or a created piggyback song. Background scenery, simple props, and/or puppets can be designed and made by the students, depending on age appropriateness. Sound effects or mood setting music should also be added.

CREATING

Large Group Student Activity

Correlation Lesson: Bringing A Book To Life[8]

In a group of four to six students, create a Correlation Lesson to enhance a children's book with music and drama. A Correlation Lesson is one in which two or more disciplines (in this case, language arts, drama and music) use or address the same materials or topics. Present the Correlation Lesson to the class and provide each student with a handout. Half of the grade will be based on colleagues' opinions of group-work skills. A sample student handout is included in Appendix 4. (Rubric on teachers' website: www.routledge.com/textbooks/9780415878234)

Connecting Activities

Connecting Music and Spelling

Spelling is a difficult subject for many students. Using all the learning modalities will assist students to become more successful. Write the words in large letters on the board (visual). Using colored markers can also be effective. Spell each word out loud, putting the letters to a "jazzy" or catchy rhythm (aural). Ask the children to clap the rhythm as they speak each letter (kinesthetic). Adding a simple melody to the rhythmic chant is also helpful. Acting out or putting movements to any word where it is appropriate can be very effective. Consistent use of all these teaching steps will enable students to be successful spellers.

Connecting Music and Writing Prompts

Grade Levels	K–4th
Language Arts Objective[1]	**5.** Students employ a wide range of strategies as they write and use different writing process elements appropriately to communicate with different audiences for a variety of purposes.
Music Objective[2]	**8. Content Standard:** Understanding relationships between music, the other arts, and disciplines outside the arts
	Achievement Standard:
	Students
	b. identify ways in which the principles and subject matter of other disciplines taught in the school are interrelated with those of music.

1 IRA/NCTE Standards for the English Language Arts
2 NATIONAL MUSIC STANDARDS, MENC

When a teacher "primes" students with previous creative experiences before a writing assignment, the resulting process and product can be much stronger. Childhood memories might remain of being asked to write poetry or a story with no advance preparation by the teacher. The frustration felt many years ago is probably still felt. When a child is properly prepared for a creative writing assignment, this frustration is replaced with anticipation. Try the following four lessons.

Lesson one. Students working in cooperative learning groups can capture in sounds the mood created in children's books. Remember to give specific directions to each group to allow maximum opportunity for a successful creative process.

CREATING

LISTENING

- What is the emotion or mood suggested by the book?
- What sounds could suggest that mood?
- What instruments could suggest the mood?
- How should the instruments be played? (Loud or soft, in combination or singly, only one sound or repeated sounds?)

Letting each group take time to experiment with capturing a mood in sound will culminate in group products to be shared with the whole class. *Home Place*,[9] by Crescent Dragonwagon, is a good book for creating a mood. Add the "mood music" at appropriate times before and during the reading of the book.

Lesson two. Songs can be used to stimulate creative writing projects. Songs such as "She'll Be Comin' Round the Mountain," "Oh! Susanna," and "Puff the Magic Dragon" tell a story. Sing the song. Allow students to choose from a list of writing prompts or create their own ideas. After singing "Puff the Magic Dragon," a list of writing prompts for students might include:

- Write about another adventure that Jackie and Puff shared together. Who did they meet?
- Describe what Honalee might look like.
- Write about the first time Puff and Jackie met.
- Describe a make-believe friend you would like to have.

Each child can create his/her own book by adding illustrations to the new story.

Songbook Selections

Get America Singing. . .Again!

P & I	"Puff the Magic Dragon" by Leonard Lipton and Peter Yarrow	34
P & I	"Oh! Susanna" by Stephen Foster	33
P & I	"She'll Be Comin' Round the Mountain" Traditional	38

SINGING

Lesson three. Another excellent idea for "priming" the creative writing experiences is to use the Music, Art and Writing Worksheet (see Appendix 5) with students. At the top, it has "Write descriptive words," the middle section is labeled "Draw a picture," the bottom section is "Write a descriptive paragraph."

Play a short programmatic music selection, such as "The Swan "(included on the CD), "Aquarium," or "The Aviary" from *Carnival of the Animals* by Saint-Saëns. Do not announce the title. Play the music through one time for each of the three sections of the paper to be completed. By incorporating music and art before the actual writing assignment, the resulting paragraph from each student should be full of creativity, adjectives, and adverbs.

LISTENING

Lesson four. As a group project, children can make up stories to go along with a musical composition. Play one of the selections on the CD without announcing the title. Divide the class into groups of three or four students and ask each group to make up a tale that goes along with the music. The groups could either write down their stories, or act them out for the class.

Connecting Musical Elements and Skills with Literature

With certain books, reading the story out loud lets the children experience the rhythms of the words. *Chicka Chicka Boom Boom*,[10] by Bill Martin, Jr. and John Archambault, is a perfect book for helping children feel rhythm. Even the title suggests rhythms to the reader. The captivating words and phrases in the book, centered on the ABCs, almost demand body movement from the listener. Several phrases repeat throughout the book. The same movement or body percussion pattern could be performed each time the repeated words are read, reinforcing the concept of same/different in music.

Several books by Caldecott Medalist Peter Spier are quite detailed and could be used in small group settings or with individual learning experiences. His *Noah's Ark*[11] is an attractive picture book that can be used to introduce folk songs about the story of Noah and the animals. *People*,[12] contains excellent paintings of people on four continents. It could be used with folk songs from each of the areas pictured.

Famous songs have inspired many authors of children's books. Several books are available about *Old MacDonald*, and Paul Zelinski has published *The Wheels on the Bus* as a pop-up book. Simply having these books on display in the primary classroom can stimulate interest in reading for some children. Often in intermediate music classes, the children play these tunes on recorder. Inviting these children to perform for your class is a way to give recognition to the music program, and to spread positive public relations in the school.

The Very Busy Spider[13] by Eric Carle can be enjoyed by primary students for its intriguing story and wonderful illustrations. From a musical perspective, the book is in rondo form. By creating and adding various body percussion patterns to each part of the story, students can hear as well as see the rondo form.

Connecting Music with Bilingual and English Language Learner (ELL) Instruction

Tantalizing Tidbit of Research

Several aspects of music education, such as the focus on rhythmic or pitch (contour) aspects of language processing in vocal music, contribute to commonalities between music and language teaching. The use of songs, not surprisingly, directly enhances pronunciation, grammatical structure, vocabulary, and idiomatic expressions as well as a wide variety in speed of delivery, phrasing, and linking of ideas.

Anne S. Lowe (1995)[14]

It is helpful for children who have limited English language experience to work with songs, games, poems/rhymes, and to have stories read to them until they have assimilated the syntax of the language. Sing simple American folk songs with ELL students. Pick songs with a chorus or refrain that repeats many times throughout the song. Jump rope rhymes and chants are also good to use.

Songbook Selections

Get America Singing. . .Again!

Teacher Bob Lake states "there is strong evidence supporting the use of music in the ESL classroom. Language and music are tied together in brain processing by pitch, rhythm and by symmetrical phrasing. Music can help familiarize students with connections and provides a fun way to acquire English."[15]

Singing songs is one of the best ways to set the mood and provide connections to American holidays. However, some children might not be familiar with the holiday. Have other students explain, for instance, that Halloween is when children dress up in costumes and attend parties. Have the children describe to the class the celebrations they have in their native cultures.

Books about Latino/Hispanic culture could be enhanced by music activities. *New Shoes for Silvia*,[16] by Johanna Hurwitz, includes some Spanish words and could be a lead-in to the rhythmic chant of the poem "New Shoes" by Frida Wolfe.

New shoes, new shoes,
Red and pink and blue shoes,
Which ones would you choose,
If you could buy?

The story could be told in a verse that the children create, interspersed with the first verse of "New Shoes" used as a refrain. The sounds of shoes walking could be played on found sounds or on percussion instruments borrowed from the music room.

The poem could also be learned in Spanish. In teaching this creative rhythmic lesson about shoes, the Spanish text could be interspersed with the English text for the rhythmic composition.

Zapatos nuevos, Zapatos nuevos,
Zapatos rojo, y rosa, azul
¿Cual escogerias
Si pudieras comprar lo?

This activity could be expanded to include other languages that are spoken by the students in the classroom.

In the same way, an excellent activity to reinforce English language acquisition in ELL Spanish-speaking students is to sing songs in Spanish and then with English translations. Or, sing songs originally written in English and then with Spanish translations.

SINGING

Books as Learning Facilitators

We miss golden opportunities in the elementary classroom by not utilizing children's books for more than story time after lunch. Books facilitate powerful learning experiences for the children. They teach fluency and reading skills. They help children make connections between sounds of words and reading of words. Music and literacy complement each other. Teaching with children's literature can stimulate creative thinking by transferring words to sounds and by capturing feelings through sounds. Musical learning about form and repetition and instrument recognition can also take place. Children can learn about other cultures and become better listeners as well. Peruse the children's section at a bookstore to see that a rich array of books is waiting to open the way for outstanding interdisciplinary learning.

Look in Appendix 3 for a list of recommended books from many different sources. This list contains a fabulous music-related Learning Library of books to use in the classroom!

Thinking It Through

In a small group, discuss the meaning of the following quotes. Identify specific classroom activities that could spring from each of these ideas:

"Music and language share many attributes. Both are primarily auditory-based forms of communication."
Daniel J. Levitin and Anna K. Tirovolas, McGill University

"The limits of my language mean the limits of my world."
Ludwig Wittgenstein, Austrian-British philosopher

"Music is the universal language of humankind."
Henry Wadsworth Longfellow, American educator and poet

Suggestions for Further Study

This Is Your Brain On Music: The Science of a Human Obsession (2006) by Daniel Levitin, published by Dutton Adult.

Listen to Learn: Using American Music to Teach Language Arts and Social Studies (2004) by Teri Tibbett, published by Jossey-Bass. The Native American unit is especially interesting. For Grades 5–8.

The Kennedy Center Arts Edge website provides many excellent materials to explore.

This website includes the following resources:

1. Arts-integrated lesson plans. Filters that can be used on the 338 lessons on this site include:

    *   Arts subjects—all arts subjects, dance, music, theater, visual arts.
    *   Other subjects—all other subjects, foreign language, language, arts, math, physical education, science, social studies, technology.
    *   Grade levels—all grades, K–4, 5–8, 9–12.

2. The National Standards in all the arts areas, K–12, are given.
3. Web links are also provided to excellent sources for teacher and student research.
4. An outstanding group of "How-To's" is also included—articles that give tips on assessment, classroom management, and other relevant topics.

Read *GarageBand Mechanics* by Dan Schmidt, published by FTC Publishing. Learn more about the easy use of this amazing program.

Listen to the CD *¡Canta mi Son! (Sing my song)—Learn Spanish through the World of Mariachi!* (2009) by Juanita Ulloa (Juanita Newland Ulloa). Record Label: Vocal Power Productions. It contains appropriate mariachi songs for students. Separate Spanish pronunciation tracks are included.

Explore *Singin', Sweatin', and Storytime: Literature-based Movement and Music for the Young Child* (2009) by Rebecca E. Hamik and Catherine (Cat) M. Wilson. Co-published by Rowman & Littlefield Education and MENC. This book combines literature, music, and movement to teach primary children. All 170 lessons are based on the national music and physical education standards. Each lesson has a story for the teacher to read to the children, a music activity, and a physical activity. Lessons include basic music and physical education skills as well as lessons that teach students about staying healthy, good character, citizenship, holidays, and world cultures.

Find some good action songs in Spanish in *Diez Deditos and Other Play Rhymes and Action Songs from Latin America* (2002) by Jose-Luis Orozco; illustrated by Elisa Kleven. Published by Puffin.

Recommended Student Books

Cleary, Brian P. (2005). *Dearly, Nearly, Insincerely: What is an Adverb?* (B. Gable, Illus.). Minneapolis, MN: Lerner.
Introduces adverbs through rhyming, rhythmic text.

Crow, Kristyn. (2008). *Bedtime in the Swamp.* (M. Pamintuan, Illus.). New York: HarperCollins.
A simple rhyming storyline, and a repetitive refrain are used in a swampy tale.

Dragonwagon, Crescent. (1993). *Home Place.* (J. Pinkney, Illus.). New York: Aladdin.
A girl and her family discover an old home place, and find hints to the past.

Fleischman, Paul. (2006). *Big Talk Poems for Four Voices.* (B. Giacobbe, Illus.). Cambridge, MA: Candlewick Press.
Poems to be read by four different children.

Spier, Peter. (1992). *Noah's Ark.* (Peter Spier, Illus.). New York: Dragonfly Books.
Illustrations of the story of Noah's Ark.

Spier, Peter. (1988). *People.* (Peter Spier, Illus.). Garden City, NY: Doubleday.
Books for Young Readers.

Yarrow, Peter, and Lipton, Lenny. (2007). *Puff, The Magic Dragon.* (Eric Puybaret, Illus.). New York: Sterling.
Wonderful illustrations bring the song to life.

CHAPTER 8 | **USING MUSIC TO ENHANCE LEARNING IN SCIENCE**

Creative Activities

Making use of music to help students learn and retain information in the science curriculum can produce excellent results.

CREATING

SINGING

Creating Piggyback Science Songs

A group of intermediate children can write their own piggyback science songs as a good short-term assessment of what the students are retaining. After a unit on a selected science topic, assign the students to groups and have them create songs using the information they learned during the unit. This song-writing exercise is an ideal outcomes-based assessment of student knowledge as well.

- Choose a science topic. These can include health, nutrition, the body, stars, the organs, and functions of the organs, magnets, plants, measuring, and so forth.
- Have the students select a tune from the following list or one of their favorites:

  - "Jingle Bells" (verse and chorus required)
  - "Twinkle, Twinkle"
  - "Do Your Ears Hang Low"
  - "On Top of Old Smokey"
  - "Row, Row, Row Your Boat"
  - "Down in the Valley"
  - "Home on the Range"
  - "You Are My Sunshine"

- Have the students rewrite the words with lyrics describing the science topic:

  1. Brainstorm and list words about the topic.
  2. Arrange these words to fit the rhythm of the tune selected—matching the number of syllables in each line works best.
  3. Try to "make sense" with the words selected.
  4. Try to rhyme the verses to match the original song.
  5. Perform for each other!

Having students create their own words to remember specific science (or math, language, social studies) information is an excellent example of an arts-infused activity with objectives from music and the other subjects being practiced. In the process of doing this activity, not only are the facts being orally reviewed by the children as they try to fit them into the melody and rhythm of the song, but clapping the rhythm would be required (a music objective), singing the melody without words would be required (a music objective), and rhyming words would need to be pointed out and created (a language arts activity).

SINGING

LISTENING

Creating Bubble Music

Grade Levels	1st–4th
Science Objective[1]	**B. Physical Science**
	E.B. 1 Properties of objects and materials
	a. Objects have many observable properties, including size, weight, shape, color, temperature, and the ability to react with other substances

122

Music Objective[2] **3. Content Standard: Improvising melodies, variations, and accompaniments**

d. Students improvise short songs and instrumental pieces, using a variety of sound sources, including traditional sounds, nontraditional sounds available in the classroom, body sounds, and sounds produced by electronic means

1 NATIONAL SCIENCE STANDARDS, the National Academies Press
2 NATIONAL MUSIC STANDARDS, MENC

A favorite activity for children of all ages is blowing bubbles. How many of us can remember getting a jar of bubbles at a birthday party and standing around blowing bubbles with our friends? Trying to blow the largest bubble before it burst, then watching it float to the ground, sometimes staying there for a second or two before it popped, was part of the fun. By combining a creative activity using words, poetry, and music with science, a complete learning unit could be developed including spelling words, reading, art, and design. Torrance Levels of Creative Thinking are noted where appropriate. This activity can be modified for use with fifth- and sixth-grade students.

1. Have several bottles of bubbles, purchased or teacher-made (see recipes that follow).
2. Let several children take turns blowing bubbles while the other class members observe the way the bubbles look and move. Then switch roles.
3. Have the children give adjectives describing the bubbles. List them on the board. (*Fluent* level of creative thinking, see page 99.) Allow this activity to go on for several minutes, until you have at least 20 terms on the board. At first the words will be simple, such as "round," "wet," "clear." Encourage the children to think of different ways to say "round," and different ways to describe how the bubbles look and move. There will be quite a list generated.
4. At this point have several instruments or found sounds displayed that might make bubble music. (Use lots of metal sounds, such as pot lids, finger cymbals, triangles, and bells capable of producing sounds that relate to how the bubbles look and move.) (*Flexible, Original, Elaborative* levels of creative thinking, see page 99.)
5. Let several children make the music, randomly and quietly, remembering that the bubbles aren't always in sight. They seem to come in streams and float down to the floor, popping along the way. Take turns until all the students have had a turn. (*Original* and *Elaborative* levels of creative thinking.)
6. While the "bubble music" is being created, other children should be encouraged to write a poem about the bubbles, using words from the list if they wish. The atmosphere in the room will be very quiet. The children will be making "bubble music" while others write. No voices are allowed in order to create good concentration. (*Original* and *Elaborative* levels of creative thinking.)
7. The quality of the poetry can be amazingly high. The music can be recorded and played during parent/teacher conferences while showing the poetry written by the children. (*Evaluative* level of creative thinking, see page 99.)
8. Include science exploration about the composition of bubbles in the unit.

Recipes for Bubbles and Super Bubbles

Bubbles	Super Bubbles
1 part dishwashing detergent	2 parts dishwashing detergent
10 parts water	4 parts glycerin
0.25 parts glycerin or light corn syrup	1 part light corn syrup

Body Bubbles

The body bubble, made with a hula-hoop and a child's small plastic wading pool, brings bubble making to a completely new level. Have a child stand in the wading pool, with feet inside the hula-hoop. Then pull the hula-hoop up over the child, making a very large body-encasing bubble.

Bubble-blowing Devices

No matter what the shape of the bubble wand, the bubbles will be round. Another science experiment featuring problem solving and exploration could be to examine different devices for wands and rate the effectiveness. A coat hanger bent into a circle works. Plastic cutouts from milk jugs or heavy twine tied in a circle on a stick also make usable bubble blower wands.

Creating Sound Waves and Instrumental Sounds

PLAYING

LISTENING

Grade Levels	1st–4th
Science Objective[1]	**B. Physical Science**
	E.B. 2 Position and motion of objects
	d. Sound is produced by vibrating objects. The pitch of the sound can be varied by changing the rate of vibration.
Music Objective[2]	**2. Content Standard: Performing on instruments, alone and with others, a varied repertoire of music**
	b. Students perform easy melodic patterns accurately and independently on melodic classroom instruments

1 NATIONAL SCIENCE STANDARDS, the National Academies Press
2 NATIONAL MUSIC STANDARDS, MENC

Sound is produced by vibrations and sound waves. The study of music, the aural art, is a logical place to study sound.

The students can complete many experiments demonstrating the relationship of length to vibration to sound. Students love the experiment of hitting a tuning fork and sticking it into a tub of water to "see" vibration. (Hint: put the tuning fork into the tub at an angle to get a really big splash.) Rubber bands around a tissue box and the same length rubber band around a larger box show the difference in length and sound. Students also enjoy creating the rubber-band box "cello" with wider and thinner "strings" to produce

124

different pitches. Drinking straws cut in various lengths and blown across demonstrate the concept as well. Blowing across the mouth of pharmacy bottles holding different amounts of water also can be used. (Using pharmacy bottles with measurements on the sides helps children measure the amount of water more accurately.) A collection of ice-tea bottles can be arranged to play a scale created by the amount of water filling each one. Students selecting a variety of examples of length and sound experiments can prove their hypothesis that length affects pitch.

Palm Pipes[5] and Music

Another successful experience with the concept of length to pitch uses PVC pipe available at hardware and home stores. PVC pipe cut in different lengths makes different sounds when hit in the palm of the hand. The longer the pipe, the lower the sound. Use half inch PVC pipe.

PLAYING

LISTENING

Note	Length of ½" PVC pipe
F	23.60 cm
G	21.00 cm
A	18.75 cm
B flat	17.50 cm
C	15.80 cm
D	14.00 cm
E	12.50 cm
F	11.80 cm
G	10.50 cm
A	9.40 cm
B flat	9.20 cm
C	7.90 cm
D	7.00 cm
E	6.25 cm
F	5.90 cm

Students should be able to play the following tunes, using the pipes. They need to play the notes in the rhythm of the melody.

"America"

f   f   g   e   f   g   a   a   b♭   a g f
My coun-try 'tis   of thee, Sweet land of   li-ber-ty,

g f   e f   c   c   c   c   b♭   a
Of thee   I sing. Land where   my fath- ers   died,

b♭   b♭   b♭   b♭   a   g   a   b♭ a   g f   a b♭ c
Land   of   the   Pil -   grim's pride, From eve -   ry - moun-tain-side,

d b♭   a   g   f
let -   -   free-dom ring.

"Yankee Doodle"

C   C   D   E   C   E   D   C   C   D   E   C   B
Yan - kee Doo-dle went   to town,   Rid- ing   on   a   pon- y

C   C D   E   F   E   D   C   B   G   A   B   C   C
Stuck   a fea - ther in   his cap and called it   "Mac-a - ro - ni,"

A   B   A   G   A   B   C   G   A   G   F   E   G
Yan- kee Doo-dle Keep   it   up, Yan - kee Doo -dle Dan-dy

A   B   A   G   A   B   C   A   G   C   B   D   C   C
Mind   the mu - sic and the   step and   with the girls be   han-dy.

Note: As an alternative to using PVC pipe, Boomwhackers (different lengths of brightly colored plastic tubes) can be purchased. These instruments also have a series of additional parts that can help change register, which can be another science lesson.

CREATING

LISTENING

Creating with Animals and Music

Grade Levels	2nd–4th
Science Objective[1]	**C. Life Science**
	E.C. 1. Characteristics of Organisms
	a. Organisms have basic needs. For example, animals need air, water, and food
Music Objective[2]	**4. Content Standard: Composing and arranging music within specified guidelines**
	b. Students create and arrange short songs and instrumental pieces within specified guidelines

1 NATIONAL SCIENCE STANDARDS, the National Academies Press
2 NATIONAL MUSIC STANDARDS, MENC

Small animal pictures can become the catalyst for musical rhythmic compositions that start with facts about the various animals.

1. Students pick four different pictures from a sack. (This activity works well with cooperative learning groups.) The students then list facts about each of their animals using books from the library, information from the internet, and additional resource materials. For example, the list for camel might include:

    *   Has humps
    *   Can go long periods without water

- Walks well in sand
- Carries heavy loads.

2. Children then create a four-measure rhythmic chant incorporating the facts from the list about each of their four animals. Groups choose one animal chant as the A section of a rondo, another animal chant as the B section, and the two other animal chants as C and D. Performance of each group's rondo (ABACADA) makes a wonderful closure to a unit on animals. (See page 41 on Form for additional information.)

Additional sources for animal names and terms to use in rhythmic compositions include:

- List the animals which are athletic team mascots (Kansas State University Wildcats, Chicago Bears, LSU Tigers, Texas University Longhorns, and Texas State University Bobcats are a few).
- Learn the terms indicating a group of animals of one type (a gaggle of geese or school of fish).
- Study the habitats and habits of different animals (a den or lair, nocturnal?).

Connecting Activities

Connecting Animals and Music

The study of animals with students should include listening opportunities as well.

LISTENING

Listening Activity

Carnival of the Animals by Saint-Saëns describes different animals in sound. Excellent *Carnival of the Animals* books with illustrations and CDs of all 14 music selections are available. Good musical connections can be made with relation to size of animal and pitch used in the music, or size of animal and dynamic level heard.

Read about the composer and the composition, and then listen to "The Elephant" from *Carnival of the Animals* by Saint-Saëns.

The Composer

Camille Saint-Saëns, (1835–1921) came from a French peasant family and was a gifted musician, even as a child. His father died when the boy was young, and his mother was always protective and dominating, and had no musical knowledge. Fortunately, he had an aunt who played piano. She became his first teacher. His gifts developed rapidly. It was said that he could play all the difficult Beethoven piano sonatas from memory when he was just ten years old. Even though he was an excellent performer, he is best known today for his skills as a composer. He died at the age of 86 after a difficult trip to Algeria.

The Composition

Saint-Saëns composed the *Carnival of the Animals* in Austria in 1886 as a joke for a Mardi Gras concert.

Except for the section called "Le Cygne" ("The Swan"), he withdrew the piece after just a few performances and wouldn't allow it to be published until after his death. The suite depicts various animals—elephants, roosters, donkeys, lions, fish, turtles, kangaroos, birds, and even extinct animals in the form of fossils—with the orchestra creating animal sounds and humorous effects. When he died, his will allowed *Carnival of the Animals* to be published and it has since become one of his most performed compositions.

The "Elephant" is in a slow triple meter. Imagine during the ABA form how an elephant might dance to this piece. Focus attention on the instrument featured (string bass), low pitch, and size of an elephant.

Each section is short, which makes it very suitable for children's attention spans. Playing a section without telling the animal makes a fun guessing game.

Listening Selection

"The Elephant" from *Carnival of the Animals* by Saint-Saëns

CD Track 9

Teaching Tip

Place the names of three animals on the board. Play a section of the music and have children decide on the correct animal. The music describes the animals with sound, which makes this a good listening "work out" as well as a study of animals. Once the animal is correctly named, discuss the environment in which it lives. Then have students move to the music, reflecting the animal's movements.

Fourteen sections are included in *Carnival of the Animals*:

1. "Introduction and Royal March of the Lion"—the music portrays the king of the animals, the lion, as he walks along, as in a royal presentation. Listeners can also hear the lion's roar.
2. "Hens and Cocks"—the music sounds like chickens pecking and scratching as they walk around. The rooster crowing is imitated by the music, and the listener can detect short, staccato notes.
3. "Wild Burros (Asses)"—the music depicts these animals as fast running, "wild" creatures.
4. "Tortoises"—Saint-Saëns shows his humor with this section. Offenbach's "Can-Can" melody, normally played very fast, and often as accompaniment to dancers performing the very energetic dance, is now used to portray the clumsy and slow turtle.
5. "The Elephant"—the music is a waltz, again a bit of humor about the large heavy animal.
6. "Kangaroos"—children love this section because it makes them think of the jumping Australian animal. They have great fun acting like kangaroos jumping around the floor.
7. "The Aquarium"—very peaceful music that reminds the listener of what it feels like to watch fish in an aquarium. It is interesting that Saint-Saëns includes this selection in a "carnival of animals!"
8. "Personages with Long Ears"—the music is quite a contrast to the peaceful watery aquarium as it pictures donkeys with sound.
9. "The Cuckoo in the Forest"—the music portrays the bird in the trees that sings out "cuckoo."
10. "The Aviary"—a musical picture of walking through the birds housed in an aviary at a zoo.

11. "Pianists"—again, Saint-Saëns makes his listener ask, "What is he doing? Pianists as animals?"

12. "Fossils"—a musical parody by Saint-Saëns as he uses very familiar tunes including what we know as "Twinkle, Twinkle Little Star" (French know it as "Ah, vous dirais-je, Maman"), a bit of a Rossini aria from *The Barber of Seville* ("Una voce poco fa"), and his own *Danse Macabre* where we hear skeletons dancing. He was telling the listener that these very familiar melodies were like fossils in a museum.

13. "The Swan"—the music describes a swan floating gracefully on a smooth pond.

14. "Finale"—the high-spirited ending recaps snippets from the various sections of the piece. Listeners must pay careful attention because the musical hints of the lion, fossils, wild asses, hens and cocks, kangaroos, cuckoo, and pianists go past very quickly in the music. Ending chords remind us of "Personages with Long Ears."

Connecting Life Science and Music

Grade Levels	1st– 4th
Science Objective[1]	**C. Life Science**
	E.C. 1. Characteristics of Organisms
	b. Each plant or animal has different structures that serve different functions in growth, survival, and reproduction. For example, humans have distinct body structures for walking, holding, seeing, and talking.
Music Objective[2]	**4. Content Standard: Composing and arranging music within specified guidelines**
	b. Students create and arrange short songs and instrumental pieces within specified guidelines

1 NATIONAL SCIENCE STANDARDS, the National Academies Press
2 NATIONAL MUSIC STANDARDS, MENC

When studying the body, children have a better chance of retaining more of the information by creating a sound composition using the terms learned. An example for primary students would be the following activity:

CREATING

Introduction:	Our body, our body—a smooth running machine
Ostinato:	Pump Blood Pump (clap) (Repeat until Coda)
A section:	Circulatory System Heart pumps Veins carry Arteries return—
B section:	Heart, two chambers Valves—connect

> Blood—circulates
> (Crescendo gradually during the B section)

A section: Repeat

Coda: Keep it working! Exercise!
              Keep it working! Exercise!

Ideas for Extending the Lesson

A complete program could be produced about the body. Children could trace around each other on large sheets of paper, coloring in facial features and drawing the shape of the organs inside their bodies. Large zip lock bags can contain the "intestines" which are really pieces of yarn cut to the actual length of a child's intestine. The heart could be shown in its actual size and location. All the systems of the body—circulatory, digestive, nervous, and skeletal—could be demonstrated on these cutouts with overlays.

Ask the children to create rhythmic chants similar to the one above describing the various systems of the body and then present the information to parents or other grade levels in school. This musical presentation makes a delightful "Back to School Night" for parents, and it is effective instruction as well. The children will hold on to the information much longer than if a worksheet or notebook is the teaching method used because of their active engagement.

Another bonus is that the activity also serves as an evaluation of the unit. As the children write the chants, the teacher can evaluate their understanding of terms and functions of the body.

One of the Berenstain Bear books, *The Berenstain Bears and Too Much Junk Food*, would be helpful with younger students. Brother and Sister Bear discuss the body systems, and drawings of the body are included.

Songs such as "Head and Shoulders, Baby" and "Mi cuerpo" reinforce the parts of the body for students. Even the old game song "Hokey Pokey" teaches right hand, left hand, right foot, and so forth, again, reinforcing the parts of the body. The traditional song "Dry Bones" musically tells a simplistic order of the connection of the bones. Add them to the presentation!

SINGING

Songbook Selections

Appendix

P	"Mi cuerpo" (My Body) Hispanic folksong	195
P & I	"Head and Shoulders, Baby" (Hombres y cabeza) African street game	197
I	"Dry Bones" African American spiritual	203

Connecting the Four Seasons and Music

Grade Levels	2nd–4th
Science Objective[1]	**D. Earth and Space Science**
	E.D. 3 Changes in earth and sky
	b. Weather changes from day to day and over the seasons
Music Objective[2]	**6. Content Standard: Listening to, analyzing, and describing music**
	b. Students demonstrate perceptual skills by moving, by answering questions about, and by describing aural examples of music of various styles representing diverse cultures

1 NATIONAL SCIENCE STANDARDS, the National Academies Press
2 NATIONAL MUSIC STANDARDS, MENC

One interesting aspect of the study of science involves learning about the four seasons and understanding that it is the tilt of the earth's axis that causes the seasons. One important part of this study is to explore weather changes that occur in summer, fall, winter, and spring. A famous composer of the Baroque period, Antonio Vivaldi, wrote music for a solo violinist and a small string orchestra that portrays the earth at these four different times of the year. The composition is suitably named *The Four Seasons*.

LISTENING

Have the intermediate students help list on the board what they would think a musical piece written to describe springtime would sound like. Words such as "birds singing," "light and airy," "peaceful," might be listed. After they hear Vivaldi's first movement, "Spring," go back to the list and compare the items to how the piece actually sounded.

Listening Activities

Read about the composer and the composition, and then listen to "Spring" from *The Four Seasons* by Vivaldi while following the Listening Map.

The Composer

Italian composer Antonio Vivaldi (1678–1741) was called "The Red Priest" because of his vivid red hair. Vivaldi's father was a self-taught musician who gave his son a love for music, and taught him to play the violin. The son very quickly became an even better violinist than his father. In fact, the two of them were, for a time, a tourist attraction, performing as a "Father and Son" duo in the streets and squares of Venice. Antonio soon was renowned as a virtuoso solo violinist, dazzling all who heard him play.

He also wanted to compose music, but in those times, the only way to make a living as a musician was to be attached to the Church. So Vivaldi became a priest, and was appointed music master at the Ospedale della Pietà, an orphanage for young girls in Venice. It was here, writing pieces for his young students, that Vivaldi's compositional talent flourished. In spite of a severe asthma condition, he lived into his sixties, and composed hundreds of works, many of which are still performed today.

The Composition

The Four Seasons, a set of pieces written for string orchestra, is a popular "classic." The composer, Antonio Vivaldi, who lived during the Baroque period, was one of the first composers to write "program music," or music that tells a story or describes a picture or scene. The composer based these string pieces on sonnets about winter, summer, spring, and autumn.

Write Vivaldi's "Spring Sonnet" on the board. This sonnet was written to show what each section of the music is describing. After listening, discuss with the class how well Vivaldi met his goal of using the orchestra to describe spring. List the specific instruments of the string family that were used in this example of "program music."

Springtime[6] is upon us.
The birds celebrate her return with festive song, and murmuring streams are softly caressed by the breezes.
Thunderstorms, those heralds of Spring, roar, casting their dark mantle over heaven.
Then they die away to silence, and the birds take up their charming songs once more.

Listening Selection

1st Movement, "Spring" from *The Four Seasons* by Vivaldi   CD Track 2
Listening Map   Appendix, p. 63

The study of storms is an important part of the study of weather. Several composers have written music about storms. Vivaldi's *The Four Seasons* includes a longer musical "storm" in the Presto or 3rd Movement from "Summer." In the opera *William Tell* by Rossini, a storm is depicted by the music. Grofé included a movement called "Cloud Burst" in his *Grand Canyon Suite*. Beethoven integrated a "storm" into his Symphony No. 6 in F Major (Pastorale). The students will enjoy listening to these dramatic musical compositions. Asking students to answer how the composers made the music sound like storms would include discussions of tone color and dynamics. Intersperse listening to these musical selections with the scientific study of weather connected to each of the seasons.

A great introduction to a study of weather would be to have the students make a "sound storm." Begin with one or two students snapping their fingers, and gradually adding all the students snapping their fingers. This sounds like rain falling. Then have a few students change from finger snapping to patting their hands on their thighs. Continue to add in more and more students patting their hands until all are making the sound of rain falling hard, like the sound of a storm. Then gradually have the students change from the hand patting to snapping fingers, making the sound of raindrops. Finally, have more students stop making sounds until only a few are snapping fingers, making the sound of the rain beginning to stop.

Connecting the Planetary System and Music

Grade Levels	5th–6th
Science Objective[1]	**D. Earth and Space Science**
	M.D. 3 Earth in the solar system
	a. The earth is the third planet from the sun in a system that includes the moon, the sun, seven other planets and their moons, and smaller objects, such as asteroids and comets.
Music Objective[2]	**6. Content Standard: Listening to, analyzing, and describing music**
	a. Students describe specific music events in a given aural example, using appropriate terminology.

1 NATIONAL SCIENCE STANDARDS, the National Academies Press.
2 NATIONAL MUSIC STANDARDS, MENC

Planets are celestial bodies that give off no light of their own. They merely reflect the light of their star. A group of planets revolving around a star is called a "planetary system" or solar system.

Our planetary system has eight planets that revolve around our sun. The inner ones—Mercury, Venus, Earth, and Mars—are made of rock. The outer ones—Jupiter, Saturn, Uranus, and Neptune—are made mainly of gas.

Intermediate students will be very interested in the music English composer Gustav Holst wrote between 1914 and 1916 to describe each planet (except Earth and Pluto). He combined them into his work titled *The Planets.*

LISTENING

Each of the movements of *The Planets* is appealing. "Mars, the Bringer of War" has been included in this book because of its great rhythmic interest.

Listening Activities

Read about the composer and the composition, and then listen to "Mars, the Bringer of War" from *The Planets* by Holst while following the Listening Map. Have students describe specific instruments heard, themes that were repeated, and rhythmic features of the music.

The Composer

Gustav Holst (1874–1934) lived his entire life in England. During his life, he was known primarily as a teacher. He has since become recognized as one of Britain's finest composers. His large-scale orchestral works, such as *The Planets*, helped build that reputation. He was one of the first composers to use the new technologies of sound recording that took his music to a wider audience than could go to concerts.

133

The Composition

A fascination with astronomy and astrology led Holst to write the orchestral suite *The Planets*. What is Mar's connection to war? The planet's reddish color is caused by rust (iron oxide) in the soil. Because the red planet's color reminded ancient astronomers of blood, they named the planet after their god of war (Mars was the Roman god of war). Mars's two moons also have names that relate to war: *Phobos* means "fear," and *Deimos* means "panic."

Listen for the three main themes in the music. Also, see if you can hear the $\frac{5}{4}$ meter.

LISTENING

Listening Selection

"Mars, the Bringer of War" from *The Planets* by Holst   CD Track 19

Listening Map   Appendix, p. 271

A New Scientific Experiment

Wise teachers employ a variety of methods to enhance student learning, and using music to improve the study of science will open doors to understanding for students. Plus, engaging the mind in new ways is really the perfect scientific experiment. Try this theory, and watch the transformation begin.

> Music helps students learn about science in extended ways. The mind is opened to learning about science in different ways through the use of music.

Perhaps keep a log of which students seem more attentive when relating the study of science to some aspect of music, as mentioned in the activities suggested in Chapter 7. Notate the interesting comments from students, and the extended learning about scientific methods that are evidenced in the classroom. Experiencing science lessons with music entwined would be an ideal approach for many students, and it may be surprising which students seem to progress more quickly with this approach. Some students who never seem interested in the sciences might be drawn to the topic when using music as the learning vehicle. Enjoy this scientific experiment with the students.

Thinking It Through

In a small group, choose one or two of the activities in this chapter. Discuss modifications that could be made to use these activities in different grade levels. Share with the other groups.

Suggestions for Further Study

Check out the website www.physicssongs.org. Dr. Walter Smith, Associate Professor of Physics at Haverford College, maintains the website and posts songs that people have written about science. Smith uses folk tunes and familiar melodies ("Sweet Betsy from Pike," "Old Dan Tucker") and adds new words. He has found that he is not alone and that many people enjoy using music to learn science. In using a web search engine and typing in "Science Songs," over 6400 "hits" came up.

A few more wonderful science and music websites include:

- www.songsforteaching.com/sciencesongs.htm
  Songs about measuring, growing seeds, the digestive system, the seasons, and numerous other science topics are included.
- http://faculty.washington.edu/chudler/songs.html
  This website includes wonderful songs like "Brain of Mine" to the tune of "Twinkle, Twinkle Little Star," "The Dendrite Song" to the tune of "Clementine," and other clever songs to help us learn about the brain.
- www.youtube.com/watch?v=05ip-N0H1Ig
  This is a marvelous performance by a choir that begins with the complete "rain storm" performed with hands and feet that is described in this chapter.

Many resources for teaching science and music can be found on the Marco Polo Educational website, www.marcopolo-education.org, by clicking on the Arts Edge icon. Very helpful teacher resources include lesson plans, rubrics for evaluation of student learning, and extensions of the lessons.

Watch the DVD *Isaac Asimov-Voyage to the Outer Planets* (2003). The idea of combining images of the planets from NASA with passages from Holst's *The Planets* was a good one!

Recommended Student Books

Barner, Bob. (1996). *Dem Bones*. San Francisco: Chronicle Books.
Clever anatomy lesson with great illustrations is based on the gospel song.

Brett, Jan. (1997). *The Twelve Days of Christmas*. New York: Putnam & Grosset Group.
Lavish illustrations of the book show various levels of meaning in the words of the song, which count from 1 to 12.

Denne, Ben. (2001). *The Usborne Internet-Linked First Encyclopedia of Seas and Oceans*. New York: Scholastic.
First reference book that explains different aspects of today's world.

Elliot, Doug. (2008). *Crawdads, Doodlebugs and Greasy Greens*. Asheville, NC: Native Ground Music.
Songs, stories, and lore celebrating the natural world.

Locker, Thomas. (2002). *Water Dance*. San Diego: Voyager Books.
A wonderful combination of science and art, paintings show each step in the water circle with haiku-like text and explanations.

Peek, Merle. (1981). *Roll Over.* New York: Houghton Mifflin/Clarion Books.
Great illustrations depicting the words of the song.

Scieszka, Jon. (1995). *Math Curse.* New York: Viking.
After being told that you can think of almost anything as a math problem, a girl starts thinking of everything
   in that way.

Stott, Carole. (2003). *I Wonder Why Stars Twinkle.* New York: Kingfisher Books.
Questions and answers about space.

CHAPTER 9 | USING MUSIC TO ENHANCE LEARNING IN MATH

Why We Should Involve Our Students in Musical Math Activities

"There is a causal link between music and spatial intelligence (the ability to perceive the world accurately and to form mental pictures of things). This kind of intelligence, by which one can visualize various elements that should go together, is critical to the sort of thinking necessary for everything from solving advanced mathematics problems to being able to pack a book-bag with everything that will be needed for the day."

Benefits of Music Education[1]

"The very best engineers and technical designers in the Silicon Valley industry are, nearly without exception, practicing musicians."

Grant Venerable, author of The Paradox of the Silicon Savior[2]

"The pleasure we obtain from music comes from counting, but counting unconsciously. Music is nothing but unconscious arithmetic."

Gottfried Wilhelm Leibniz, German mathematician[3]

Much of music is mathematical. Although it is a simplified form of arithmetic, counting in sets of two, three, four, and higher are used consistently in performing music. When teaching the values of rhythmic notation, we develop and reinforce the concepts of addition, subtraction, multiplication, division, and fractions.

The notes in music are divisions of a whole and have certain numbers of beats. Measures in music are intended to include the correct number of beats according to the meter signature. The staff has five lines and four spaces. Melody in music is often patterns of sound. Harmony is two or more tones sounding together. Thus, using music to enhance math in the elementary school is a logical combination.

Connecting/Reinforcing Activities

Grade Levels	K–2nd
Math Objective[1]	**Number and Operations Standard** All students should connect number words and numerals to the quantities they represent, using various physical models and representations; **Understand meanings of operations and how they relate to one another** All students should understand the effects of adding and subtracting whole numbers;
Music Objective[2]	**1. Content Standard: Singing, alone and with others, a varied repertoire of music** a. Students sing independently, on pitch and in rhythm, with appropriate timbre, diction, and posture, and maintain a steady tempo.

1 Principals and Standards for School Mathematics, NCTM
2 NATIONAL MUSIC STANDARDS, MENC

Counting

Note

The melodies for most of the songs in this chapter can be heard at www.kididdles.com.

Many children's songs include counting. As children sing these songs, they are reinforcing their understanding of counting, and they are learning about their American heritage through music.

SINGING

One, Two, Tie (or Buckle) My Shoe
One, two, tie my shoe,
Three, four, shut the door,
Five, six, pick up sticks,
Seven, eight, lay them straight,
Nine, ten, a big fat hen.

Singing this simple song while holding up the correct number of fingers is a great time-filler to use before lining up for lunch or recess. Thinking the song silently is an easy way to encourage children to walk down the hall quietly. They continue to hold up the appropriate fingers as they sing silently—another good use of audiation.

The original version used "buckle my shoe." Older children can be asked what that meant, and why did someone substitute the words "tie my shoe"? These discussions require higher-level thinking skills. Students in upper grades can be assigned to small groups to create a more modern version of the chant. They might choose to substitute more current wording for a 21st-century rhyme. They could use higher numbers or exponents or multiplication to make this activity more challenging, both mathematically and linguistically. (The melody is notated on page 31.)

Subtraction

"Ten in the Bed," "Five Little Monkeys," "Alice the Camel," and "Five Green and Speckled Frogs" all deal with subtraction.

Ten in the Bed
There were ten in the bed
And the little one said "Roll over, roll over,"
And they all rolled over and one fell out.

In "Ten in the Bed," the little one says "roll over," and one falls out, leaving nine. The song continues until the little one is alone in the bed with lots of room, and comfortably sings "good night." Children, sitting in a circle, holding cards with a number on each, become part of the math game. When the group sings "there were nine. . ." the child holding the nine card stands up, and so forth.

Nursery rhymes, jump rope chants, and folk tales include counting and subtraction, and can reinforce these numerical concepts for children.

SINGING

Songbook Selection

Appendix

P   "Ten in the Bed" Traditional   186

Five Little Monkeys
Five little monkeys jumping on the bed
One fell off and bumped his head
Called for the doctor, the doctor said,
"No little monkeys jumping on the bed!"

The chant can be continued, subtracting with each repetition—four little monkeys, three, and so forth until "no little monkeys" are left. Hand puppets, paper sack puppets, and finger puppets can be made or purchased commercially to use with this chant.

Alice The Camel (or "Allison's Camel")
Alice the camel has ten humps

Alice the camel has ten humps
Alice the camel has ten humps,
So go, Alice, go! Boom Boom Boom.

When the number is sung in "Alice The Camel," children hold up the correct number of fingers. So in the first verse, all ten fingers are held. On the words, "go, Alice, go," they punch their hands rhythmically out in front of them three times, once on each word. On the "Boom Boom Boom" part, the children bump hips with the child on each side in the circle, once on each boom. This takes some teaching of self-control to keep them from bumping too rambunctiously and sending the neighbor child to the floor. If the class can't handle the bumping at first, just have them put their hands on their hips and shift their hips to the right and left. On each verse, subtract one "hump," so that the song is sung with nine, eight, and so forth, with children holding up the correct number of fingers with each verse. The song ends with zero, "Alice the camel has NO humps." Children make a zero with their fingers on this last verse, which ends with the sung words, "'cause Alice is a horse, of course!" This song is a favorite of the primary grades, and they think the ending is a hysterically funny joke.

SINGING

Songbook Selection

Appendix

P   "Alice The Camel" Traditional   187

Five Green and Speckled Frogs
Five green and speckled frogs, sat on a speckled log,
Eating some most delicious bugs—*Yum, yum!*
One jumped into the pool,
Where it was nice and cool.
Then there were four green speckled frogs—*Glub, glub!*

Children sing this song, motioning with their hands in a circular pattern on their stomachs, on the "yum" parts, and holding their noses on the "Glub, glub." Again, after the frog jumps into the water, children must subtract and find the number of frogs left on the log. The final verse ends with "And then there were no green speckled frogs! "*Glub, glub!*"

SINGING

Songbook Selection

Appendix

P   "Five Green and Speckled Frogs" Traditional   188

Addition

This Old Man
This old man, he played one,
He played knick-knack on my thumb,
With a knick-knack paddy whack, give a dog a bone,
This old man came rolling home.

Each verse of the song adds a number, with new rhyming words, always ending with the "knick knack paddy whack" lines. Other verses can use the following words, although many versions exist because folk music comes from an aural tradition.

Two	shoe
Three	knee
Four	door
Five	jive
Six	sticks
Seven	heaven
Eight	gate
Nine	shine
Ten	hen

Singing includes holding the correct number of fingers up for each verse, and making up a hand-jive part for the last two lines. Try snapping fingers on the "knick knack," patting the knees with alternating hands on "paddy whack," and doing the motion of tossing a bone over one shoulder for the "give a. . ." part. Then make a rolling motion with both hands on "rolling home."

SINGING

Songbook Selection

Appendix

P	"This Old Man" Traditional	189

Many CDs are available with songs for learning a variety of subjects, including math. Hap Palmer has written many creative, useful CDs that help children learn. As stated on his website, "Hap Palmer is an innovator in the use of music and movement to teach skills and encourage the use of imagination."[4] Among his award-winning musical recordings which teach math are: *Two Little Sounds: Fun with Phonics and Number*, *Singing Multiplication Tables*, and *Multiplication Mountain*.

Multiplication

Tantalizing Tidbit of Research

In psychological research, music and rhythm have been shown to benefit the rote memorization process. When various types of verbal information (e.g., multiplication tables, spelling lists) have been presented simultaneously with music, memorization has been enhanced (Gfeller, 1983; Schuster and Mouzon, 1982).[5]

Grade Levels	3rd–5th
Math Objective[1]	**Understand meanings of operations and how they relate to one another**
	All students should understand the effects of multiplying and dividing whole numbers;
Music Objective[2]	**1. Content Standard: Singing, alone and with others, a varied repertoire of music**
	a. Students sing independently, on pitch and in rhythm, with appropriate timbre, diction, and posture, and maintain a steady tempo.

1 Principals and Standards for School Mathematics, NCTM
2 NATIONAL MUSIC STANDARDS, MENC

SINGING

Many classroom teachers have found that using piggyback songs to practice multiplication tables and skip-counting is very effective. Here is a suggested list:

3s   To the tune of "London Bridge" ("Three times one is three, three times two is six, three times three is nine, three times four is twelve.")
4s   To the tune of "Bingo"
6s   To the tune of "Happy Birthday"
7s   To the tune of "Row, Row, Row Your Boat"
8s   To the tune of "Mary Had A Little Lamb"
9s   To the tune of "99 Bottles of Pop"

Prediction

Grade Levels	K–2nd
Math Objective[1]	**Develop and evaluate inferences and predictions that are based on data**
	All students should discuss events related to students' experiences as likely or unlikely.
Music Objective[2]	**1. Content Standard: Singing, alone and with others, a varied repertoire of music**
	a. Students sing independently, on pitch and in rhythm, with appropriate timbre, diction, and posture, and maintain a steady tempo.

1 Principals and Standards for School Mathematics, NCTM
2 NATIONAL MUSIC STANDARDS, MENC

"Three Little Pigs" is the much loved children's story about the pigs who build their houses, only one of which withstands the "huffing and puffing" of the big, bad wolf. The story teaches many lessons, including work ethic and making wise decisions, but it can also be used to practice prediction.

What happens to the first house, thrown up very quickly by the first pig, when it is blown on? How many houses are left standing? Where are the other two pigs going? Good discussions with the children bring a better understanding of the three original houses, with suggestions as to why only one was left standing.

Find a great song that tells the whole "Three Little Pigs" story to the tune of "This Old Man" at www.geocities.com/EnchantedForest/Cottage/3192/3littlepigs.html.

SINGING

Patterns

Grade Levels	K–5th
Math Objective[1]	**Understand patterns, relations, and functions**
	K–2nd All students should recognize, describe, and extend patterns such as sequences of sounds and shapes or simple numeric patterns and translate from one representation to another;
	3rd–5th All students should represent and analyze patterns and functions, using words, tables, and graphs.
Music Objective[2]	**6. Content Standard: Listening to, analyzing, and describing music**
	a. Students identify simple music forms when presented aurally

1 Principals and Standards for School Mathematics, NCTM
2 NATIONAL MUSIC STANDARDS, MENC

143

Music has repeating patterns that children can discover both aurally and visually. Rhythm patterns are often repeated within a song, as are melodic patterns. When looking at and listening to music, help the students discover these repeating patterns. Discuss and practice predicting and sequencing when students create their own musical patterns.

Find the repeated rhythmic and melodic patterns in "America."

SINGING

Songbook Selection

Get America Singing. . .Again!

| P & I | "America" Traditional melody with words by Samuel Smith | 8 |

Fractions

Grade Levels	3rd–5th

Math Objective[1]

Number and Operations Standard

All student should develop understanding of fractions as parts of unit wholes, as parts of a collection, as locations on number lines, and as divisions of whole numbers;

Music Objective[2]

5. Content Standard: Reading and notating music

a. Read whole, half, dotted half, quarter, and eighth notes and rests in $\frac{2}{4}$, $\frac{3}{4}$, and $\frac{4}{4}$ meter signatures

1 Principals and Standards for School Mathematics, NCTM
2 NATIONAL MUSIC STANDARDS, MENC

The notational system for music is based on a numerical structure, so it is filled with opportunities for mathematical/musical learning. The traditional notation used for writing music includes numerical values and fractions.

As a review, in $\frac{4}{4}$ meter signature the following number of beats is given to each note:

Whole note	4 beats
Half note	2 beats
Quarter note	1 beat
Eighth note	½ beat
Sixteenth note	¼ beat

The half note is one half of a whole note, thus the name "half note." All the notes listed above have the same system. The quarter is one fourth of a whole, the eighth is one eighth of a whole, and so forth. Working with eighth, quarter, half, and whole notes in reading and performing rhythms produces a sense of proportions.

144

Many teachers draw pie charts showing the relationship of the different notes to the whole, and have students try to learn the fractions of the whole. Most students struggle with this concept. Expecting students in the first or second grades to understand fractions, such as a quarter note represents one fourth of a whole note, is not a good plan. Piaget's research gives us the answer (see page 19). According to Piaget, the preoperational child cannot understand such concepts as fractions of the whole. Of course, these are generalizations of the student's learning abilities, and there are "exceptions to the rule."

Musical Math Problems

Math problems could be stated using musical challenges. For example:

- The end result is 9½. Represent this total using musical notation.
- Think of words to represent meter in 3s (bas-ket-ball, bloom-ing rose, ten-nis team, cho-co-late). Chant the words softly while listening to a piece in the meter of 3s (triple meter).
- Think of words to represent meter in 4s (high school foot-ball, cats rule dogs drool, cap-puc-ci-no). Chant the words softly while listening to a piece in the meter of 4s (quadruple meter).
- Bounce a ball to show meter in 2s, 3s, or 4s. Get a partner and work out a game showing all three sets of beats while bouncing the ball to each other. Sing a song in each of the meters while bouncing the ball.
- Clap a steady beat while listening to a musical selection. Count how many beats in 10 seconds. Challenge students to figure out how many were in a minute, in 10 minutes, etc.

CREATING

LISTENING

SINGING

Games for Note Duration and Rhythm

Teaching Note Duration Through Movement

MOVING

One successful plan for working with note names involves body movement.

- Have large sketches of the notes on poster boards.
- Have the students move according to the note that is being displayed on the easel or on the board. Change the poster after the students do the correct movement.
- Let one child play a steady beat on a drum.
- For a whole note, students will step on beat one and bend their knees three times to indicate the four-beat value of the whole note.
- For the half note, step and bend, showing the two-beat value.
- The quarter note, often called the walking note, is shown by one step for each beat.
- Show the eighth note by jogging, two steps to a beat.

Clapping Note Duration Game

Students can also say and clap the note names as part of the learning of the number of beats or counts for each note. Use the following game:

Say	As We	Do
Whole note, three, four		Clap once and keep hands clasped, moving them downward a few inches on beats two, three, and four
Half note		Clap and clasp on beat two
Quarter (said to the beat)		Clap once on each quarter note, thus the clap goes with the "quar" syllable of the word "quarter."
Eighth note OR two eighths		Clapping on each word, thus, two claps per beat.

This game works well, except for the quarter note plan. The word "quarter" has two syllables and the quarter note only gets one beat. That can be confusing for some students. Some teachers say "quart" for the quarter note to avoid the misunderstanding.

Reading Rhythmic Notation

Students can read lines of notation using this game. The following line of notation would be read:

Quarter Two eighths Half-note Quarter Quarter Two eighths Quarter

Then, they can write the rhythms mathematically. The line would be written:

$$\tfrac{1}{4} + \tfrac{1}{8} + \tfrac{1}{8} + \tfrac{1}{2} = 1 \ + \ (\tfrac{1}{4} + \tfrac{1}{4} + \tfrac{1}{8} + \tfrac{1}{8} + \tfrac{1}{4}) = 2$$

Student Project

SINGING

Rhythmic Notation Project

Sing "Simple Gifts" from *Get America Singing. . .Again!*, page 39. Next, clap the rhythm of the melody. Finally, add up the rhythmic notation mathematically for each line, then for the whole song. What is the total?

Rhythm patterns can be represented using Cuisenaire rods. The longest rod would represent the whole note, the half note would be presented as a rod half as long as the whole note rod, the quarter note would be quarter of the length of the longest rod, and so forth.

Mathematical Descriptions of Instruments

A method of classifying instruments that is successful for organizing instruments from all areas of the world includes the labels of Idiophones, Membranophones, Chordophones, Aerophones and Electrophones. These classifications correspond well to the mathematical description of the source of the sound the instruments produce. The first four categories are based on a Hindu system dating back more than two thousand years that divides instruments into four similar groups.

- *Idiophones*: where the body of a vibrating instrument produces the sound. Instruments in this category are made of material such as metal or wood capable of producing sound by shaking as with a rattle, rubbing as with a glass harmonica, striking as with gongs or bells, or plucking as with a Jew's harp.
- *Membranophones*: where the vibration of a stretched membrane produces the sound. These instruments are mainly drums or instruments that make sound by hitting, plucking or tapping a stretched skin. It also includes "singing" membranes such as the kazoo.
- *Chordophones*: where one or more vibrating strings produce the sound. This category includes stringed instruments that can play several tones simultaneously, such as a violin, harp, piano, zither or auto-harp.
- *Aerophones*: where a vibrating column of air produces the sound. These instruments require air to be blown, and include the woodwind orchestral instruments such as the flute, and brass orchestral instruments such as the trumpet. This category also includes ethnic instruments such as a whistle, conch shell or bone flute.
- *Electrophones*: where the sound is produced primarily by electrical or electronic means. This category includes the modern electronic synthesizer as well as sound generated by a computer program.

Mathematicians work with the components that determine the nature of the sound coming from a musical instrument. The set of resonant frequencies making up the spectrum of the sound is one of these components. "Wave equations" are used to determine how and why instruments make their distinctive sounds.[6]

Have students explore the sound of each of the four original instrument categories by making and performing on their own simple instruments.

Making Simple Rhythm Instruments[7]

Idiophones

To make shakers, use any of the following types of containers:

- Plastic Easter egg
- Empty plastic tubs with lids
- Dried gourd—very authentic and easy to grow in many places.

Fill the containers with popcorn kernels, pebbles, nuts or seeds. The sound will vary depending on the filler used.

To make a glass xylophone, fill some tall glasses with different amounts of water. The more water in the glass, the lower the pitch will be. Having less water in the glass will raise the pitch. To play, gently strike the glasses with a metal spoon.

Membranophones

A kazoo, which you play by humming into it, is simple to make. Use a square of waxed paper or tissue paper, and either put it onto one end of a cardboard tube with rubber bands, or fold it over the teeth of a small comb.

The following make useful drums:

- Empty plastic tubs (such as margarine or ice cream tubs) with the lids on—the bigger the tub, the better.
- A sheet of canvas, plastic, rubber, or waxed paper stretched very taut over the lip of a wooden bowl or a clay flowerpot, held in place by strong tape, heavy rubber bands, or strong cord.
- An empty cylindrical oatmeal box with a lid.

To make beaters, secure one of the following onto the end of a stick, a long pencil, or a short length of dowel:

- A large wooden bead wrapped with yarn or string.
- A rubber ball or "superball" wrapped with yarn or string.
- A cork.

Or wrap many rubber bands around one end of the stick.

Chordophones

Stretch rubber bands between nails, or thumbtacks, or around tubs or shoeboxes. A traditional wash tub bass, made using a small metal tub, broom handle, and thick string, is easy to create.

Aerophones

Blow across the lip of a glass jug or bottle.

Thinking It Through

Read and discuss the following excerpt from *Music With the Brain In Mind* by Eric Jensen.[8] Then name three different music activities that could be useful before math time in the classroom.

> Studying adults, Lawrence Parsons of the University of Texas at San Antonio's Health Science Research Imaging Center found that auditory rhythm, but not melody/harmony, enhanced both visualization and mental rotation, and that dynamic abstract visual stimuli enhanced both, as well.
>
> The results were approximately the same for auditory and visual rhythm primers as they were for Mozart. This study suggests that either auditory rhythm or rhythmic visual stimuli can lead to short-term enhancement of mental rotation—a useful spatial-temporal skill (the skills crucial for greater success in subjects like math and science). The study also suggests that music in general (Mozart's music in particular) is effective because it possesses multiple lines of rhythmic streams . . . and more complex rhythmic sounds lead to even greater enhancement than very simple rhythmic sounds.

Suggestions for Further Study

Read *Music With the Brain In Mind* (2000) by Eric Jensen, published by Corwin Press, to learn more about brain research as it relates to music and cognition. The book also provides strategies for incorporating music into teaching at all levels.

Read *Musicophilia: Tales of Music and the Brain* (2007) by neurologist Oliver Sacks, published by Picador, to learn more about the concept that humans are truly a "musical species."

Two good websites are available where the lyrics and the recorded song for many traditional children's songs can be found for free. Explore the KIDiddles website at www.kididdles.com to listen most of the songs used in this chapter. Another good resource is http://freekidsmusic.com.

Explore all the money-counting songs on www.mrsjonesroom.com/songs/money.html.

Recommended Student Books

Brett, Jan. (1997). *The Twelve Days of Christmas*. New York: Putnam & Grosset Group.
Lavish illustrations of the book show various levels of meaning in the words of the song, which count from
    1 to 12.

Peek, Merle. (1981). *Roll Over.* New York: Houghton Mifflin/Clarion Books.
Great illustrations depicting the words of the song.

Scieszka, Jon. (1995). *Math Curse.* New York: Viking.
After being told that you can think of almost anything as a math problem, a girl starts thinking of everything
    in that way.

CHAPTER 10 | **USING MUSIC TO ENHANCE LEARNING IN SOCIAL STUDIES**

Why We Should Involve Our Students in Multicultural Music Activities

"A study of the arts provides children with an internal glimpse of other cultures and teaches them to be empathetic toward the people of these cultures. This development of compassion and empathy, as opposed to development of greed and a "me first" attitude, provides a bridge across cultural chasms that leads to respect of other races at an early age."

Benefits of Music Education[1]

"The history of a people is found in its songs."

George Jellinek, author and authority on opera[2]

"Folk Music is the original melody of man, it is the musical mirror of the world."

Friedrich Nietzsche, German philosopher[3]

"The arts are the signature of a nation."

Joan Mondale, appointed by President Carter as the honorary chairperson of the Federal Council on the Arts and Humanities[4]

"The recommendation to start teaching music from world cultures as early as possible seems advisable, given that ethnic awareness emerges at about age four. Once positive or negative attitudes are formed, they tend to increase with age."

Elisa Macedo Dekaney and Deborah A. Cunningham[5]

The Importance of Teaching World Music

The goals and objectives for most elementary schools include understanding other cultures as well as our own American culture. Most state standards in elementary education, as part of their goals or outcome statements, include global understanding or knowledge of other cultures and historical eras. The arts provide perfect means for exploring other peoples and historical periods. What remains from any lost civilization is the art, and no culture or group of people has ever existed that did not have music.

One important reason for the study of World music to be included in schools is that students need to learn that the music of our Western culture is only one of the many musical styles that exist around the world.

Other important points are made in the introduction to the *National Standards for Arts Education*:

The cultural diversity of America is a vast resource for arts education and should be used to help students understand themselves and others. The visual, traditional and performing arts provide a variety of lenses for examining the cultures and artistic contributions of our nation and others around the world. Students should learn that each has its own history and heroes. Subject matter from diverse historical periods, styles, forms, and cultures should be used to develop basic knowledge and skills in the various art disciplines.[6]

Singing songs and performing the dances of many countries helps children understand other cultures. Incorporating World music into units highlighting specific countries is an excellent way for classroom teachers to integrate music into the curriculum.

Student Project (individual and small group)

Watch *Pulse: A Stomp Odyssey* DVD

Take notes on this vibrant musical sound journey around the world, a celebration of music, dance and cultures. Note the countries featured (including the United States), and the basic kinds of dance and music performed in each location. What musical surprise is revealed in the last section of the film?

Using the *Pulse: A Stomp Odyssey* CD, listen carefully to the following examples of World music. In small groups, discuss the commonalities and differences in the music.

How does the music show that the world is connected in many ways we may not be able to see?

1. Flamenco dancer Eva la Yerbabuena in Granada, Spain (Flamenco track)
2. A religious festival in Kerala, India (Keralan Procession track)
3. The Timbalada band in Salvador de Bahia, Brazil (Candyall Beat track)

Note: A Teacher's Guide for *Pulse: A Stomp Odyssey* is available online at http://pulsethemovie.com with lesson plans, resource websites, worksheets, and student projects in the subjects of Music, Dance, English (Language Arts), Math, Science, and Social Studies.

Connecting Our American Story to America's Music: Our "Multimusical Culture"[7]

Multiculturalism is a familiar concept for teachers. Colleges structure courses devoted to teaching about people from backgrounds different from our own, and school districts sponsor workshops and in-services for teachers on the topic. Americans are proud of their diverse roots. Cities such as Chicago are famous for their neighborhood festivals celebrating the different nationalities represented by the citizenry.

Music is common, but unique to every culture on earth. When studying our American "multimusical culture," awareness of the world around us is raised.

It almost seems that teaching about multiculturalism is often more successful than teaching about our own native culture and country, America. In order for children to truly learn about our world, they need to know about our own country and culture in addition to knowing about countries and cultures around the world. We in education must be on a dual track, making sure we teach our students about America, our history, our heroes, and our culture, along with exposing students to the people of the world.

Our world is shrinking, due in part to ready access to media and technology. Every night on the news we watch people from all over the world. Even wars fought on other continents are televised for instant viewing. We type in a web address and instantly are connected to sites filled with information about other nations, other cultures, World music—just any imaginable international topic is available.

Music activities featuring folk dance, ethnic instruments, and cultural uses are included in all the music textbooks available for use in our schools. Music stores have large inventories of folk music. Music from other nationalities or cultures is readily available through school supply catalogues and companies (see Appendix 3, page 220) As with most new things, getting started is the hardest part.

Multicultural Student Populations

Starting with the background of children in the class is a logical beginning. Often family members are more than willing to visit the class to share music from their native country. Any one classroom of students will represent an amazing diversity, and encouraging them to discover their cultural origins can be an extraordinarily meaningful family project.

Where do we come from? America is a country of immigrants. Almost every person can trace ancestors back to another part of the world. Here is a breakdown of America's ancestry if it were a village of 100 in the year 2000:[8]

German	15
Irish	11
African	9
English	9
Mexican	7
Italian	6
Polish	3
French	3

* There would also be 1 Scotch-Irish, 1 Swedish, and 26 of other backgrounds.

One teacher, Janet Armstead from Kansas, sends a note home at the beginning of every year asking if any families represent other cultures. She invites them to send CDs of music representing those cultures. By starting with the cultures of the children in class, and then progressing to other, more distant countries and cultures, multicultural studies seem less daunting and more manageable for both teacher and pupils.

Enjoy singing the multicultural materials included in the *Get America Singing. . .Again!* songbook, and the Songbook in the Appendix.

Songbook Selections

Get America Singing. . .Again!

P & I	"De colores" Mexican folk song	13
P & I	"Sakura" Japanese folk song	37
I	"Shalom Chaverim" Traditional Hebrew folk song	37
P & I	"This Little Light of Mine" African American Spiritual	47
I	"Lift Ev'ry Voice and Sing" by James W. and J. Rosamond Johnson	28

Appendix

P	"Acitrón" Spanish stone-passing game	194
P	"A la rueda rueda" ('Round and 'Round) Latin American folk song	196
I	"Chíu, Chíu, Chíu" Uruguyan folk song	199
I	"Si me dan pasteles" (When You Bring *Pasteles*) Puerto Rican folk song	200

Enhancing Multicultural Awareness Through Children's Literature and Music

Grade Levels	5th–6th
Social Studies Objective[1]	**1. Culture**
	Social studies programs should include experiences that provide for the study of culture and cultural diversity.
Music Objective[2]	**4. Content Standard:** Composing and arranging music within specified guidelines
	Achievement Standard: Students a. compose short pieces within specified guidelines, demonstrating how the elements of music are used to achieve unity and variety, tension and release, and balance

1 NCSS Curriculum Standards for Social Studies
2 NATIONAL MUSIC STANDARDS, MENC

CREATING

SINGING

A wonderful book for expanding the awareness of the African American culture is *Talking Eggs* by Robert D. San Souci with pictures by Jerry Pinkney. It is a 1989 Caldecott Honor Book. This fascinating adaptation of a Creole folk tale is set in rural Louisiana. It tells the story of Blanche, a child with a "spirit of do-right" and her sister Rose who is selfish and mean. This book could provide the libretto for an opera performed by an elementary class. This opera performance could be sung by improvisation in only one class period, or it could be composed and presented in "real opera" format for the school or parents. Set design, costuming, lighting, and staging would be hands-on learning. The performers could be children in the class or puppets created by class members. A memorable operatic event taking a variety of forms could be the result—all from reading one book in class.

Grade Levels	K–4th
Social Studies Objective[1]	**III People, Places and Times**
	Social studies programs should include experiences that provide for the study of people, places, and environments.
Music Objective[2]	**4. Content Standard:** Composing and arranging music within specified guidelines
	Achievement Standard:
	Students a. create and arrange music to accompany readings or dramatizations

1 NCSS Curriculum Standards for Social Studies
2 NATIONAL MUSIC STANDARDS, MENC

PLAYING

LISTENING

Several books are available for sharing the Native American culture. It is simple and effective to add instruments to the reading of *Hiawatha* by Henry Wadsworth Longfellow with pictures by Susan Jeffers, an artfully illustrated section from the original poem. *The Legend of the Indian Paintbrush*, retold and illustrated by Tomie DePaola, can serve as a wonderful introduction to a listening experience with American Indian music. Several available recordings of authentic Native American music include the following: *Songs, Chants and Flute Music of the American Indian*, *Tribal Songs of the American Indian*, and *Authentic Music of the American Indian*, all by various artists and all available through Amazon.com.

Grade Levels	K–4th
Social Studies Objective[1]	**I Culture**
	Social studies programs should include experiences that provide for the study of culture and cultural diversity.
Music Objective[2]	**4. Content Standard:** Composing and arranging music within specified guidelines
	Achievement Standard:

Students
b. create and arrange short songs and instrumental pieces within specified guidelines
c. use a variety of sound sources when composing

1 NCSS Curriculum Standards for Social Studies
2 NATIONAL MUSIC STANDARDS, MENC

At the Crossroads by Rachel Isadora is an energetic tale of South African children waiting for their dads to come home from working in the mines. At one point in the story, the children make up a lively musical piece using some instruments they have. The book, while describing another culture, could also be used as a starting point for students to create their own composition using found sounds or instruments.

CREATING

Grade Levels	3rd–4th
Social Studies Objective[1]	**II Time, Continuity, and Change**
	Social studies programs should include experiences that provide for the study of the ways human beings view themselves in and over time.
Music Objective	**9. Content Standard:** Understanding music in relation to history and culture
	Achievement Standard:
	Students
	a. identify by genre or style aural examples of music from various historical periods and cultures

1 NCSS Curriculum Standards for Social Studies
2 NATIONAL MUSIC STANDARDS, MENC

Listening Activities

American multicultural composers enrich the classical, or art music of America. Read about the composers and the compositions featured below, and then listen to two pieces, both written in the first half of the 20th century: a Cuban American, Ernesto Lecuona, wrote the first, which is full of Latin rhythms and melodies; a famous African American composer, William Grant Still, wrote the other selection that features a banjo sitting in with the orchestra.

"Malagueña": The Composer

Born and raised in Cuba, Ernesto Lecuona (1895–1963) first won international fame as a concert pianist. He went on to also be known for his composing and conducting skills. He wrote music for many films and theater productions. In 1942, his biggest popular song hit, from the movie of the same name, "Always in My Heart" ("*Siempre en mi Corazon*") was nominated for an Oscar for Best Song.

The Composition

Lecuona's piano music is an important and very significant contribution to 20th-century music. In all, the composer wrote 176 pieces for piano solo. Among the most famous are the six that comprise the *Andalucía Suite Espagnole,* including "Malagueña." American composer and arranger Ferde Grofe created the orchestral arrangement of "Malagueña" that you will hear.

Symphony No. 1 ("Afro-American"): The Composer[9]

William Grant Still (1895–1978) was a pioneer. He was one of the first successful African American composers of classical music. Still loved music, and learned violin as a teenager. His mother wanted him to become a doctor, but his stepfather encouraged his interest in music.

Still made a good living arranging and performing music for dance clubs. Many of his works (such as Symphony No. 1) reflect his experience as a jazz musician. However, he was trained in classical composition, and wrote symphonic works, ballets, film scores, chamber music, and vocal works. Composer George Gershwin, a friend, said Still's music had a distinct "American sound."

The Composition[10]

Symphony No. 1 ("Afro-American") is full of jazz chords and syncopation, and was one of the first symphonic works written in a jazz or blues style. Still said this about writing Symphony No. 1: "I knew I wanted to write a symphony; I knew that it had to be an American work; and I wanted to demonstrate how the blues . . . could be elevated to the highest musical level." The third movement is lively, with a joyful "gospel" feeling. It's almost dance-like, a very happy piece even in the more stern-sounding minor section. There are several themes. However, the first, light-hearted theme is heard all the way through. How many times is it heard?

LISTENING

Listening Selections

"Malagueña" (*Andalucía Suite Espagnole*) by Lecuona   CD Track 22
3rd Movement, Symphony No. 1 ("Afro-American") by Still   CD Track 17

Connecting Music to the Study of American History

When the class is studying a particular period of history, play music by composers who were active during this time period. For instance, if the subject is 20th-century America, the students could listen to the works mentioned above plus music by Aaron Copland.

Music of the Wars

Grade Levels	K–4th
Social Studies Objective[1]	**VI Power, Authority, and Governance**
	Social studies programs should include experiences that provide for the study of how people create and change structures of power, authority, and governance.
Music Objective[2]	**9. Content Standard:** Understanding music in relation to history and culture
	Achievement Standard:
	Students a. identify by genre or style aural examples of music from various historical periods and cultures

1 NCSS Curriculum Standards for Social Studies
2 NATIONAL MUSIC STANDARDS, MENC

Music can help retell history. Each war had music associated with it. The following chart can be the start of a research projects to help students learn more about military history.

Revolutionary War	"Yankee Doodle" "Chester" from *New England Triptych* by W. Schuman (A hymn adopted as a Revolutionary War marching song)
War of 1812	"Battle of New Orleans" (A popular song in the 1960s) "Star Spangled Banner"
Civil War	"When Johnny Comes Marching Home Again" "I Wish I Was in Dixie" "Battle Hymn of the Republic"
World War I	"Caisson Song" "Over There" "It's A Long, Long Way to Tipperary"
World War II	"Don't Sit Under the Apple Tree with Anyone Else But Me" "Boogie Woogie Bugle Boy" "Sentimental Journey"
Vietnam War	"Where Have All the Flowers Gone?" "If I Had a Hammer"
Hostages in Iran, 1979	"Tie a Yellow Ribbon 'Round the Old Oak Tree"
Operation Desert Storm, 1991	"God Bless the U.S.A."

LISTENING

Sing the songs linked to historical periods in American history that are included in the *Get America Singing. . .Again!* songbook.

SINGING

Songbook Selections

Get America Singing. . .Again!

I	"Battle Hymn of the Republic" by Julia Ward Howe and William Steffe	10
I	"If I Had a Hammer" by Lee Hays and Peter Seeger	26
I	"God Bless the U.S.A." by Lee Greenwood	19

LISTENING

The American Indian wars are another important part of our history. In her book *Listen to Learn: Using American Music To Teach Language Arts and Social Studies*,[11] Teri Tibbett links music with history, such as the Ghost Dance that took place before the Massacre at Wounded Knee in the late 1800s. The dancers performed the dance as a healing ritual, but "the military perceived it as a war dance," she says. "It made them nervous—and the massacre followed." Hearing the music that accompanied the Ghost Dance (included on the CD that goes with the Tibbett book) can bring history alive for students. By considering their own reactions to the music, students can gain a better understanding of how the military interpreted the Ghost Dance and the dancers' intentions.

Popular Folk Songs of America's History

Grade Levels	3rd–4th
Social Studies Objective[1]	**II Time, Continuity, and Change**
	Social studies programs should include experiences that provide for the study of the ways human beings view themselves in and over time.
Music Objective[2]	**9. Content Standard:** Understanding music in relation to history and culture
	Achievement Standard:
	Students a. identify by genre or style aural examples of music from various historical periods and cultures

1 NCSS Curriculum Standards for Social Studies
2 NATIONAL MUSIC STANDARDS, MENC

The music of our country includes folk songs (songs handed down with no known composer) and patriotic compositions that every child living in America should know. Many schools have "sing-alongs" in the gym with all the children in the school together singing the folk songs and patriotic songs of our country. These events build a great sense of community within the school.

Dr. Marilyn Ward, in her doctoral dissertation from the University of Florida in 2004, surveyed each state for inclusion of folk music in the curriculum. The state most likely to teach folk music is Nebraska, with Kansas a close second, and the state most likely not to teach folk music is California. She discovered through her research the disturbing information that Americans no longer know our own folk music. We need to educate our students about this vital and important part of our cultural heritage. Sing the American folk songs, defined as traditional music with no known composer, that are included in the *Get America Singing. . .Again!* songbook.

SINGING

Songbook Selections

Get America Singing. . .Again!

P & I	"Home on the Range" Traditional cowboy song	23
P & I	"I've Been Working on the Railroad" Traditional American folk song	24
P & I	"She'll Be Comin' 'Round the Mountain" Traditional	38
I	"Shenandoah" Traditional Sea Chantey	39
P & I	"Simple Gifts" Traditional Shaker hymn	39

Wonderful songs are often composed in a folk song style. Here are some of the best that are included in the *Get America Singing. . .Again!* songbook. Enjoy singing them!

SINGING

Songbook Selections

Get America Singing. . .Again!

I	"Green, Green Grass of Home" by Curly Putman	20
P & I	"Oh! Susanna" by Stephen Foster	33
I	"If I Had a Hammer" by Lee Hays and Pete Seeger	26

American Patriotic Music

Grade Levels	K–4th
Social Studies Objective[1]	**I Culture**
	Social studies programs should include experiences that provide for the study of culture and cultural diversity.
Music Objective[2]	**8. Content Standard:** Understanding relationships between music, the other arts, and disciplines outside the arts
	Achievement Standard:
	Students
	b. identify ways in which the principles and subject matter of other disciplines taught in the school are interrelated with those of music

1 NCSS Curriculum Standards for Social Studies
2 NATIONAL MUSIC STANDARDS, MENC

Teaching music of our country is an aural key to our past, and a way to experience history in a "now" time frame. Songs sung today can be the same as songs sung 100 years ago. History becomes more "alive" when approached through music. A teaching approach to expand this section would be an investigation of what makes a song patriotic and to look at anthems and patriotic songs from other cultures.

The National Anthem

SINGING

LISTENING

Reading the books *The Star Spangled Banner* by Peter Spier, and *The Dawn's Early Light* by Steven Kroll can provide children a clearer understanding of the text of the songs.

The story of the writing of the "Star-Spangled Banner" by Francis Scott Key is not only a story of patriotism, but one of friendship, too. The British had captured Francis Scott Key's friend Dr. Beanes, a dedicated physician helping both the Americans and the British during the war of 1812. Key, a lawyer determined to gain his friend's freedom, went to the British battle ship anchored in the Baltimore bay where Beanes was being held to demand his release. After Key boarded the British ship to plead his friend's case, the battle at Fort McHenry began, thus forcing him to remain on board the ship. The long night he and Dr. Beanes spent watching the raging battle from the deck of the ship, and the eventual American victory, led him to write the words of our national anthem.

All Americans and students studying in American schools need to be familiar with the words to the national anthem, and should know the story behind the song. Out of respect, students should stand and sing the song, just as Americans would stand for another country's national anthem.

MENC, the national association for music educators, developed a project to encourage all teachers to "Get American Singing" our national anthem. A press release provides the following information:

About the National Anthem Project 2004–2007

In response to a 2004 Harris Interactive survey that showed two out of three Americans didn't know the words to our national anthem, MENC: The National Association for Music Education created the

"National Anthem Project: Restoring America's Voice" campaign in March 2005 to re-teach the anthem while raising awareness of the importance of school music.

The National Anthem Project officially culminated in a grand finale in Washington, DC, in June 2007, after celebrating music education through community anthem sings and special events at road shows in each state.

MENC continues to encourage communities to celebrate school music by singing the Anthem together on National Anthem Day, September 14. Always sing "The Star Spangled Banner" while standing.

Songbook Selection

Get America Singing. . .Again!

| I | "The Star Spangled Banner" by Key and Smith | 44 |

SINGING

The Stars and Stripes Forever

"The Stars and Stripes Forever" is the best known and most often performed march written for band. It is so popular in the United States that it is often included in the list of American National Music and is called our official National March.

Listening Activities

LISTENING

PLAYING

Read about the composer and the composition, and then listen to "The Stars and Stripes Forever" by Sousa while following the Listening Map. Sing the words given below during the trio. On a second listening, play rhythm instruments as indicated on the map.

The Composer[12]

John Philip Sousa (1854–1932) was born in Washington, DC. Following his father's interests, he learned to play many instruments, and eventually joined the Marine Band. In 1880, Sousa re-enlisted and became the conductor and principal composer of the United States Marine Band. He composed 136 marches during his lifetime, earning him the title of "March King." Among his marches is "Semper Fidelis" ("Always Faithful"), which became the Marine Corps' official march. To enhance band performances, he invented a larger version of the orchestral tuba so the upward facing bell would create a full warm tone. This new tuba is called the sousaphone. As a conductor, he wore a new pair of white gloves for every performance. Sousa died on March 6, 1932. The last piece he conducted was "The Stars and Stripes Forever."

The Composition[13]

Sousa liked "The Stars and Stripes Forever" so much that he usually planned it as a rousing encore at the end of performances. The piece is written in standard march form: first strain, second strain, trio and break. The trio tune of "The Stars and Stripes Forever" is very catchy, and Sousa wrote words so everyone could sing along.

> Hurrah for the flag of the free!
> May it wave as our standard forever,
> The gem of the land and the sea,
> The banner of the right.
>
> Let despots remember the day
> When our fathers with mighty endeavor
> Proclaimed as they marched to the fray
> That by their might and by their right
> It waves forever.

LISTENING

Listening Selection

March "The Stars and Stripes Forever" by Sousa

CD Track 18

When Johnny Comes Marching Home

LISTENING

The tune of this Civil War song is used for the theme and variations in *American Salute*, a 20th-century instrumental composition by Martin Gould. The theme, "When Johnny Comes Marching Home" is heard first in the bass clarinet and bassoon, playing softly. The varied theme is played eight more times, with each variation changing to keep the listener's attention. Theme and variation form can be effectively taught by using different kinds of soda cans or potato chips (see page 42).

Yankee Doodle

SINGING

This is the theme of several children's books that can be read as a class. The song was actually sung by the British soldiers to make fun of the colonist rebels who were fighting during the War of Independence. These "rag-tag" fighters were in stark contrast to the British regiments who wore their bright red uniforms, and were skilled in fighting in rows. The American rebels wore whatever they could find, and fought in nontraditional ways, hiding behind trees to ambush the more highly trained British army. What was intended as a musical insult became a favorite song of the American rebels, often sung to taunt the British!

America the Beautiful

The words to this song were originally written by Katherine Lee Bates as a poem. Ms. Bates was traveling from her home in Massachusetts, where she taught at Wellesley College, to teach a summer course at

Colorado College. She traveled by train, going first to Chicago to attend the Columbian Exposition in 1893, then on to Colorado. Throughout the trip, she experienced the different parts of the country, and became aware of the beauty and variety of the land and its people. When in Colorado, she took a trip up to the top of Pikes Peak and later wrote:

> One day some of the other teachers and I decided to go on a trip to 14,000-foot Pikes Peak. We hired a prairie wagon. Near the top we had to leave the wagon and go the rest of the way on mules. I was very tired. But when I saw the view, I felt great joy. All the wonder of America seemed displayed there, with the sea-like expanse.

Katharine Lee Bates wrote the original version of "America the Beautiful" in 1893. She wrote the second version in 1904 and her final version was written in 1913. Many people started putting the poem to music so it could be sung. One tune used was "Auld Lang Syne" before the tune we now recognize, "Materna," composed by Samuel A. Ward in 1882, became the accepted version. "Materna" was composed nearly a decade before the poem was written.

Katharine Lee Bates never realized or wanted any royalties from her work, but she retained the copyright to maintain the integrity of her written verses. In essence, she gave the song to the American people.

Elementary school libraries should have several books about "America the Beautiful," as well as other books about patriotic songs.

This Land Is Your Land

This is a great song to use with a unit on the geography of the United States. After the students learn the song, hand out maps of the U.S. In partners, have the students map a route for a trip across the country from the "redwood forests" to the "Gulf Stream waters," or from California to New York City. After drawing the route, students could write up journal entries that list each city and state they would pass through.

SINGING

Songbook Selections

Get America Singing. . .Again!

P & I	"America the Beautiful" by Bates and Ward	9
P & I	"America (My Country 'Tis of Thee)" Traditional Melody with Words by Samuel Smith	8
I	"God Bless America" by Berlin	18
P & I	"This Land Is Your Land" by Woody Guthrie	42
I	"Lift Ev'ry Voice and Sing" by James W. and J. Rosamond Johnson	28

Music Unique to America

Slave Songs

Grade Levels	K–4th
Social Studies Objective[1]	**I Culture**
	Social studies programs should include experiences that provide for the study of culture and cultural diversity.
Music Objective[2]	**1. Content Standard:** Singing, alone and with others, a varied repertoire of music
	Achievement Standard:
	Students
	c. sing music representing diverse genres and cultures, with expression appropriate for the work being performed

1 NCSS Curriculum Standards for Social Studies
2 NATIONAL MUSIC STANDARDS, MENC

The years of slavery in the early centuries of the United States can be documented by a study of spirituals. The incredibly beautiful genre of folk music given us by the slaves is a great life lesson. Slavery, a dark and horrific part of our American history, produced the art form of Negro spirituals. Are we sorry that slavery happened? Yes!

Yet we cannot change history. What we can do is learn from the example set for us by the slaves—from great difficulty, they created a living, beautiful art form.

"Swing Low, Sweet Chariot" depicts the faith held by the slaves that someday they would be transported to heaven from this life of toil and trouble. As they worked in the fields, they would sing together. One can only imagine the hope and courage these songs gave to the slaves as they toiled in the fields. Sometimes the songs had a "call and response" form. A leader would sing a line, such as "Swing low, sweet chariot," which was the "call." Then the others would answer, singing "Comin' for to carry me home," which was the "response." In the elementary classroom, children could act out this musically, with one child being the caller and the rest singing the response. They could draw pictures of the field workers with their hoes and plants growing. The children could experience eating a "hoe cake" which was corn bread made in the field from corn meal and water, patted into a little cake, and baked over an open fire on the metal end of the hoe.

Sing this famous spiritual as a "call and response" song.

SINGING

> ## Songbook Selection
>
> Get America Singing. . .Again!
>
> P & I   "Swing Low, Sweet Chariot" African American Spiritual   41

PBS has created a wonderful series and website, *Slavery and the Making of America*.[14] This series reminds us that slave songs, usually divided into religious, work, and recreational groupings, provided the origin for jazz, gospel, and blues music. What a heritage for us all!

The lyrics of "Follow the Drinking Gourd" told slaves planning to run away how to escape to the North by night. They were to find the Big Dipper in the sky, represented in the song by the image of a "Drinking Gourd," and move during the dark of night in that direction. Of course, the overseers and landowners were unaware of the double meaning of the beautiful music they were hearing as the slaves were singing in the fields.

The use of a gourd for drinking also is descriptive of the life of a slave. In the fields, gourds grew wild, often around fence posts. These gourds could be hollowed out, dried, and then used as a dipper to get water. While the slaves were working in the fields, they kept their dippers, which were light weight and had a natural long handle, with them so they could get water from a bucket or creek or pump. Elementary students, by singing the beautiful song together, are linked to the history of the Underground Railroad.

The Underground Railroad is the symbolic name given to the routes slaves traveled from safe house to safe house until they reached freedom. Music played a big role as songs gave coded instructions for the routes to follow and warned of dangers along the way. The songs also encouraged slaves to join the Underground Railroad, provided inspiration and support for the long journey to the North, and celebrated the end of a successful trip to freedom.

Jazz

Grade Levels	3rd–6th
Social Studies Objective[1]	**I Culture**
	Social studies programs should include experiences that provide for the study of culture and cultural diversity.
Music Objective[2]	**9. Content Standard:** Understanding music in relation to history and culture
	K–4th
	Achievement Standard:
	Students a. identify by genre or style aural examples of music from various historical periods and cultures
	5th–8th
	Achievement Standard:
	Students b. classify by genre and style (and, if applicable, by historical period, composer, and title) a varied body of exemplary (that is, high-quality and characteristic) musical works and explain the characteristics that cause each work to be considered exemplary

1 NCSS Curriculum Standards for Social Studies
2 NATIONAL MUSIC STANDARDS, MENC

New Orleans at the turn of the 20th-century is considered the home of the truly American art form of jazz, and even today one can visit Preservation Jazz Hall and experience the joy of early New Orleans Jazz. The development of this unique musical style occurred almost simultaneously in other American cities such as Kansas City, Saint Louis, and Chicago. Elements from West African black folk music developed in the Americas and joined with European popular music of the 19th century to become the syncopated rhythms of ragtime and minor chords characteristic of the blues. An interesting note is that early blues, gospel, and jazz were aural traditions, and that many of the most skilled musicians didn't read music.

LISTENING

Jazz has the unique aspect of improvisation, where musicians perform solos and make up the music as they play. At one point in our history, jazz was considered inappropriate music to be studied. Now, musicians realize how much musical skill and theoretical understanding is required to be a jazz musician. Jazz influenced European musicians and composers such as Debussy, Milliau, and Stravinsky.

Find a recording of a favorite jazz piece and reflect on the influences of slave songs as you listen.

The Blues

The blues tell in song of the hard times African American people lived through in the early 20th century, and continue to be composed and sung today. Hard work, money woes, bad bosses, and lost love are all themes sung about in the blues. The music of the blues is unique because it starts with a sad theme, but is infused with a sense of beauty and fun. The Blues are the basis for a great deal of popular music performed today.

CREATING

SINGING

Children can write their own 12-bar blues lyrics, but they must select a topic that gives them "the blues." Homework, tests, something about themselves, such as being slow to get up in the morning, might be the topic of the blues. B. B. King is an American blues icon of our musical culture, who sings the blues with his guitar he named "Lucille." The teacher could play something from B. B. King, and the children could do reports on his life and music.

African American Spirituals/Gospel Music

The African American culture taught us a lot about living through hard times with grace, beauty, and dignity. The African American faith continued to be expressed through music. Gospel music to this day is a vital American musical genre. Large gospel festivals are held throughout America, with different groups presenting gospel music.

Usually the festivals include choirs who often wear robes, soloists, choreography with the singers moving as they sing, and an element of improvisation from the solo performers.

In June of 2009, in Austin, Texas, a different kind of gospel festival was held. "Rock My Soul: A Celebration of the African American Spiritual" was held featuring the professional choir, Conspirare. Over 200 singers, from elementary students to experienced professional singers, performed a 90-minute salute to this historical song form. Conspirare's director, Craig Helle Johnson, said, "This [music] is about deep, hard human expression. It's a human song."

Experience this special "human song" as you sing the following spirituals in the *Get America Singing . . .Again!* songbook.

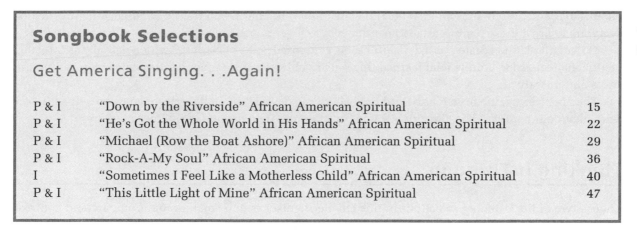

Songbook Selections

Get America Singing. . .Again!

P & I	"Down by the Riverside" African American Spiritual	15
P & I	"He's Got the Whole World in His Hands" African American Spiritual	22
P & I	"Michael (Row the Boat Ashore)" African American Spiritual	29
P & I	"Rock-A-My Soul" African American Spiritual	36
I	"Sometimes I Feel Like a Motherless Child" African American Spiritual	40
P & I	"This Little Light of Mine" African American Spiritual	47

Holiday Music

Music is part of our celebrations. Christmas carols help us celebrate the Christian holiday. Songs about Santa Claus help us celebrate the tradition of the jolly elf leaving gifts and toys for the boys and girls. The music of Hanukah and Kwanzaa can also be enjoyed in a Winter Celebrations unit. This music is appropriate to be sung in the public schools of America if it is taught for musical reasons or for historic/cultural study.

Christmas in the Big House, Christmas in the Quarters by Patricia and Frederick McKissack is a children's book that depicts Christmas in the 1880s in Virginia. It shows what the holiday celebration would have been like for the slaves and for the slave owners. One of the traditions described is the cakewalk. We think of cakewalks as something done at the elementary school carnival where people walk in a circle to music, and stop on a number when the music stops. Numbers are drawn from a bowl, and the person on the winning number gets the cake. In the African American tradition, couples dance to the music, and the dancers with the most unique, interesting dance moves win the cake. Usually the older members of the group, those less likely to be among the dancers, are the judges.

The French composer Debussy composed a musical cakewalk, "Golliwog's Cakewalk," for a collection of music, *Children's Suite*, written for his daughter. The golliwog was one of her stuffed toys. The children in an elementary class can do a cakewalk to Debussy's music, either the elementary carnival type or the historic type, after reading the book.

A recommended resource *Highlighting the Holidays* by Jeff Kriske and Randy DeLelles includes songs, poems, and dances that can be used within appropriate holiday plays during the school year. For K–sixth graders (suggested grade levels given for each activity), it contains materials for Columbus, Halloween, Thanksgiving, Hanukah, Christmas, Valentine's Day, Chinese New Year, St. Patrick's Day, Easter, and May Day.

Other Resources

A creative approach to helping students memorize dates and facts is putting the required information into piggyback songs that the students create themselves. The information will easily be recalled at test time! Writing raps is another excellent way to involve student creativity with learning and memorizing information. One example would be to have small groups create a rap to explain each amendment included in

SINGING

the Bill of Rights. When presented to the full class, this would be an entertaining and meaningful way for everyone to learn these ten important amendments.

"Fifty Nifty United States" is a delightful song, composed by Ray Charles,[15] which lists all the 50 states in alphabetical order. Adults who learned this song as children still remember the states by recalling the lyrics and melody.

The music magazine from Plank Road Publishers, *Music K-8*,[16] often has raps or songs to help children learn about our country. The "President's Rap" is a popular item presented by this company.

Thinking It Through

Choose two of the listening selections in this chapter to discuss in a small group. Compare and contrast the musical styles, and use of music elements. Discuss how the backgrounds of the composers affected their compositions.

Suggestions for Further Study

Read *Listen to Learn: Using American Music to Teach Language Arts and Social Studies* (2004) by Teri Tibbett. Published by Jossey-Bass.
The Native American unit is especially interesting.

Read *If America Were a Village: A Book about the People of the United States* (2009) by David J. Smith. Published by Kids Can Press.
Written for intermediate students, this is a snapshot—past, present, future—to help define America for children.

Listen to the CD *¡Canta mi Son! (Sing My Song)—Learn Spanish through the World of Mariachi!* (2009) Juanita Ulloa (Juanita Newland Ulloa). Record Label: Vocal Power Productions.
Includes appropriate mariachi songs for teachers and students. Spanish pronunciation tracks included.

Recommended Student Books

Bates, Katherine Lee. (1993). *America the Beautiful.* (N. Waldman, Illus.). New York: Macmillan/McGraw Hill.
Illustrations of the lyrics to the song.

Bates, Katherine Lee. (2004). *America the Beautiful: A Pop-up Book.* (R. Sabuda, Illus.). New York: Little Simon.
Illustrations of the lyrics to the song.

Bunting, Eve. (1998). *Going Home.* (D. Diaz, Illus.). New York: HarperCollins.
Pictures an immigrant family visiting their old hometown in Mexico.

Campbell, Patricia Shehan, Williamson, Sue, and Pierre Perron. (1997). *Traditional Songs of Singing Cultures: A World Sampler.* Miami: Warner Bros. Publications.
Songs from around the world. Good information about music and culture. Teaching ideas and CD included.

Catrow, David. (2005). *We the Kids.* New York: Puffin.
Illustrations of the preamble of the US Constitution. The special wording is made memorable and fun.

Crow, Kristyn. (2008). *Cool Daddy Rat.* (M. Lester, Illus). New York: Putnam Juvenile.
Read-aloud, rhyming text with a swingin' beat.

DePaola, Tomie. (1988). *The Legend of the Indian Paintbrush.* (T. DePaola, Illus.). New York: Putnam.
A rhythmic retelling of an Indian legend.

Dragonwagon, Crescent. (1993). *Home Place.* (J. Pinkney, Illus.). New York: Aladdin.
A girl and her family discover an old home place, and find hints to the past.

Ehrhardt, Karen. (2006). *This Jazz Man.* (R. G. Roth, Illus.). Orlando: Harcourt.
Alternate lyrics to the tune of "This Old Man." This book introduces famous African American jazz musicians. Biographies in the back.

Erbsen, Wayne. (1993). *Front Porch Old-Time Songs, Jokes and Stories.* Asheville, NC: Native Ground Music.
Forty-eight great sing-along favorites. Includes information about the music.

Fox, Mem. (2007). *Whoever You Are.* (L. Staub, Illus.). Orlando: Voyager Books.
Fox has created a simple refrain to celebrate human connections.

Guthrie, Woody. (2008). *This Land is Your Land.* (K. Jakobsen, Illus.). Boston: Little, Brown.
Illustrations of the folk song.

Hopkinson, Deborah. (1995). *Sweet Clara and the Freedom Quilt.* New York: Dragonfly Books.
Story of a courageous young slave girl is based on a true event.

Iqus, Toyomi. (1998). *I See the Rhythm.* (M. Wood, Illus.). San Francisco: Children's Book Press.
Picture-book history of African American music from African origins and slave songs through rap. Text is lines from the songs.

Kroll, Steven. (2000). *By the Dawn's Early Light.* (D. Andreaseen, Illus.). New York: Scholastic.
Story of the events leading to the writing of our National Anthem.

Krull, Kathleen. (2003). *I Hear America Singing! Folk Songs for American Families.* (A. Garns, Illus.). New York: Knopf.
Collection of American folk songs for children. Beautiful illustrations and brief information about the songs. CD included. Formerly published as *Gonna Sing my Head Off!*

Kushner, Tony. (2003). *Brundibar.* (M. Sendak, Illus.). New York: Hyperion Books for Children.
A picture book based on the Czech opera originally performed by the children of Terezin Concentration Camp.

Locker, Thomas. (2002). *Water Dance.* San Diego: Voyager Books.
A wonderful combination of Science and Art, paintings show each step in the water cycle with haiku-like text explanations.

Longfellow, Henry Wadsworth. (1996). *Hiawatha.* (S. Jeffers, Illus.). New York: Puffin.
The telling of Hiawatha's early years as he learns the ways of American Indians from his grandmother.

Myers, Walter Dean. (2003). *Blues Journey.* (C. Myers, Illus.). New York: Holiday House.
Call-and-response, blues-inspired poetry for older students.

Pinkney, Andrea Davis. (1999). *Duke Ellington*. (B. Pinkney, Illus.). New York: Hyperion Books.
A view into who Duke Ellington was and what he did for the musical world.

Pinkney, Andrea Davis. (2002). *Ella Fitzgerald: The Tale of a Vocal Virtuosa*. (B. Pinkney, Illus.). New York: Hyperion Books.
A cat tells the story of The First Lady of Song with a rhythmical beat.

Robinson, Sandra Chisholm. (1994). *The Rainstick, A Fable*. Guilford, CT: TwoDot.
History, myths, and traditions of West Africa come to life in this book.

San Souci, Robert D. (1989). *Talking Eggs*. (J. Pinkney. Illus.). New York: Dial Books for Young Readers.
Creole folk tale with a strong heroine and magic.

Sherr, Lynn. (2001). *America the Beautiful: The Stirring True Story Behind Our Nation's Favorite Song*. New York: Public Affairs.
A history of Katherine Lee Bate's life, and what led her to write the poem.

Spier, Peter. (1992). *The Star Spangled Banner*. (P. Spier, Illus.). New York: Dragonfly Books.
Illustrated version of the writing of our National Anthem.

Winter, Jeanette. (1992). *Follow the Drinking Gourd*. New York: Dragonfly Books.
Shows how the song holds directions for following the Underground Railroad to freedom.

CHAPTER 11 | RELATING MUSIC TO THE OTHER ARTS

How to Relate the Arts

Each of the arts uses unique materials and elements. For example:

- Music composers use elements such as melody, rhythm, form, tone color, tempo and harmony to organize sounds across time.
- Visual artists use elements of design such as color, line, texture, form, and space to organize their work in media such as clay, wood and oil paint on canvas.

- Actors in drama focus on elements of acting including body language, emotion, levels, staging, and gesture, and include some elements of the other arts, such as tempo, tone color, time, and space.
- Dancers work with the elements of movement (locomoter, nonlocomotor, leading/following), time, space, energy (strong/light, sharp/smooth), and body (shape, parts) to express themselves.

The arts—music, visual art, drama, photography, architecture, poetry, sculpture, and dance—also contain many similar qualities. Relating them through the use of common principals for study is an effective teaching strategy, and helps students compare, contrast, and discover ways to use higher-level thinking skills.

One of the most commonly used methods to study related arts is through shared historic time periods. While this approach can be interesting, Dr. Bennett Reimer,[6] noted music educator, emphasizes that finding art products with similar characteristics for study provides a more valid, authentic learning experience for students.

Tantalizing Tidbit of Research

A collection of research finds that learning in the arts may be uniquely able to boost learning and achievement for young children, students from economically disadvantaged circumstances, and students needing remedial instruction. Arts education helps close the achievement gap, improves academic skills essential for reading and language development, and advances students' motivation to learn.

Critical Links: Learning in the Arts and Student Academic and Social Development (2002)

A book by the Arts Education Partnership finds that schools with large populations of students in economic poverty—often places of frustration and failure for students and teachers alike—can be transformed into vibrant and successful centers of learning and community life when the arts are infused into their culture and curriculum.

Stevenson and Deasy (2005)[7]

Common Principals Among the Art Forms

The arts all make use of unity, variety and balance (UVB) strategies to enhance the aesthetic qualities of their medium. Music, visual art, sculpture, photography, dance, architecture, poetry, and drama all utilize repetition and contrast to achieve balance in their art form, and to make it interesting to the viewer, the listener, or the audience.

Color in visual art can be repeated, while movements in dance can achieve repetition. Colors of the costumes worn by dancers can be both a unifying and a contrasting technique. Color in music is achieved by the different sounds of the instruments, called tone color. Texture can be used to achieve variety in sculpture or in visual art through the way the stone is cut away or by the brush strokes used to apply the paint. Texture in music refers to the thick or thin sounds of the music achieved through the sounds produced by the various instruments, the number of instruments playing at one time, and by the dynamic qualities of the sounds.

Discussing the different art forms can be problematic, as demonstrated by the terms "color" and "texture" in the paragraph above. Part of the reason for this ambiguity or difficulty in using words to describe the arts is inherent in all art because art is often created to provide meaning without the use of words. Some philosophers believe that art gives meaning to life in ways that words can never do. Words are inadequate when describing emotions such as love. Yet, art can capture feelings for us. When one relates a piece of music to an event in life, hearing that music again always transports the person back to that time or event, even if it happened 40 years ago, and it does so in a matter of seconds.

Art is believed by some to be exemplary, an example or illustration, of life. Life has movement, it has hard times and good times, and it is filled with emotional experiences. Art reflects life. Good life has variety, but not so much as to make us feel harried or unsure. Our world has seasons, which provide variety to our lives while at the same time making life unified through predicted repetition year after year. We have night and day, again providing a unifying aspect to life and variety to our days. Art does the same. Life at its best has balance. We don't want to go through final examinations all the time, which would be too stressful. But, we don't want to spend all our time with no stress, which would be boring. The arts reflect this. They provide tension and release, again picturing life for us. We certainly don't want to repeat the same day over and over as in the movie *Groundhog Day*. Music that repeated the same tune over and over again would not be interesting to our ears. Composers and performers know how to achieve variety, even within repetition.

Focusing on having the students discover the common principles among the art forms they are studying will produce interesting experiences and pointed discussions. These common principles include:

Unity—Variety—Balance
Repetition—Contrast
Tension—Release
Smooth—Jagged

Helping students discover the information brought to us through the arts is often a missing part of education. Yet our children, our youth, seek experiences that bring excitement to their lives. The arts can provide a positive outlet for emotional experience.

Learning about the arts makes youngsters aware of the differences among us, again reflected through the arts. The arts are unique, each piece of art bringing us different information.

Through the study of the arts, children can begin to realize that different can be good. Because of the differences, particular music or visual art or dance or drama works become valued parts of our world.

We are not all the same, nor is art all the same. We are tall and short and young and old and all made up with different colors of skin and different appearances. We have blue eyes and brown eyes and hazel eyes and green eyes, and zillions of different combinations of colors and shapes of eyes. We have brown, blond, red, grey, and black hair and it can be curly or straight and all sorts of combinations in between. We have big feet and little feet and long arms and shorter arms and all different body types. Our mouths are wide or narrow with lips of different thicknesses, and we speak differently. What a great variety of people we have in this world!

Each of us is *different*, and that is good. The arts in education teach this well. As a teacher, use and enjoy the study of the arts in the classroom!

SINGING

Songbook Selection
Get America Singing. . .Again!
P & I   "Over My Head" African American Spiritual   34

The Other Arts and Music

Art and Music

Finding music and visual art with similar characteristics for study can lead to very rich learning experiences for students.

LISTENING

Mussorgsky's Pictures

The Russian composer Modest Mussorgsky created *Pictures at an Exhibition* as "A Remembrance of Viktor Hartmann" in 1874. When Mussorgsky's good friend, artist and architect Viktor Hartmann, died suddenly at age 39, an exhibition of over 400 of his works was held in the Academy of Fine Arts in St. Petersburg. After reviewing this exhibition, Mussorgsky quickly created his *Pictures* as an imaginary tour of an art collection. Selections based on Hartmann's drawings and watercolors include: "Gnome", "The Old Castle," "Tuileries" (a Parisian park where children are playing), "Bydlo" (cattle), "Ballet of the Unhatched Chicks," "Samuel Goldenberg and Schmuyle" (conversation between a wealthy man and a beggar), "The Market Place at Limogenes" (French housewives argue at the market), "Catacombs," "The Hut on Fowl's Legs" (about a witch), and "The Great Gate at Kiev". The music, composed for piano, but often heard in orchestrated versions, offers opportunities for dramatization and visualization. Reflecting this very expressive music by creating art works or by acting out different selections can be very successful intermediate student activities.

Impressionistic Art and Music

The Impressionistic period is one historic time frame that allows visual art and music to be justifiably explored together. Both visual art and music from the end of the 19th century through the beginning of the 20th century were moving beyond capturing images and sounds as they had been done previously.

After the invention of photography, which made exact imagery possible, artists were less concerned with creating realistic images. They were seeking new ways to visually represent their world.

The artists of the period, including Renoir and Monet, were finding ways to make their art more of an "impression" of the visual. Using colors and light and painting techniques, they created hazy, vague, indistinct images resulting in a whole new type of art.

At the same time, music was moving beyond the traditional sounds made by large orchestral pieces, which often used heavy brass instrumentation. The composers were striving for sounds that were new and different. Claude Debussy (1862–1918), a French composer, was exploring a new musical sound. He favored wind and string instruments, with a thin texture. The harp was a favorite instrument of the time. The musical results were an aural correlation to the visual representation of the Impressionist painters.

174

One of Debussy's famous orchestral compositions, *Prélude à l'après-midi d'un faune* (Prelude to the Afternoon of a Faun), is a good piece for children to hear. Listening to this piece is like looking through a window with a sheer curtain. The children can describe how Debussy achieved this hazy, indistinct feel from the music (using lighter sounding instruments such as the flute, clarinet, violin, harp; having fewer instruments playing at certain points in the music). Asking the following questions helps them discover the essence of Impressionist music:

- What is the faun (a mythical creature) doing? (Many think the answer is "peeking out from the woods," or "softly and quietly walking toward a meadow.")
- What sounds make us have this image of the faun? (Solo wind instruments, the harp, lots of woodwinds and strings.)
- What is similar between Debussy's music and Impressionistic paintings? (Show a print of Renoir's *Girl with Watering Can* or of one of Monet's *Water Lilies* paintings.)
- Guide the students to see the lighter colors used, the lack of distinct lines, the haziness of the images.
- Both art and music created a feeling of hazy, indistinct imagery. Music through instrumentation and dynamics; art through color and light and brush techniques.

An obvious intermediate class activity would be to paint or color an impressionistic artwork as Debussy's *Prélude à l'après-midi d'un faune* is playing in the background. Display the results in a wall collage opposite a display of famous Impressionist art works. Students could do reports on the historic period, or on one of the artists or musicians of this era.

Abstract Art and Music

Another successful activity for intermediate students can involve using technology to assist students in creating a piece of music to express a piece of abstract art. A project designed by skilled elementary music teacher Debbie Tannert in Austin, Texas involves groups of three students. Each group chooses from three very different abstract paintings brought to the classroom (check with the art teacher or your school library). Paintings by Wassily Kandinsky, Paul Klee, and Pablo Picasso work well. Arrange for time at the computer where each group can use GarageBand (or another program) to create music to reflect their chosen painting. This activity can be an excellent addition to your class podcast. Put the three pieces of art on the podcast, and then each group's composition. Parents can have the experience of guessing which picture their child was describing with his or her music.

The "Colors" of Music

Play one of the selections from this book's CD. Don't let anyone know its title. Have Grade 2–6 students write down adjectives to point out various qualities of the work. Is it fast or slow, loud or soft, angry or relaxed? Do you think the composer is telling a story with his music? Ask students to draw a picture of what they think the music expresses as they hear the music again. Compare students' works after the drawings are finished. Discuss the various colors used by students to show different aspects of the sound of the music.

175

Jazz-Related Art, Music, and Literature

Another excellent activity connecting music and art with similar characteristics can easily include literature. Students are usually very interested in jazz, the only uniquely American style of music.

An extraordinary African American author, Langston Hughes, provides a remarkable experience relating music and art in his *The First Book of Rhythm*.[8] Follow his simple directions and let students learn how to relate the rhythm in music to the rhythm in art:

> Take a crayon or pencil and a sheet of paper and start a line upward. Let it go up into a curve, and you will have rhythm. Then try a wavy line and you will see how the line itself seems to move. Rhythm comes from movement. The motion of your pencil makes your line. When you lift your pencil as you finish, the rhythm of your line on the paper will be the rhythm of your hand in motion. There is no rhythm in the world without movement first.

LISTENING

He then gives examples of various types of lines to draw. Reading portions of his *The First Book of Jazz*, contained in the same volume, will give students even more ideas for their art project. Culminate this activity by letting intermediate students create "artistic rhythm" artworks as they listen to a very rhythmic jazz selection, such as "Take the A Train" by Ellington and Strayhorn.

Individual Student Activity

Using information given by Langston Hughes, create a rhythmic art piece that reflects a jazz selection.

Kristen Crow has written a marvelous book that lets primary and intermediate students experience one special aspect of jazz—*scat singing*, which is done using nonsense syllables. Her book, *Cool Daddy Rat*,[9] lends itself to the echo method. Read the book, which tells the story of a jazz musician in New York City, and use different voices for each character. Have the students snap or pat the steady beat, and echo on the "scat" lines as they occur in the book. The students will enjoy the story, the experience of "scatting," and the wonderful artwork by Mike Lester.

Continuing the jazz-related theme, read *Ben's Trumpet*, written and illustrated by Rachel Isadora. Featuring amazing black-and-white art, this Caldecott Honor book is an imaginative story of a boy growing up in the 1930s. It introduces the instruments of a jazz ensemble. Reading the book also offers a historical perspective on life in a different era. This book could lead to learning about the life of Louis Armstrong, who grew up in racially segregated New Orleans in about the same time period as the one reflected in the book. Armstrong, known as Satchmo because he could fill his cheeks with air making them look like satchels when he played the trumpet, became one of the world's best-loved performers. His singing is heard on the song "What a Wonderful World," which can be used as a very special music and art experience for children. Tony Bennett, famous American pop singer, said, "The bottom line of any country is, what did we contribute to the world? We contributed Louis Armstrong."

Individual Student Activity

Divide up the following list so that someone draws a picture to represent each phrase. As you draw, listen to Louis Armstrong perform.

"What A Wonderful World"   CD Track 20

1. Draw a picture of trees with green leaves.
2. Draw a picture of red roses.
3. Draw a picture of flowers blooming.
4. Draw a picture of you and a friend.
5. Draw a picture of "thinking to yourself."
6. Draw a picture of a wonderful world.
7. Draw a picture of blue sky.
8. Draw a picture of white clouds.
9. Draw a picture of a bright, sunny day.
10. Draw a picture of a dark night.
11. Draw a picture of you thinking about yourself.
12. Draw a picture of a wonderful world.
13. Draw a picture of the colors of the rainbow.
14. Draw a picture of the rainbow in the sky.
15. Draw a picture of faces of different types of people.
16. Draw a picture of different kinds of people walking past each other.
17. Draw a picture of friends shaking hands.
18. Draw a picture of friends saying, "How do you do."
19. Write the words, "I Love You," and decorate the paper around them.
20. Draw a picture of a baby crying.
21. Draw a picture of a child growing.
22. Draw a picture of a school.
23. Draw a picture of you thinking to yourself.
24. Draw a picture of a wonderful world.
25. Draw a picture of you thinking to yourself.
26. Draw a picture of a wonderful world.
27. Write the words "Oh, Yes," and decorate the paper around the words.

After the artwork is completed, students can stand in a circle as the recording of "Wonderful World" is played. At the appropriate time in the music, each child holds up the picture. Sheryl Maklary, master Kindergarten teacher in Katy, Texas, binds the pictures into a classroom book that is placed at a listening center with the song on CD.

Slides can also be made of the pictures, and used in a slide show for Back to School Night, or the pictures can be scanned into a computer or digitally photographed for use with a multimedia production.

This activity can be part of an assembly program with several projectors being used at the same time. All the classes of one grade level can do the activity and have several pictures of the same phrase shown, so that three or four images project at the same time. Have the children standing on raisers, singing the song "What a Wonderful World," and there won't be a dry eye in the crowd! This entire lesson can be modified to be appropriate for students in K–sixth grade.

Architecture and Music

Anderson Hall at Kansas State University

- Notice the three sections of the building.
- What is the form of this building?
- How does the building show the form?
- Compare with how music shows form.

This building on the K-State campus is an ABA form, demonstrated by the similar wings on either end of the structure, with the taller section in the middle. What piece of music comes to mind as a good example of this same ABA form?

The windows, another element of this building, are a good example of the principle of repetition and contrast. Some have an arched top, where others are rectangular. Beside the main door are two windows on either side, each with the arched design. Above those windows are rectangular shaped windows, an excellent example of achieving contrast and repetition and balance in design.

Music does the same thing. Handel's "Hallelujah Chorus" from *Messiah* is an excellent example of the principle of repetition and contrast (see page 173). It has repetition of melodic themes, which are used to unify the work and achieve balance. The composer achieves variety and contrast by changing these themes, using different vocal tone colors, inserting different melodies, and by combining two of the melodic themes together. Handel is a master of using repetition and contrast. Listen again to hear unity, variety, and balance (UVB) in the musical elements of this famous selection. This is an excellent experience for intermediate students.

Listening Selection

LISTENING

"Hallelujah Chorus" (*Messiah*) by Handel   CD Track 3

Dance and Music

LISTENING

The Red Pony Suite by Aaron Copland includes a section "Walk to the Bunkhouse" where the rhythms are contrasted very clearly. Students in Grades 2–5 can be grouped and assigned to one of the sections: jagged, smooth, or strings.

- After the students have been introduced to the lesson, listen to the selection, pointing out each of the three sections.
- Have each group explore possible movement patterns before deciding on a movement that shows what the music of its section sounds like.
- Play the music, having the groups move to demonstrate their selected movement while the music is playing. The rule is that groups can only move when their music is playing. Strings group moves during "strings sections," jagged group moves during the "jagged" music sections, and smooth group moves only during the "smooth" sections of music.

Attending a performance of the *Nutcracker* ballet by Tchaikovsky during the winter holiday season is a wonderful opportunity to have elementary children of all ages experience an authentic example of music and movement together. Many ballet companies have performances for school-age children, and teachers can write grants to fund the attendance. For schools located in areas far from actual performances, many videos of the *Nutcracker* are available for purchase and can substitute for a live performance. The children can observe how the dancers' movements illustrate the music. Choreography for the dancers reflects UVB. Dancers achieve UVB through the levels of the movements, which are sometimes low and sometimes high on toes; the location on the stage of the dancers shows UVB, as does their group movement (in a circle or in pairs) contrasted with a more scattered plan with dancers individually moving. Dance is a beautiful art form.

Drama and Music

Watching a scene from a movie, once without the sound followed immediately by a viewing with sound, is a dramatic demonstration of how much music enhances the dramatic effect of the movie.

LISTENING

Watching the opening scene from *Forrest Gump,* where the feather drifts through the air, is a great selection for this activity for intermediate students. The sensation of watching without sound almost makes this scene trite, whereas the addition of the music draws the viewer into the drama.

Exploring operas, such as *The Magic Flute* by Mozart, are wonderful demonstrations of the power of combining drama, music, art (stage scenery and costumes), and dance in such productions.

179

Poetry and Music

Poetry and music can be an excellent combination to use in putting together simple grade-level programs for parents. Each class can recite a poem—from an established poet or written by a student—followed by all the classes singing a song with a similar theme. Themes come from the curriculum—for example, animals students have studied in science (animal songs are easy to find), geography (songs about people, places), or a holiday/celebration. For variety, try to have rhythm instruments added to at least two of the songs, and include others songs with games or dances that can be showcased. Sing at least one song with motions; for example, "Deep in the Heart of Texas" is always a crowd pleaser if it can be worked into your theme. Simple student costumes such as special "hats" can add visual interest.

Thinking It Through

In a small group, choose a painting, a poem, a YouTube clip from a movie or play, and a music selection to bring to class to compare and contrast. Use these terms in your discussion:

Unity—Variety—Balance
Repetition—Contrast
Tension—Release
Smooth—Jagged

Share your discussion with the class.

Suggestions for Further Study

Explore *Works for Children and Young Adults: Poetry, Fiction, and Other Writing* by Langston Hughes (Dianne Johnson, editor) to learn more from his *First Book of Rhythms* and *The First Book of Jazz*, which are both included in this volume.

Read *POPS: A Life of Louis Armstrong* (2009) by Terry Teachout, published by Houghton Mifflin Harcourt. This biography of Satchmo describes him as "an innovator who changed the face of his art form, an endlessly inventive pioneer whose discovery of his own voice helped remake 20th-century culture."

Recommended Student Books

Celenza, Anna Harwell. (2006). *Pictures at an Exhibition.* (J. Kitchel, Illus.). Watertown, MA: Charlesbridge Publishing.
The story follows three Russian friends, Mussorgsky, Hartmann, and Stasov up to the events that were the inspiration for the orchestral piece.

Geslin, Campbell. (2004). *Elena's Serenade.* (A. Juan, Illus.). New York: Atheneum Books for Young Readers.
A young Mexican girl discovers music on her journey to become a glassblower.

Hughes, Langston. (2003). *Works for Children and Young Adults: Poetry, Fiction, and Other Writing.* (D. Johnson, ed.). Columbia, MO: University of Missouri Press.

Excellent stories, poems, and short books written by a famous African American author. Includes *The First Book of Rhythms*, and *The First Book of Jazz*.

Kimmel, Eric A. (2006). *A Horn for Louis*. New York: Random House.
An account of how Louis Armstrong got his first trumpet.

Lach, William. (2006). *Can You Hear It?* New York: Abrams Books for Young Readers.
Introduces students to great music through great works of art. The book has a brief introduction of orchestral instruments and composers. CD included.

McDonough, Yona Zeldis. (2003). *Who Was Wolfgang Amadeus Mozart?* (J. O'Brien and N. Harrison, Illus.). New York: Grosset & Dunlap.
A chapter book about Mozart plus a few "extras" on opera and the evolution of musical instruments, and a timeline.

Weiss, George David and Thiele, Bob. (2005). *What a Wonderful World.* (A. Bryan, Illus.). New York: Atheneum Books for Young Readers.
Illustrations of the song.

CHAPTER 12 | FAVORITE TEACHING TIPS

Lagniappe for the Teacher

Lagniappe is a term used by the Cajun French culture meaning "a little bit more." A bakery in Lafayette, Louisiana, in the heart of Cajun country, might give an extra cookie or two with an order of a dozen. A home decorating store has the practice of giving a little gift, perhaps small hand soaps or a bookmark, just for *lagniappe*.

This chapter contains ideas that are little extras to help you succeed as a teacher. Try them out with your lessons. Make your own list. Keep implementing good teaching practices and watch yourself grow in confidence and skill as a teacher.

Videotape Yourself Teaching

A student teacher dramatically developed his teaching skill during his semester of student teaching. The change was impressive, leading to the question, "How did you do it?" His answer: "I videotaped myself teaching everyday. At night, I would watch and find the points in my teaching that I didn't like. I would correct them the next day, and go through the whole process again."

You may not have time to tape everyday, but once a week should be achievable. The results will be terrific growth in teaching skill, especially valuable at the beginning of your teaching career. With developments in technology, you could set up the camera on your laptop and tape interactions with students or small groups and evaluate these teaching times as well.

Things to be aware of when you watch yourself on video:

- Eye contact with the students. Are you really paying attention to students when they ask you a question?
- Are you visually sweeping the class periodically during the lesson to make sure students are on task? A common problem of the beginning teacher is unawareness of students off task in the back row!
- Only ask a question when you really want an answer. Don't ask unnecessary questions, such as "Would you like to play the drums today?" This type of question opens the door for students to yell out. If you really want the children to play drums, just state "We are going to play drums today."

- Make sure you give many students opportunities to take part in the learning. One student teacher asked a little boy who was usually very disruptive in class to handle a special task. He was thrilled to get the chance, and he told her later that it was the "best day of his life." Giving children a second chance may change their whole attitude about learning.

- Are you walking around as you teach? Don't stand in just one place. Walk among the desks or around the groups of children. It keeps the discipline problems in check and it allows you to see what individual students are doing.

- Make sure you have a visual, an aural, and a kinesthetic activity for each lesson. Children learn through seeing, hearing, and doing. Also keep Howard Gardner's Multiple Intelligences theory in mind as you plan lessons. Give each of your students the best chance to learn.

- How are your transitions, when you move from one activity to the next? These are danger spots for the beginning teacher who is inexperienced in keeping students engaged even when moving from one part of the lesson to the next. Questions such as "What was the main thing we learned from reading that paragraph?" can keep students attentive while you are shifting to a new activity.

- Are you speaking loudly enough and projecting your voice so that the children can hear? And conversely, are you varying the level of your voice to keep the children attentively listening?

- Do the children look bored? You may need to add variety to your lesson. Remember that music is a great key to success! Bring in a CD player and play a variety of music at different times during the day. During artwork or seatwork, music can lift the atmosphere in the classroom. Remember the power of moving to classical music selections as a break during work periods.

- Are you accepting children's comments? Do you make them feel valued by your reaction? Watch that you do not look irritated at some children, even if they do "drive you nuts" by their actions. You are there to help them learn acceptable behavior.

- Do you have classroom organization, where appropriate responses are spelled out, and where behavior has consequences? Do you consistently apply the rules?

- Are your questions *making the children think*? Questioning so that the answers are beyond "yes/no" is a mark of an experienced and skilled teacher. One former student puts a list of questions on the board before the lesson starts. She writes the questions with a marker on a large piece of brightly colored construction paper and uses a magnet to attach them to the board. The list of questions helps her keep focused on key points of the lesson, and gives the children something to read and look at as she directs their attention to significant information they need to learn.

Welcome to the profession of teaching. We never stop learning and getting better. Watching yourself teach, although painful at times, is like using an all-purpose plant food on plants. It helps you "grow fast" in your skill level.

Reinforce the Behavior You Want to See Again

A beginning teacher trying to get the class focused on the lesson often has the tendency to talk to the ones who are not yet "with her." She might say things such as, "Denise, are you having a problem with Seth?" or "Row three, you are not listening." The authors would like to recommend an alternate approach.

This approach focuses on the use of positive reinforcement to increase learning, and includes methods that encourage learning positively rather than punitively or negatively. Positive reinforcement affects many aspects of the classroom: discipline, classroom management, structuring lessons, questioning skills, and a host of other issues about teaching.

The basis of this approach is to focus on the children who are doing something correctly. Teacher statements could be, "Wow, Susan is ready to begin class. She is sitting tall and listening," and "That group three is really following directions perfectly. I am so lucky to have them in my class." Rather than the "drill sergeant" in class, become the encourager for learning.

Keys to Teaching Success

Keys come in such an extensive variety of shapes, sizes, and functions today. In the time of knights and castles surrounded by moats, keys were heavy, large, and made of hand-forged iron. Some keys are very small, such as the ones used to open a small chest or jewelry box. Some, such as the plastic ones used to open a hotel room, don't even look like keys any more. The object of a key, however, is still to open or to start something.

With most aspects of life, we learn what works for us by trial and error. Learning to walk doesn't mean a baby just stands up and walks perfectly right away. It involves a little one going through a lot of falling and getting up again, and repeating the process over and over before walking is perfected. Learning is a process, and the process includes failure before success is finally achieved. Learning to teach is no different.

We try something in the classroom, and if it works, we use it again. If it doesn't bring the desired result, we modify or totally change the method. We try another "key." This trial and error approach is useful with teaching. Try a teaching strategy that you have observed or thought of yourself. If it doesn't work, analyze where the malfunction occurred. Design an alternate strategy for that part of the teaching plan. Try it again. You can always bring the children into this trial and error phase, asking for suggestions from the class.

Your path to teaching success may be different from your friend's or your mentor teacher's, or your administrator's. Beginning teachers have to find the *keys* that work for them. Although this can be rather frustrating, it is also the reason teaching can be such a rewarding profession. It is never stagnant or dull, new things to learn are always around us as teachers, and each class is different. Teachers constantly have to try out new and different ways to reach their students. Authentic teaching is pulsing with life, always growing and changing, and full of learning for the students and for the teacher.

The importance of eye contact with the children cannot be overstated. It makes them more accountable for both learning and behavior. Training yourself to be observant of the students is another enormous key to teaching success.

In a biography of Laura Bush's life, she said "Teaching is a noble profession," and she is right! Mrs. Bush was a teacher and then a librarian, and one of her desires is to encourage others to become teachers because it is noble work.

A teacher's life is spent helping others learn to succeed. Even as you are trying out new keys, searching for teaching successes yourself, your goal is to help your students learn more effectively. A teacher's desire is for the students to gain knowledge, information, skills, behaviors, and facts that enable these individuals to become productive members of society. We want our students to be those thriving people. Yes, teaching is a noble profession.

Astute teachers will use the natural childhood love of music to their advantage, and let it help them teach. Best wishes to every new teacher as they become part of the "noble profession."

Tantalizing Tidbit of Research

Students with High Levels of Arts Involvement Are Less Likely To Drop Out of School by Grade 10

1.4% Drop Out Rate

High Arts Involvement

4.8% Drop Out Rate

Low Arts Involvement

Longitudinal data of 25,000 students demonstrate that involvement in the arts is linked to higher academic performance, increased standardized test scores, more community service and lower drop out rates (see chart above). These cognitive and developmental benefits are reaped by students regardless of their socioeconomic status.

Dr. James S. Catterall, Graduate School of Education and Information Studies, UCLA[1]

APPENDIX 1 | **SONGBOOK**

Rhythmic Singing Games

Ten In The Bed

Traditional

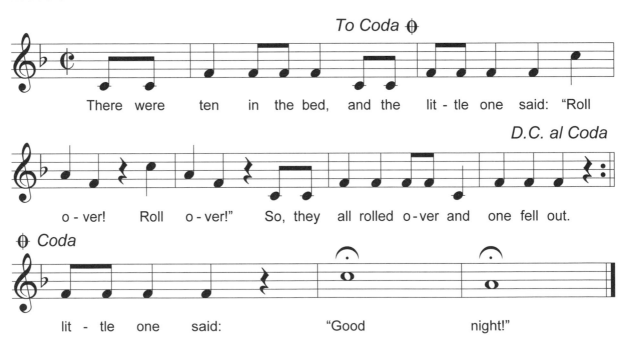

There were ten in the bed, and the lit - tle one said: "Roll o - ver! Roll o - ver!" So, they all rolled o - ver and one fell out. lit - tle one said: "Good night!"

There were nine in the bed,
and the little one said: "Roll over! Roll over!"
So, they all rolled over and one fell out. . .

There were eight in the bed,
and the little one said: "Roll over! Roll over!"
So, they all rolled over and one fell out. . .

There were seven in the bed,
and the little one said: "Roll over! Roll over!"
So, they all rolled over and one fell out. . .

There were six in the bed,
and the little one said: "Roll over! Roll over!"
So, they all rolled over and one fell out. . .

There were five in the bed,
and the little one said: "Roll over! Roll over!"
So, they all rolled over and one fell out. . .

There were four in the bed,
and the little one said: "Roll over! Roll over!"
So, they all rolled over and one fell out. . .

There were three in the bed,
and the little one said: "Roll over! Roll over!"
So, they all rolled over and one fell out. . .

There were two in the bed,
and the little one said: "Roll over! Roll over!"
So, they all rolled over and one fell out. . .

There was one in the bed,
and the little one said: "Good night!"
(sung softly and slowly).

Alice The Camel

Traditional

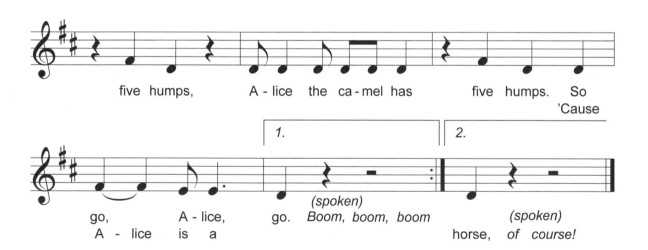

Alice the camel has four humps.
Alice the camel has four humps.
Alice the camel has four humps.
So go, Alice, go. *Boom boom boom.*

Alice the camel has three humps.
Alice the camel has three humps.
Alice the camel has three humps.
So go, Alice, go. *Boom boom boom.*

Alice the camel has two humps.
Alice the camel has two humps.
Alice the camel has two humps.
So go, Alice, go. *Boom boom boom.*

Alice the camel has one hump.
Alice the camel has one hump.
Alice the camel has one hump.
So go, Alice, go. *Boom boom boom.*

Alice the camel has no humps.
Alice the camel has no humps.
Alice the camel has no humps.
'Cause Alice is a horse, of course! (spoken)

Five Green and Speckled Frogs

Traditional

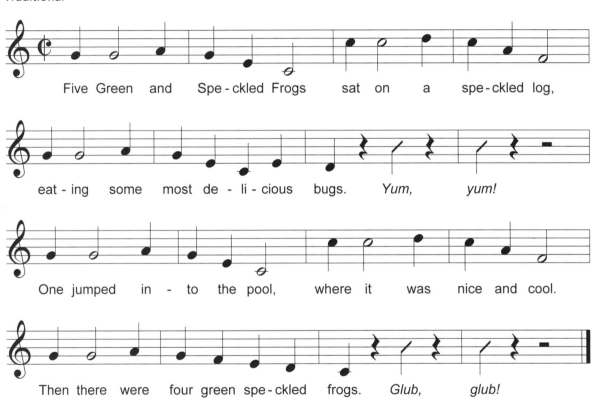

Five Green and Spe-ckled Frogs sat on a spe-ckled log,
eat-ing some most de-li-cious bugs. *Yum, yum!*
One jumped in-to the pool, where it was nice and cool.
Then there were four green spe-ckled frogs. *Glub, glub!*

Four Green and Speckled Frogs,
sat on a speckled log,
eating some most delicious bugs. *Yum. Yum.*
One jumped into the pool,
where it was nice and cool.
Then there were three green speckled frogs.
　　Glub glub.

Three Green and Speckled Frogs,
sat on a speckled log,
eating some most delicious bugs. *Yum. Yum.*
One jumped into the pool,
where it was nice and cool.
Then there were two green speckled frogs.
　　Glub glub.

Two Green and Speckled Frogs,
sat on a speckled log,
eating some most delicious bugs. *Yum. Yum.*
One jumped into the pool,
where it was nice and cool.
Then there were one green speckled frogs.
  Glub glub.

One Green and Speckled Frog,
sat on a speckled log,
eating some most delicious bugs. *Yum. Yum.*
It jumped into the pool,
where it was nice and cool.
Then there were no green speckled frogs.
  Glub glub.

This Old Man

Traditional

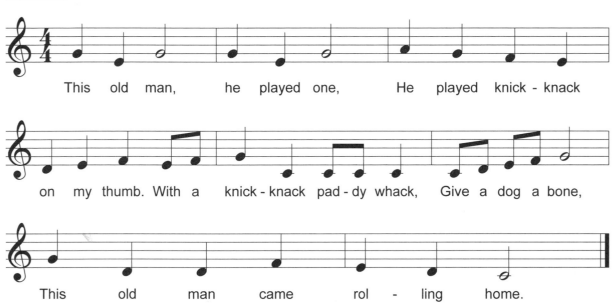

This old man, he played two,
He played knick-knack on my shoe,
With a knick-knack paddy whack,
Give a dog a bone,
This old man came rolling home.

This old man, he played four,
He played knick-knack on my door,
With a knick-knack paddy whack,
Give a dog a bone,
This old man came rolling home.

This old man, he played three,
He played knick-knack on my knee,
With a knick-knack paddy whack,
Give a dog a bone,
This old man came rolling home.

This old man, he played five,
He played knick-knack on my jive,
With a knick-knack paddy whack,
Give a dog a bone,
This old man came rolling home.

(See page 141 for additional verses)

Teddy Bear, Teddy Bear

Traditional

Ted-dy bear, ted-dy bear, turn a-round,— ted-dy bear, ted-dy bear,

touch the ground,— ted-dy bear, ted-dy bear, show your shoe,—

ted - dy bear, ted - dy bear, that will do.

"Hey There, Neighbor"

Traditional

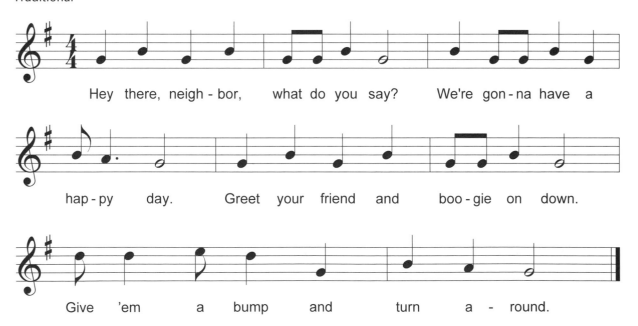

Hey there, neigh-bor, what do you say? We're gon-na have a

hap-py day. Greet your friend and boo-gie on down.

Give 'em a bump and turn a-round.

Partner Game

Line 1   Shake hands.
Line 2   "Happy hands" to right, then left, up by head.
Line 3   Flat handclaps up and down, then "boogie on down."
Line 4   Follow words.

Miss Mary Mack

African American Clapping Game Song

Partner Game

Pairs of children are in a double circle formation performing the hand-clap motions to each phrase. Change partner as the inner circle moves after each verse. Don't drop the steady beat!

Cross arms on shoulders
Pat thighs
Clap own hands
Clap partner's right hand
Clap own hands
Clap partner's left hand
Clap own hands
Clap partner's two hands
(Repeat entire pattern)

Bow Wow Wow

Traditional

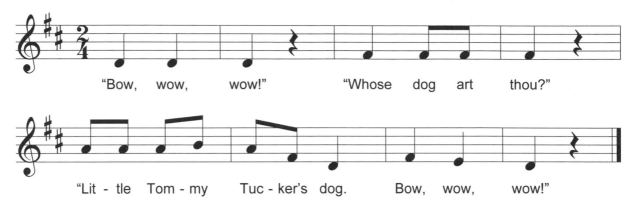

"Bow, wow, wow!" "Whose dog art thou?"

"Lit - tle Tom - my Tuc - ker's dog. Bow, wow, wow!"

Partner Game

Have the students form a single circle and count off by 2s. All the "1s" face right, and all the "2s" face left, so that each child is facing a partner.

Line 1   Stamp three times (alternating feet).
Line 2   Clap three times, and then join hands with partner.
Line 3   Change places with partner in three steps, then drop hands.
Line 4   Jump-turn halfway around to face a new partner.

(Repeat pattern until everyone is back with his/her original partner.)

Song Maps

"Home On The Range" Song Map

Tap with the steady beat three times on each side of every box as you sing the song.

"Oh, What a Beautiful Mornin'" Song Map

Tap each picture on the steady beat as you sing the song. Begin tapping on "bright."

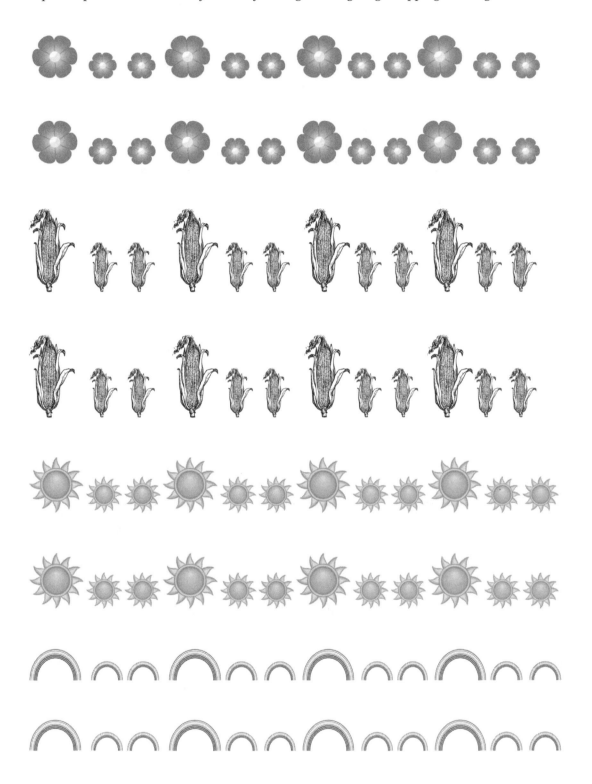

Songs in Spanish and English

From *Musica para todas* Primary and Intermediate Songbooks, Mollie Tower, senior author. (Recordings of all these songs are available with the songbooks from Macmillan/McGraw Hill.)

Acitrón

Spanish Stone-Passing Game

A - ci - trón   de   un   fan - dan - go, zan - go,   zan - go, sa - ba - ré.

Sa - ba - ré   de   far - an - de - la, con su   tri - qui, tri - qui tran.

Have the students sit in a circle and give each student a beanbag (lemon). As the song begins, students use their right hand to pick up their beanbag from the floor in front of them and put it down on the floor in front of their neighbor to the right on the steady beat.

Bate, Bate (Stir, Stir)

Mexican Game

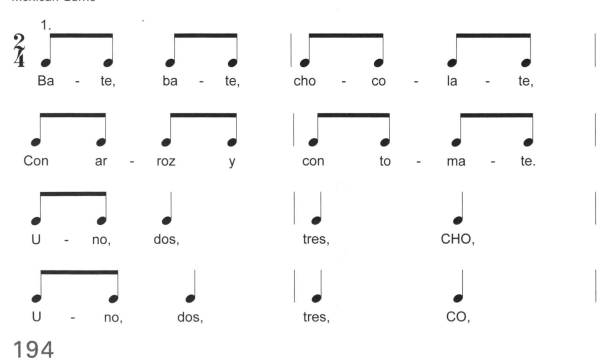

Ba - te,   ba - te,   cho - co - la - te,

Con   ar - roz   y   con   to - ma - te.

U - no,   dos,   tres,   CHO,

U - no,   dos,   tres,   CO,

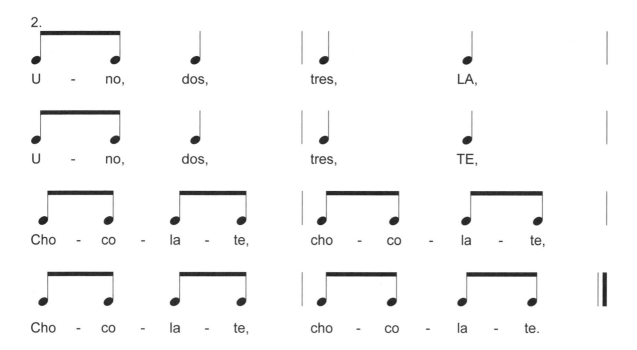

2.

U - no, dos, tres, LA,

U - no, dos, tres, TE,

Cho - co - la - te, cho - co - la - te,

Cho - co - la - te, cho - co - la - te.

Children in Mexico often drink hot chocolate with breakfast. They stir it with a special utensil called a *molinillo* that is held between the hands and rotated back and forth. During this chant, have students rub their palms together and pretend to "stir" the chocolate with a molinillo. If possible, bring a molinillo to class to show them. Next, do a partner handclap game with the chant.

Beats 1–8   On the beat, clap right hands, own hands, left hands, own hands, right hands, own hands, both hands, own hands.

Beats 9–24   Pat legs on *uno, dos, tres*. Touch partner's hands high overhead on *cho*. Repeat three times.

Beats 25–32 Join hands with partner, lean back slightly, and quickly take small steps around in a circle.

Mi cuerpo (My Body)

Hispanic Folk Song. English version by MMH

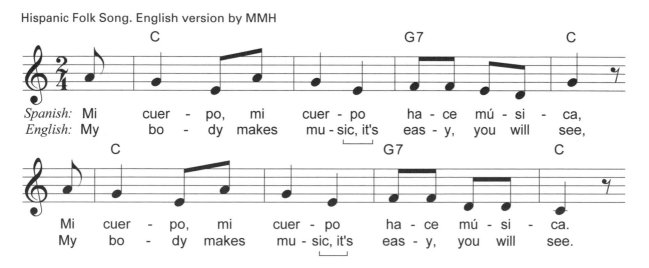

Spanish: Mi cuer - po, mi cuer - po ha - ce mú - si - ca,
English: My bo - dy makes mu - sic, it's eas - y, you will see,

Mi cuer - po, mi cuer - po ha - ce mú - si - ca.
My bo - dy makes mu - sic, it's eas - y, you will see.

195

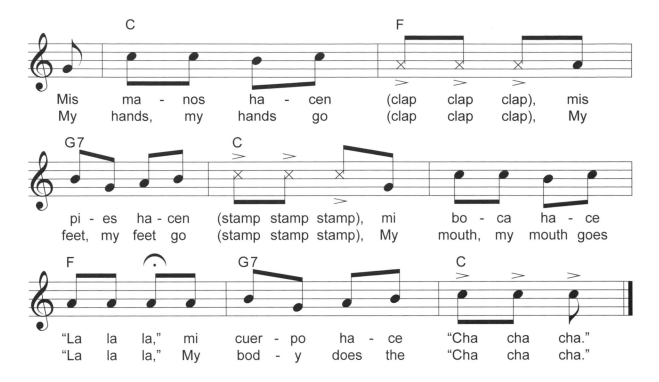

Mis   ma - nos ha - cen   (clap clap clap), mis
My   hands,   my   hands go   (clap clap clap), My

pi - es ha - cen (stamp stamp stamp), mi   bo - ca ha - ce
feet,   my   feet go (stamp stamp stamp), My   mouth, my   mouth goes

"La la la," mi   cuer - po ha - ce   "Cha cha cha."
"La la la," My   bod - y   does the   "Cha cha cha."

Sing the song while adding the clapping, stamping, and dancing movements indicated in the lyrics.

A la rueda rueda ('Round and 'Round)

Latin American Folk Song. English version by MMH

Spanish: A   la rue - da   rue - da,   pan y ca - ne - la;
English: 'Round and 'round and   'round, sweet cin-na - mon and   sweet rolls.

to - ma tu chi - ni - ta,   é - cha - la a la es cue - la;
Take your lit - tle child, and   send her to the   school - room.

si   no quie - re ir.   é - cha - la a dor - mir
If   she will not go,   may - be she's a - sleep!

196

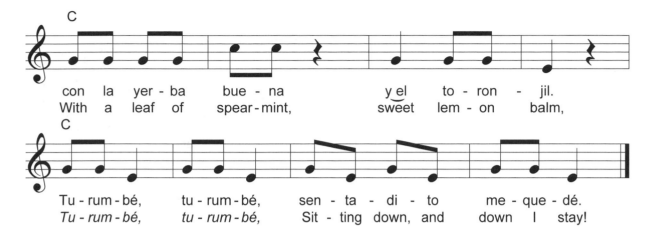

con la yer - ba bue - na y el to - ron - jil.
With a leaf of spear - mint, sweet lem - on balm,

Tu - rum - bé, tu - rum - bé, sen - ta - di - to me - que - dé.
Tu - rum - bé, *tu - rum - bé,* Sit - ting down, and down I stay!

Act out the words in a singing game. Have students form a circle.

Beats 1–16	Walk in a circle, holding hands.
Beats 17–20	Stop and shake a finger back and forth four times.
Beats 21–24	Pretend to sleep.
Beats 25–29	Shake a pretend leaf.
Beats 30–40	On the beat: clap own hands, pat legs—repeat three times, then crouch on the floor for four beats.

Head and Shoulders, Baby (Hombres y cabeza)

African American Street Game As Sung by René Boyer-White
Spanish Version by MMH

Spanish: 1. Hom - bros y ca - be - za, u - no, dos, tres.
English: 1. Head and shoul - ders, ba - by, one,___ two, three.
Spanish: 2. Ro - di - lla y to - bi - llo, u - no, dos, tres.
English: 2. Knee and an - kle, ba - by, one,___ two, three.

Hom - bros y ca - be - za, u - no, dos, tres.
Head and shoul - ders, ba - by, one,___ two, three.
Ro - di - lla y to - bi - llo, u - no, dos, tres.
Knee and an - kle, ba - by, one,___ two, three.

197

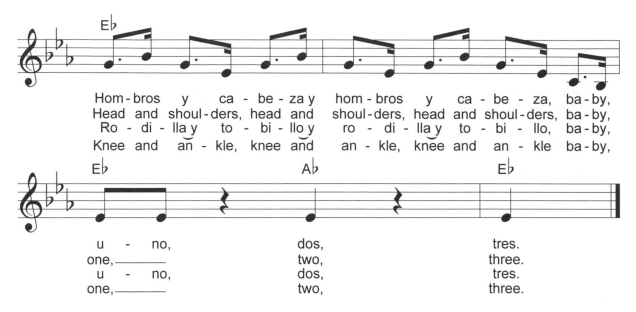

Hom - bros   y   ca - be - za y   hom - bros   y   ca - be - za,   ba - by,
Head   and   shoul - ders,   head   and   shoul - ders,   head   and   shoul - ders,   ba - by,
Ro - di - lla y   to - bi - llo y   ro - di - lla y   to - bi - llo,   ba - by,
Knee   and   an - kle,   knee   and   an - kle,   knee   and   an - kle   ba - by,

u - no,   dos,   tres.
one,_____   two,   three.
u - no,   dos,   tres.
one,_____   two,   three.

3. Ordeña la vaca . . .   3. Milk the cow . . .
4. Tira la pelota . . .   4. Throw the ball . . .

Have the students do a handclap, changing partner game with this song. Form two circles—one inside the other. Partners are facing each other. Tap the mentioned body parts or perform the actions described by the words when sung. On *unos, dos, tres*, pat right hands with partner, clap, pat left hands, clap, pat both hands. When singing the song in English, add a clap on the word "baby" each time. Reposition the inside circle quickly after each verse so students move to a new partner. Don't drop the beat!

De allacito carnavalito (The Carnival is coming)

Argentine Folk Song. English Version by MMH

Spanish: De a - lla - ci - to,   de a - lla - ci - to,   ya   vie - ne el   car - na - va - li - to;
English: Ev' - ry - one there   is___   com - ing   down   to   the   *car - na - va - li - to.*

To - dos ba - jan   en   pa - re - ja,   yo voy ban - jan - do so - li - to.
Ev' - ry - one comes down   in   cou - ples,   I   am   a   lone - ly___   so - lo.

198

This is a very short and fun song to sing. To add a partner changing game, line up in two lines with partners facing each other. During the first line of the song, partners do a "pat right, clap, pat left, clap" hand-clap pattern. (Note the repeat sign.) On the second line of the song, the lines of students step back to form an "alley." The first person in line 1 moves down the "alley" doing any movement he or she chooses, while the other students clap to the steady beat. Line 1 shifts, and when the partners form again everyone has a new partner to repeat the game.

Chíu, Chíu, Chíu

Uruguayan Folk Song. English Version by MMH

Spanish: Can - ta, can - ta, pa - ja - ri - to.____ Can - ta, can - ta tu can -
English: Can - ta, can - ta, pa - ja - ri - to.____ Sing the songs that cheer me

ción, Mi - ra que la vi - da es tris - te y tu can -
so. See, my life is full of sor - row, your mer - ry

tar me a - le gra el co - ra - zón. Chí - u, chí - u, chí - u,
sing - ing sets my heart a - glow. Chí - u, chí - u, chí - u,

chí - u,____ chí - u, chí - u, chí - u, chí - u.____ Can - ta, can - ta pa - ja-
chí - u,____ chí - u, chí - u, chí - u, chí - u.____ Can - ta, can - ta pa - ja-

ri - to. Que tu can - tar me a - le gra el ca - ra - zón.
ri - to. Your mer - ry sing - ing sets my heart a - glow.

Estribillo/Refrain

Con tus got - je - os,——— con tu tri - nar, Des - pier - ta el
Your mer - ry chirp - ing;——— your roun - de - lay, You bring the

al - ba, la no - che ya se va. Con tus gor - je - os,——— con tu tri-
dawn - ing, the shad - ows fade a - way, Your mer - ry chirp - ing;——— your roun-de-

nar,——— Des - pier - ta el al - ba, la no - che ya se va.
lay.——— You bring the dawn - ing, the shad - ows fade a - way.

Have the students explore adding different instruments on the steady beat with this song.

Si me dan pasteles (When You Bring *Pasteles*)

Puerto Rican Folk Song
Arranged by Alejandro Jiménez
English Version by MMH

Parte 1/Part 1

Spanish: Si me dan pas - te - les,——— dén - me - los ca - lien - tes,———
English: When you bring *pas - te - les,*——— give me on - ly hot ones,———

Partes 2, 3/Parts 2, 3

200

This song is traditionally sung in Puerto Rico during the Christmas season, especially around January 6, which is Three Kings Day (Epiphany). Strolling carolers often perform the song and get rewarded with treats. The harmony parts are simple and beautiful. The melody can be played on recorders.

Campanas vespertinas (Evening Bells)

Music by Julio Z. Guerra
Words by Juana Guglielmi
English Version by MMH

Andante

Spanish: Las cam - pa - nad de la i - gle - sia   dan el   to - que de o - ra   ción
English: Hear the   ring - ing   of the church bells,   hear them   call - ing, hear the   sound.

Y   la   luz del   sol   que   mue - re   a o - tro   mun - do i - rá a a - lum - brar.
See the   sun - light slow - ly   dy - ing,   as the   eve - ning comes a - round.

¡Qué   dul - ce a - cen - to,   ding, ding, ding,   dong.   Su voz a -
How   sweet their   ac - cent, Ding, dong, ding,   dong!   They lift my

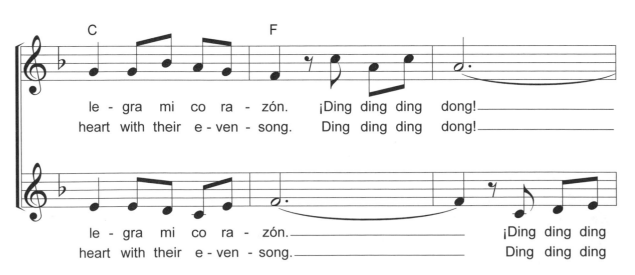

le - gra   mi   co   ra - zón.   ¡Ding ding ding   dong!_____
heart   with their   e - ven - song.   Ding ding ding   dong!_____

le - gra   mi   co   ra - zón._____   ¡Ding ding ding
heart   with their   e - ven - song._____   Ding   ding ding

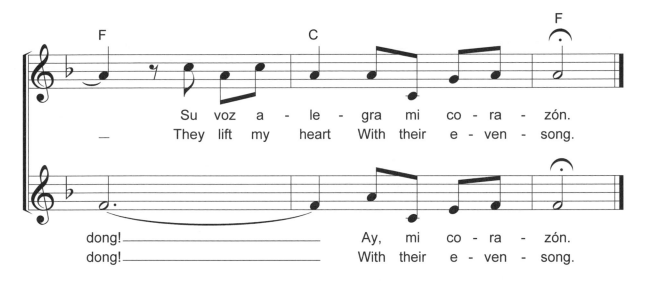

Su voz a - le - gra mi co - ra - zón.
They lift my heart With their e - ven - song.

dong! _____ Ay, mi co - ra - zón.
dong! _____ With their e - ven - song.

Have students try a gentle shuffle or waltz step with this song: step-close-step. Start on the left foot with the next pattern beginning on the right foot. The harmony part is more difficult, but beautiful when added.

Dry Bones (Hueses)

African American Spiritual. Spanish Version by MMH

Spanish: E - ze-quiel gri - tó "¡Hue - sos!" E - ze - quiel gri - tó "¡Hue - sos!"
English: E - zi - kiel cried, "Them dry bones!" E - zi - kiel cried, "Them dry bones!"

E - ze-quiel gri - tó "¡Hue - sos, y o - ye la pa - la - bra!" E -
E - zi - kiel cried, "Them dry bones, Now hear the Word of the Lord!" — E -

accelerando

la - bra!" El hue - so - del pie con la pier - na,
Lord!" — The foot bone con - nect - ed to the leg bone,

203

El hue - so de la pier - na con la ro - di - lla,
The leg bone con - nect - ed to the knee bone,

El hue - so de la ro - di - lla con la ca - de - ra,
The knee bone con - nect - ed to the hip - bone,

El hue - so de la ca - de - ra con la es - pal - da,
The hip - bone con - nect - ed to the back - bone,

El hue - so de la as - pal - da con el del hom - bro,
The back - bone con - nect - ed to the shoul - der bone,

El hue - so del hom - bro con el del cue - llo,
The shoul - der bone con - nect - ed to the neck bone,

El hue - so del cue - llo con la qui - ja - da,
The neck bone con - nect - ed to the jaw - bone,

La qui - ja - da con la ca - be - za,
The___ jaw - bone con - nec - ted to the head bone,

Y o - ye la pa - la - bra.
Now hear the Word of the Lord.___

C *allegro*

E - sos hue - sos van a ca - mi - nar, e -
Them bones, them bones gon - na walk a - round, Them

sos hue - sos van a ca - mi - nar, e - sos hue - sos van a
bones, them bones gon - na walk a - round, Them bones, them bones gon - na

ca - mi - nar, y o - ye la pa - la - bra.
walk a - round, Now hear the Word of the Lord.___

An easy movement game to add to this song is:

A section   Stand in a circle and add a pat-clap pattern to the beat.
B section   Touch the body parts as their names are sung.
C section: Walk around the circle to the beat.

205

APPENDIX 2 | RECORDER SONGBOOK

By Kay Greenhaw (www.studiokay.com/recorder)

Basic Recorder Fingering Chart

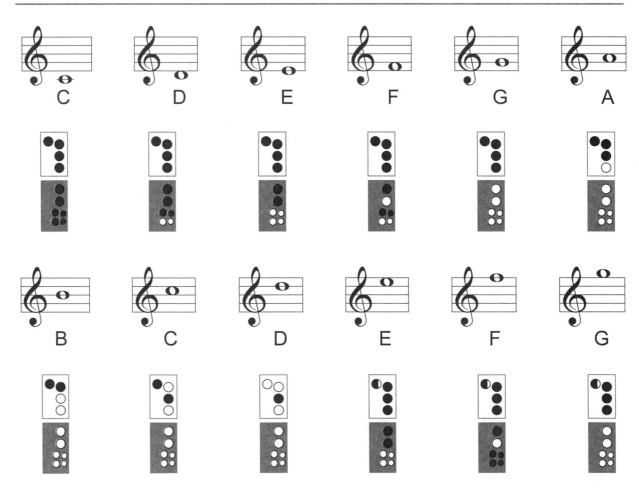

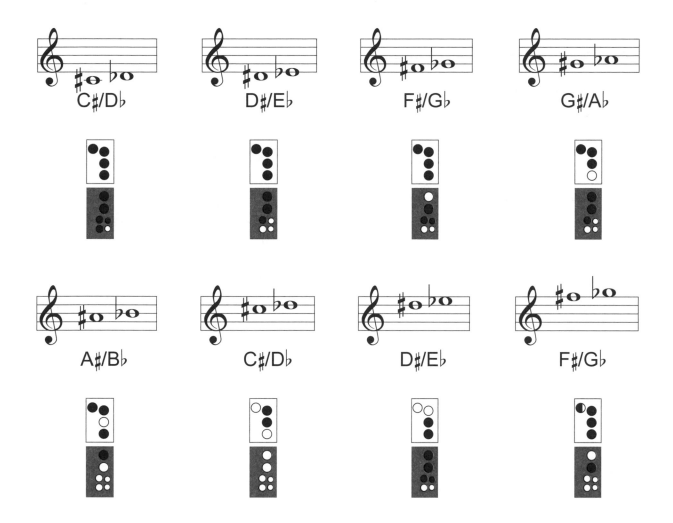

Interactive fingering charts

www.musick8kids.com/html/recorder_training.php

www.dolmetsch.com/cfingerchart.html

www.hrs.hampshire.org.uk/finger/cfinger.html

Learn B, A, and G

The "B" Song

(*Circle the quarter rest.*)

B is the first note, the ea-sy one to play. One fin-ger, one thumb, I could play all day.

The "A" Song

(Circle the Half Note.)

A is next and hard - er. Two things can go wrong.

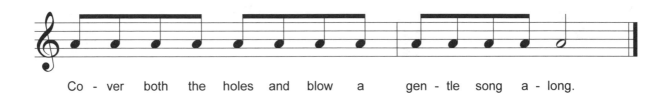

Co - ver both the holes and blow a gen - tle song a - long.

The "G" Song

(Circle the Treble Clef.)

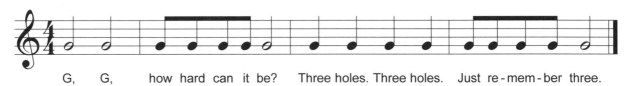

G, G, how hard can it be? Three holes. Three holes. Just re - mem - ber three.

Bag It!!

(Circle the Half Rest.)

B is the first note. B B B A is for two fin - gers don't you see?

G this is ea - sy as one two three. B A G

Hot Cross Buns

(Circle the Time Signature.)

Another BAG Song

(Circle the Key Signature.)

If you play this song cor - rect - ly and don't let the mu - sic drag, you will

learn this song so well that it will soon be in the BAG!

Nutcracker March

(Circle the Key triplet.)

Oh, let us go march-ing through this land. Oh, let us go march - ing through this land.

Moonlight

(How many beats are in each measure? _____.)

Mary Had A Little Lamb

(Circle the steps.)

Long Legged Sailor

(Circle the skips.)

Have you e - ver, e - ver, e - ver in your long leg-ged life seen a

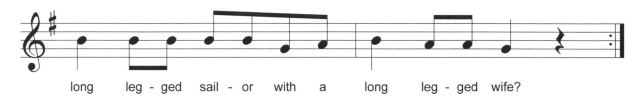

long leg - ged sail - or with a long leg - ged wife?

Good News

(Circle the syn-co-pa pattern.)

Good news, char - i - ot's a com-in' Good news, char - i - ot's a com-in'. Good

news, Char - i - ot's a com-in' and I don't want it to leave me be - hind.

From the Appendix 1 Songbook

Page 203	Dry Bones	G to B chorus only (Songbook)
Page 190	Hey There, Neighbor	G to B (leave out the high D and E) (Songbook)

Learn Low E

Skin and Bones

(Circle the repeat sign. How many beats per measure? _____.)

There was an old wo - man all skin and

bones.   Oooo   Oooo   Ooo   Oooo.

It's Raining It's Pouring

(*Circle the interval E to A.*)

It's   rain - ing   it's   pour - ing   the   old   man   is   snor - ing.

Went to bed and he   bumped his head and he   could-n't get up in the   morn - ing.

Play By Ear

A Tisket, A Tasket   AGE, begin on G

Learn Low D

The Broomstick

(*Circle the slurs. Box the tie.*)

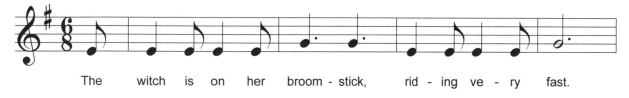

The   witch   is   on   her   broom - stick,   rid - ing ve - ry   fast.

Ooo   Ooo   Ooo   Ooo   Hal - lo - ween   at   last

Play By Ear

Old MacDonald   low D to B, begin on G

211

Learn F, Low and High C, High D (CDEFGABCD)

Jingle Bells

Play By Ear

Twinkle, Twinkle Little Star   adds F and low C, begin on low C
Row, Row, Row Your Boat   uses all notes from low C to high C, begin on low C

From *Get America Singing. . .Again!*

Page 7	Amazing Grace	C to C
Page 19	God Bless the USA	C to D
Page 32	Oh, What a Beautiful Mornin'	C to A (verse only)
Page 34	Over My Head	F to A

From the Appendix 1 Songbook

Page 194	Acitrón	D to B
Page 195	Mi cuerpo	C to C
Page 196	A la rueda rueda	E to C
Page 189	This Old Man	C to A
Page 190	Teddy Bear, Teddy Bear	C to A
Page 192	Bow Wow Wow	C to A

Learn B♭

From *Get America Singing. . .Again!*

Page 13	De colores	C to C (B♭)
Page 23	Home on the Range	C to C (B♭)
Page 39	Simple Gifts	C to C (B♭)

From the Appendix 1 Songbook

| Page 202 | Campanas vespertinas | C to C (B♭) | Melody and harmony |

Learn F♯

From *Get America Singing. . .Again!*

Page 29	Michael (Row the Boat Ashore)	D to B (F♯)
Page 33	Oh! Susanna	D to B (F♯)
Page 36	Rock-A-My Soul	D to C (F♯)
Page 42	This Land Is Your Land	D to C (F♯)

From the Appendix 1 Songbook

| Page 200 | Si me dan pasteles | E to C (F♯) | Melody only |
| Page 194 | Miss Mary Mack | D to G (F♯) |

Add More Notes For More Difficult Songs

From *Get America Singing. . .Again!*

| Page 11 | Blue Skies | C to D♭ (add B♭ and high D♭) |
| Page 47 | This Little Light of Mine | D to C (add A♯) |

APPENDIX 3 | **RESOURCES**

Benefits of Music Education

1. Early musical training helps develop brain areas involved in language and reasoning. It is thought that brain development continues for many years after birth. Recent studies have clearly indicated that musical training physically develops the part of the left side of the brain known to be involved with processing language, and can actually wire the brain's circuits in specific ways. Linking familiar songs to new information can also help imprint information on young minds.

2. There is also a causal link between music and spatial intelligence (the ability to perceive the world accurately and to form mental pictures of things). This kind of intelligence, by which one can visualize various elements that should go together, is critical to the sort of thinking necessary for everything from solving advanced mathematics problems to being able to pack a book-bag with everything that will be needed for the day.

3. Students of the arts learn to think creatively and to solve problems by imagining various solutions, rejecting outdated rules and assumptions. Questions about the arts do not have only one right answer.

4. Recent studies show that students who study the arts are more successful on standardized tests such as the SAT. They also achieve higher grades in high school.

5. A study of the arts provides children with an internal glimpse of other cultures and teaches them to be empathetic toward the people of these cultures. This development of compassion and empathy, as opposed to development of greed and a "me first" attitude, provides a bridge across cultural chasms that leads to respect of other races at an early age.

6. Students of music learn craftsmanship as they study how details are put together painstakingly and what constitutes good, as opposed to mediocre, work. These standards, when applied to a student's own work, demand a new level of excellence and require students to stretch their inner resources.

7. In music, a mistake is a mistake; the instrument is in tune or not, the notes are well played or not, the entrance is made or not. It is only by much hard work that a successful performance is possible. Through music study, students learn the value of sustained effort to achieve excellence and the concrete rewards of hard work.

8. Music study enhances teamwork skills and discipline. In order for an orchestra to sound good, all players must work together harmoniously toward a single goal, the performance, and must commit to learning music, attending rehearsals, and practicing.

9. Music provides children with a means of self-expression. Now that there is relative security in the basics of existence, the challenge is to make life meaningful and to reach for a higher stage of development. Everyone needs to be in touch at some time in his life with his core, with what he is and what he feels. Self-esteem is a by-product of this self-expression.

10. Music study develops skills that are necessary in the workplace. It focuses on "doing," as opposed to observing, and teaches students how to perform, literally, anywhere in the world. Employers are looking for multi-dimensional workers with the sort of flexible and supple intellects that music education helps to create as described above. In the music classroom, students can also learn to better communicate and cooperate with one another.

11. Music performance teaches young people to conquer fear and to take risks. A little anxiety is a good thing, and something that will occur often in life. Dealing with it early and often makes it less of a problem later. Risk-taking is essential if a child is to fully develop his or her potential.

Used by permission of the author, Carolyn Phillips,
executive director of the Norwalk Youth Symphony, Connecticut.

Examples of Music Objectives

Accompaniment   The student will enhance music by adding appropriate body percussion or instrumental percussion sounds.

Dynamics   The student will learn that dynamics refers to "the different degrees of loudness and softness of sound." She or he will identify and/or perform two contrasting dynamic markings in the music.

Soft (*p-piano*)   Loud (*f-forte*)

Form   The student will identify the sections of verse/chorus, ABA, rondo, and theme and variations forms.

Melody   The student will compare the singing voice and the speaking voice and demonstrate the difference between them.

Pitch   The student will define pitch as "the highness or lowness of a sound or musical tone." She or he will learn that songs are made of different pitches, and will aurally identify the highest and lowest pitches in a song.

Rhythm   The student will define rhythm as "a combination of durations of sound and silence in music." She or he will demonstrate that there are many more sounds (ex. taps or claps) for the rhythm than there are for the steady beat by clapping the rhythm of the music.

Rhythmic Movement   The student will add rhythmic movements to the music—movements that are clearly stated in the music or creative movements.

Steady Beat   The student will demonstrate the steady feeling in a song. This steady feeling is called *steady beat* or *pulse*.

Tempo   The student will demonstrate tempo changes by clapping steady beats or a rhythm in a slow tempo and again in a faster tempo, and/or by singing a song in a slow tempo and again in a faster tempo.

Tone Color   The student will identify the different families of instruments and their tone colors (*timbre*). She or he will identify each voice type and/or key instrument's tone colors.

Finger Plays

Collected by Dr. Timy Baranoff

Finger plays have an almost magical effect on young children, particularly at the beginning of the year. If you start a finger play when children are having difficulty settling down for a direct-teach time, in just a few moments they will either be participating or be simply entranced by the words and motions. Finger plays seem to have a soothing effect on unhappy children and to give comforting reassurance to shy children.

Note: Don't overuse finger plays. They are most appreciated when used occasionally.

Animal Finger Plays

1)
My bunny's so funny,
It wiggles its nose
And then hops away on the tips of its toes.

Motions: Use index and middle finger for ears. Hold thumb and ring finger together and wiggle for nose. Use index and middle finger to hop away on tips.

2)
I had a little turtle,
It always walked so slow,
For if it walked any faster
It'd be sure to stub its toe. Ouch!

Motions: Hold left arm out and walk up it with index and middle fingers of right hand. When you come to the last word, slide your fingers down arm to hand.

3)
Here is the beehive
But where are the bees?
Hiding away where nobody sees.
Now they come creeping out of the hive
One, two, three, four, five.
BZZZZZZZZZZZZZZZZZZZZZZZZZZZZZ!

Motions: Cup the hand into a fist. Starting with thumb, extend fingers one by one as you count.

4)
Ten little kittens standing in a row,
They bow their heads to the children so.
They run to the left, they run to the right,
They stand up and stretch with all their might.

Along comes a dog who wants some fun.
Meow, meow,
Just see those kittens run.

Motions: Use ten fingers to represent kittens. Use one hand to represent dog and then ten fingers again for the running kittens.

5)
Five little chickadees
Peeping at the door.
One flew away
And then there were four.

Chorus

Chickadee, chickadee, happy and gay,
Chickadee, chickadee, fly away.
Four little chickadees
Sitting in a tree.
One flew away and then there were three.

Chorus

Three little chickadees
Looking at you.
One flew away
And then there were two.

Chorus

Two little chickadees
Sitting in the sun.
One flew away
And then there was one.

Chorus

One little chickadee
Left all alone.
It flew away
And then there were none.

Motions: Use fingers to represent five birds. Take one finger away at a time.

6)

This little froggie broke his toe,
This little froggie said, Oh, Oh, Oh!
This little froggie laughed and was glad,
This little froggie cried and was sad,
This little froggie did what he should
He hopped for a doctor as fast as he could.

Motions: Show one finger at a time as you talk about frogs.

7)

Five little bunnies sitting at the door,
One hopped away and then there were four.
Four little bunnies sitting under a tree,
One hopped away and then there were three.
Three little bunnies looking at you,
One hopped away and then there were two.
Two little bunnies sitting in the sun,
One hopped away and then there was one.
One little bunny left all alone,
It hopped away and then there were none.

Motions: Use fingers to represent five bunnies. Take one finger away at a time.

8)

This little cow eats grass,
This little cow eats hay,
This little cow drinks water,
This little cow runs away,
This little cow does nothing but lie in the grass all day.

Motions: Show one finger at a time as you talk about each cow.

9)

The Itsy Bitsy Spider went up the water spout,
Down came the rain and washed the spider out.
Out came the sun and dried up all the rain
And the Itsy Bitsy Spider
Went up the spout again.

Motions: Touch index finger of right hand to thumb of left hand, then thumb of right hand to index finger of the left hand. Repeat to show climbing motion of spider. Show the rain with big arms. Make circle with arms for sun.

Alternate versions: Change to low voice and slow, exaggerated motions for Great Big Spider. Change to a very high voice and tiny, fast motions for Eensy Weensy Spider.

10)
Funny, funny bunny, hop, hop, hop,
Funny, funny bunny, stop, stop, stop.
Funny, funny bunny, run and play.
Funny, funny bunny, don't run away.

Motions: Use index and middle fingers to show hopping motion (tips of fingers touch floor or other surface).

11)
Five little mocking birds sitting in a tree
The first one said, "What's that I see?"
The second one said, "See a lady up the street!"
The third one said, "She's putting out seeds."
The fourth one said, "Seeds are good to eat!"
The fifth one said, "Tweet, tweet, tweet, tweet!"

Motions: Show one finger at a time for each of the five birds. Start with thumb.

12)
Two little blackbirds sitting on a hill,
One named Jack, the other name Jill.
Fly away Jack; fly away, Jill,
Come back, Jack; come back, Jill.

Motions: Hold up index finger of each hand. Put one hand behind back for "Fly away, Jack" and put other hand behind back for "fly away, Jill." Bring one hand in front for "Come back, Jack" and the other in front for "come back, Jill."

13)
A little mouse hid in a hole
Quietly in a hole, shhhh!
When all was safe as safe could be,
Out popped he!

Motions: Put closed hand inside the other. Take it out and wiggle fingers.

14)
There was a bunny who lived in the woods,
It wiggled its ears like a good bunny should.

It hopped by a squirrel, it hopped by a tree,
It hopped by a duck and it hopped by me.

It stared at the squirrel, it stared at the tree,
It stared at the duck, but it made faces at me.

Motions: Place one finger at each side of your head. With the two fingers upright, move the remaining fingers of each hand up and down for "It wiggled its ears." Make hopping motions with tips of index and middle fingers on flat surface. Stop hopping while bunny stared. Wiggle nose for the last line.

15)
Three little ducks that I once knew,
Short ones, fat ones, and skinny ones too,
But the one little duck with the feather on its back
It ruled the others with its "quack, quack, quack."

Down to the river they would go
Wiggle waggle, wiggle waggle, to and fro.
But the one little duck with the feather on its back
It ruled the others with its "quack, quack, quack!"

Motions: Show three fingers. Use hands to show various sizes. For "the one little duck" show one finger and hold index and middle finger of other hand behind head. Put palms together and wiggle back and forth for ducks walking to the river.

16)
There was a turtle and it lived in a box,
It swam in a puddle and it climbed on the rocks,
It snapped at a mosquito and it snapped at a flea,
It snapped at a minnow and it snapped at me!
It caught the mosquito and it caught the flea,
It caught the minnow but it didn't catch me!

Motions: Use hands to act out snapping turtle.

17)
Here is a turkey with its tail spread wide,
It sees the farmer coming, so it's trying to hide.
It runs across the barnyard, wobble, wobble, wobble,
Talking turkey talk, gobble, gobble, gobble.

Motions: Spread fingers wide, put thumb in front for turkey's head. Hide thumb with fingers on "trying to hide." Wiggle hand back and forth for running motions.

18)
"Come, my bunnies, it's time for bed."
That's what the mother bunny said.
"But first I'll count you just to see
If you have all come back to me.
Bunny 1, bunny 2, bunny 3, so dear,
Bunny 4, bunny 5, yes you're all here.
You're the sweetest things alive
My dear little bunnies, 1, 2, 3, 4, 5."

19)
Let's go on a lion hunt. Okay? Are you afraid?
Say everything I say,
and do everything I do, okay?
Here we go, I'm not afraid. (*Children repeat*)

Tall grass! Have to go through it. Swish, swish,
swish, swish.
(*Brush sides of body with flat of hand.*)
And down the road, I'm not afraid.

Big river! Have to swim it. Swim, swim, swim, swim.
(*Continue descriptive motions here and below.*)
And down the road, I'm not afraid.

Look at the mud, have to walk through it.
Plop, plop, plop, plop.
And down the road, I'm not afraid.

Big mountain! Have to climb it.
Climb, climb, climb, climb.
And down the other side, roll, roll, roll, roll.
And down the road, I'm not afraid.

A dark cave. Let's explore it.
Walk, walk, walk, walk.
What's that I feel?
Furry back! Long tail! Big fat tummy! Two big teeth!
It's a lion! Let's get out of here!

(*Faster*) Big Mountain! Have to climb it.
Climb, climb, climb, climb.
And down the other side. Roll, roll, roll, roll.
And down the road, run, run, run!

Look at the mud, have to walk through it.
Plop, plop, plop, plop.
And down the road, run, run, run!

Big river! Have to swim it.
Swim, swim, swim, swim.
And down the road, run, run, run!

Tall grass! Have to go through it.
Swish, swish, swish, swish.
And down the road, run, run, run!
There's my house. Open the door, shut the door, up the stairs, in my room, under my bed.
Whew! I'm not afraid!

20)
I had a big rubber balloon
Almost as big as the moon.
It floated so prettily on the air
When suddenly POP! It wasn't there.

Motions: Make large circle with both arms above head. Move hands from left to right in sweeping motion. At the word "pop" clap hands together loudly.

21)
Ten little peas in a pea pod press
One grew, two grew, and so did all the rest.
They grew and they grew and they grew and they grew
And one day the pea pod POPPED!

Motions: Hold closed hands together, hiding fingers. Let one index finger come, then the other, and then all fingers. Separate closed hands and spread arms farther and farther apart as peas grow. Use softer voice on last line, and bring hands together loudly on the word "POPPED."

22)
There were five in the bed and the little one said,
"Move over, move over."
And they all rolled over and one fell out.
There were four in the bed and the little one said,
"Move over, move over."
And they all rolled over and one fell out.
There were three in the bed and the little one said,
"Move over, move over."
And they all rolled over and one fell out.
There were two in the bed and the little one side,
"Move over, move over."
And they all rolled over and one fell out.
There was one in the bed and the little one said,
"I'm lonesome, I'm lonesome."

So they all got up, got into the bed.
We're happy, we're happy.

Motions: Show five fingers; wiggle little finger for smallest child. Use left arm to motion "move over." Open hand and rotate for rolling motion.

23)
Oh, Jack in the box, so very still,
Will you come up and see me?
"Yes, I will!"

Motions: Hide face and curl up. Spring up and clap hands over head at "Yes, I will!"

Halloween Finger Plays

24)
One little, two little, three little witches
Fly over haystacks, fly over ditches,
Slide down the moon without any hitches.
Hi ho! Halloween's here.

Horned owl's hooting, it's time to go riding.
Deep in the shadows are black bats hiding,
With gay little goblins sliding, sliding.
Hi ho! Halloween's here.

Stand on your head with a lopsided wiggle,
Tickle your little black cats till they giggle,
Swish through the clouds with a higgledy-piggle.
Hi ho! Halloween's here.

Motions: Use hands to act out the rhyme.

25)
Jack-o-lantern, jack-o-lantern,
Big and yellow.
Jack-o-lantern, jack-o-lantern,
Funny fellow shining in the night,
With your candle light
Scaring all the witches
With your BOO! BOO! BOO!

Motions: Use hands to act out the rhyme.

26)
Five little pumpkins sitting on a gate,
The first one said, "It's getting late."
The second one said, "There's witches in the air."
The third one said, "I don't care."
The fourth one said, "Let's run, run, run."
The fifth one said, "It's Halloween fun."
When WOOOOOOO went the wind
And out went the light,
And away ran the jack-o-lanterns
On a Halloween night.

Music Resources: Student Books, DVDs, Teacher Books

Recommended Student Books

Specifically recommended for fourth- to sixth-grade students.

Ahlberg, Allan. (2006). *The Jolly Postman.* (J. Ahlberg, Illus.). Boston: Little, Brown.
A set of notes, postcards, and letters (included in the book) delivered to a cast of nursery rhyme characters.

Aliki. (2005). *Ah, Music.* New York: HarperCollins.
Introduction to musical elements such as rhythm, pitch, composition, and history.

Allan, Debbie. (2003). *Dancing in the Wings.* (K. Nelson, Illus.). New York: Puffin.
Sassy proves that despite her looks she can do whatever she dreams of.

Auch, Mary Jane. (1997). *Bantam of the Opera.* New York: Holiday House.
Luigi the Rooster gets his chance to sing Rigoletto when the star tenor and understudy both come down with the chickenpox.

Barner, Bob. (1996). *Dem Bones.* San Francisco: Chronicle Books.
Clever anatomy lesson with great illustrations is based on the gospel song.

Barnes, Peter W. and Barnes, Carol Shaw. (2005). *Maestro Mouse and the Mystery of the Missing Baton.* Alexandria, VA: VSP Books.
Takes children on a tour through the orchestra and around the Kennedy Center for the Performing Arts in search of a lost baton.

Bates, Katherine Lee. (1993). *America the Beautiful.* (N. Waldman, Illus.). New York: Macmillan/McGraw Hill.
Illustrations of the lyrics to the song.

Bates, Katherine Lee. (2004). *America the Beautiful: A Pop-up Book.* (R. Sabuda, Illus.). New York: Little Simon.
Illustrations of the lyrics to the song.

Beall, Pamela Conn and Hagen, Susan. (2007). *Wee Sing: The Best of Wee Sing.* New York: Price Stern Sloan.
A treasury of best-loved children's songs. Excellent CD with children singing included.

Boynton, Sandra. (2002). *Philadelphia Chickens: A Too-Illogical Zoological Musical Revue.* New York: Workman Pub.
Music with illustrations about an imaginary musical production. CD included.

Brett, Jan. (1996). *Berlioz the Bear.* (B. Giacobbe, Illus.). New York: Putnam.
The journey of an animal orchestra on their way to a concert.

Brett, Jan. (1997). *The Twelve Days of Christmas. New York:* Putnam & Grosset Group.
Lavish illustrations of the book show various levels of meaning in the words of the song, which count from 1 to 12.

*Bunting, Eve. (1998). *Going Home.* (D. Diaz, Illus.). New York: HarperCollins.
Pictures an immigrant family visiting their old hometown in Mexico.

*Burleigh, Robert. (2001). *Hoops.* (S. T. Johnson, Illus.). San Diego, CA: Voyager Books.
A book that captures the energy and poetry of a neighborhood game of basketball.

*Burns, Marilyn. (2008). *The Greedy Triangle.* New York: Scholastic Paperbacks.
An offbeat introduction to geometry as a triangle shifts into pentagons, hexagons, and so forth.

Bynum, Eboni and Jackson, Roland. (2004). *Jamari's Drum.* (B. W. Diakite, Illus.). Toronto: Groundwood Books.
An African boy saves his village by playing the Djembe.

Campbell, Patricia Shehan, Williamson, Sue, and Pierre Perron. (1997). *Traditional Songs of Singing Cultures: A World Sampler.* Miami: Warner Bros. Publications.
Songs from around the world. Good information about music and culture. Teaching ideas and CD included.

Carlson, Nancy. (2006). *Harriet's Recital.* Minneapolis: Carolrhoda Books.
About a dog that didn't want to dance in her recital but then ended up loving the experience.

* Catrow, David. (2005). *We the Kids.* New York: Puffin.
Illustrations of the preamble of the US Constitution. The special wording is made memorable and fun.

Celenza, Anna Harwell. (2006). *Pictures at an Exhibition.* (J. Kitchel, illus.). Watertown, MA: Charlesbridge Publishing.
The story follows three Russian friends, Mussorgsky, Hartmann, and Stasov, up to the events that were the inspiration for the orchestral piece.

Celenza, Anna Harwell. (2006). *Rhapsody in Blue.* (J. Kitchel, Illus.). Watertown, MA: Charlesbridge Publishing.
The story of Gershwin's creation of the rhapsody. Includes CD.

*Cleary, Brian P. (2005). *Dearly, Nearly, Insincerely: What is an Adverb?* (B. Gable, Illus.). Minneapolis, MN: Lerner.
Introduces adverbs through rhyming, rhythmic text.

*Clements, Andres. (1997). *Double Trouble in Walla Walla.* (S. Murdocca, Illus.). Brookfield, CT: The Millbrook Press.
A young girl and her teachers come down with a case of speaking in nonsense words.

Cronin, Doreen. (2006). *Dooby Dooby Moo.* (B. Lewin, Illus.). New York: Atheneum Books for Young Readers.
Farmer Brown's animals go to a talent show.

Crow, Kristyn. (2008). *Bedtime in the Swamp.* (M. Pamintuan, Illus.). New York: HarperCollins.
A simple rhyming storyline, and a repetitive refrain are used in a swampy tale.

Crow, Kristyn. (2008). *Cool Daddy Rat.* (M. Lester, Illus). New York: Putnam Juvenile.
Read-aloud, rhyming text with a swingin' beat.

Denne, Ben. (2001). *The Usborne Internet-Linked First Encyclopedia of Seas and Oceans.* New York: Scholastic.
First reference book that explains different aspects of today's world.

DePaola, Tomie. (1988). *The Legend of the Indian Paintbrush.* (T. DePaola, Illus.). New York: Putnam.
A rhythmic retelling of an Indian legend.

Dillon, Leo. (2002). *Rap a Tap Tap.* New York: Blue Sky Press.
A biography of the African American tap dancer Bill "Bojangles" Robinson.

Dragonwagon, Crescent. (1993). *Home Place.* (J. Pinkney, Illus.). New York: Aladdin.
A girl and her family discover an old home place, and find hints to the past.

Edgers, Geoff. (2006). *Who Were the Beatles?* (J. Tugeau, Illus.). New York: Grosset & Dunlap.
A chapter on each of the Beatles plus a few "extras" on Elvis, Ray Charles, the Vietnam War and the 1960s, and a timeline.

Edgers, Geoff. (2007). *Who Was Elvis Presley?* (J. O'Brien and N. Harrison, Illus.). New York: Grosset & Dunlap.
A chapter book about Elvis Presley plus a few "extras" on the Grand Ole Opry, gospel music, acoustic and electric guitars, Graceland, Elvis Jumpsuits, Las Vegas, Elvis Sightings, and a timeline.

Ehlert, Loin. (1999). *Snowballs.* Orlando: Voyager Books.
Steps in building a snowman depicted in wonderful collage illustrations.

Ehrhardt, Karen. (2006). *This Jazz Man.* (R. G. Roth, Illus.). Orlando: Harcourt.
Alternate lyrics to the tune of "This Old Man." This book introduces famous African American jazz musicians. Biographies in the back.

Elliot, Doug. (2008). *Crawdads, Doodlebugs and Greasy Greens.* Asheville, NC: Native Ground Music.
Songs, stories, and lore celebrating the natural world.

Erbsen, Wayne. (1993). *Front Porch Old-Time Songs, Jokes and Stories.* Asheville, NC: Native Ground Music.
Forty-eight great sing-along favorites. Includes information about the music.

Falconer, Ian. (2006). *Olivia Forms a Band.* New York: Atheneum Books for Young Readers.
A piglet and her mother get creative on the day of a fireworks show.

Fleischman, Paul. (2006). *Big Talk Poems for Four Voices.* (B. Giacobbe, Illus.). Cambridge, MA: Candlewick Press.
Poems to be read by four different children.

Fox, Mem. (2007). *Whoever You Are.* (L. Staub, Illus.). Orlando: Voyager Books.
Fox has created a simple refrain to celebrate human connections.

*Gerstein, Mordicai. (2007). *The Man Who Walked Between the Towers.* New York: Square Fish.
Immortalizes Philippe Petit's tightrope walk across the World Trade Towers in 1974.

Geslin, Campbell. (2004). *Elena's Serenade.* (A. Juan, Illus.). New York: Atheneum Books for Young Readers.
A young Mexican girl discovers music on her journey to become a glassblower.

*Gilman, Phoebe. (1993). *Something from Nothing.* New York: Scholastic.
A Jewish folk tale beautifully illustrated and written with rhythmic text.

Gollub, Matthew. (2000). *The Jazz Fly.* (K. Hanke, Illus.). Santa Rose, CA: Tortuga Press.
A fly gets lost on his way to a performance and gets help from other animals. CD included.

Guthrie, Woody. (2008). *This Land is Your Land.* (K. Jakobsen, Illus.). Boston: Little, Brown.
Illustrations of the folk song.

*Harness, Cheryl. (1999). *The Amazing Impossible Erie Canal.* New York: Simon and Schuster Books for Young Readers.
The history and construction of the Erie Canal comes to life with wonderful illustrations of life in 19th-century New York State.

*Henkes, Kevin. (1996). *Chrysanthemum.* New York: Mulberry Books.
A small mouse loves her name until other mice start making fun of it. This is resolved when their music teacher announces that she will be naming her daughter Chrysanthemum.

Henry, Sandi. (1999). *Kids Art Works!: Creating With Color, Design, Texture & More.* (N. Martin-Jourdenais, Illus.). Williamson Publishing.
Intermediate students will enjoy making simple creative projects to display. Information about famous artists also included.

Heyward, Dubose, Heyward, Dorothy, Gershwin, Ira, and Gershwin, George. (2002). *Summertime.* (M, Wimmer, Illus.). New York: Aladdin.
Illustrations of the Gershwin song from Porgy and Bess.

Hillenbrand, Will. (2002). *Fiddle I Fee.* San Diego: Harcourt.
A musical illustration of the folk song.

Hopkinson, Deborah. (1995). *Sweet Clara and the Freedom Quilt.* New York: Dragonfly Books.
Story of a courageous young slave girl is based on a true event.

Hughes, Langston. (2003). *Works for Children and Young Adults: Poetry, Fiction, and Other Writing.* (D. Johnson, ed.). Columbia, MO: University of Missouri Press.
Excellent stories, poems, and short books written by a famous African American author. Includes *The First Book of Rhythms*, and *The First Book of Jazz.*

Hughes, Shirley. (2004). *Ella's Big Chance: A Jazz-Age Cinderella.* New York: Simon & Schuster Books for Young Readers.
A 1920s Cinderella story with a feminist twist at the end.

Hurwitz, Johanna. (1993). *New Shoes for Silvia.* New York: HarperCollins.
A story about a girl and her shiny red shoes, set in Latin America.

Iqus, Toyomi. (1998). *I See the Rhythm.* (M. Wood, Illus.). San Francisco: Children's Book Press.
Picture-book history of African American music from African origins and slave songs through rap. Text is lines from the songs.

Isadora, Rachel. (1979). *Ben's Trumpet.* New York: Greenwillow Books.
Story of a boy growing up in the 1920s.

Isadora, Rachel. (1994) *At the Crossroads.* New York: Greenwillow Books.
A lively portrayal of young children in a South African village eagerly awaiting their fathers' homecoming after ten months of working in the mines. The celebration includes children fashioning home-made musical instruments from salvaged scraps.

Joel, Billy. (2005). *New York State of Mind.* (I. Zenou, Illus.). New York: Scholastic.
Two dogs take a tour of New York City, to the words of Billy Joel's 1992 song.

*Johnson, Stephen T. (1995). *Alphabet City.* New York: Viking.
Caldecott winner, this book draws attention to everyday objects that spell the alphabet.

Johnston, Tony and Bloom, Lloyd. (2002). *Yonder.* Salt Lake City: Gibbs Smith.
A plum tree shows the generations of a 19th-century family.

Katz, Alan and Catrow, David. (1996). *Take Me Out of the Bathtub.* New York: Margaret K. McElderry.
Silly lyrics to familiar tunes (piggyback songs).

Katz, Alan and Catrow, David. (2001). *I'm Still Here in the Bathtub.* New York: Margaret K. McElderry.
Silly lyrics to familiar tunes (piggyback songs).

Kimmel, Eric A. (2006). *A Horn for Louis.* New York: Random House.
An account of how Louis Armstrong got his first trumpet.

Kroll, Steven. (2000). *By the Dawn's Early Light.* (D. Andreaseen, Illus.). New York: Scholastic.
Story of the events leading to the writing of the American national anthem.

Krosoczka, Jarrett J. (2005). *Punk Farm.* New York: Knopf Books for Young Readers.
Follows farm animals' preparation and performance of a rock concert.

Krull, Kathleen. (2002). *Lives of the Musicians.* (K. Hewitt, Illus.). New York: Sandpiper.
Short biographies of several composers such as Beethoven, Mozart, Joplin, and Gilbert and Sullivan.

Krull, Kathleen. (2003). *I Hear America Singing! Folks Songs for American Families.* (A. Garns, Illus.).
    New York: Knopf.
Collection of American folk songs for children. Beautiful illustrations and brief information about the
    songs. CD included. Formerly published as *Gonna Sing my Head Off!*

Krull, Kathleen. (2009). *M is for Music.* (S. Innerst, Illus.). New York: Sandpiper.
An alphabetical compendium of musical words.

Kushner, Tony. (2003). *Brundibar.* (M. Sendak, Illus.). New York: Hyperion Books for Children.
A picture book based on the Czech opera originally performed by the children of Terezin Concentration
    Camp.

Lach, William. (2006). *Can You Hear It?* New York: Abrams Books for Young Readers.
Introduces students to great music through great works of art. The book has a brief introduction of orchestral
    instruments and composers. CD included.

Legge, Anne. (2008). *Veggie Friends and Fruits Too: A Children's Cookbook on Creating Healthy Snacks.*
    Booksurge.
Encouraging children's creativity by working with fruits and vegetables to create healthy snacks.

Lewis, E. B. (2005). *This Little Light of Mine.* (E. B. Lewis, Illus.). New York: Simon & Schuster Children's
    Publishing.
Illustrations of the familiar African American spiritual.

Lithgow, John. (2003). *The Remarkable Farkle McBride.* (C. F. Payne, Illus.). New York: Simon & Schuster
    Books for Young Readers.
Introduction to sections of the orchestra through a young boy trying to find "the perfect instrument."

Lithgow, John. (2007). *Carnival of the Animals.* (B. Kulikov, Illus.). New York: Simon & Schuster Books
    for Young Readers.
Story about Oliver who gets left behind after a field trip to a natural history museum. Includes a CD of
    John Lithgow narrating and a complete recording of the piece by Saint-Saëns.

Longfellow, Henry Wadsworth. (1996). *Hiawatha.* (S. Jeffers, Illus.). New York: Puffin.
The telling of Hiawatha's early years as he learns the ways of American Indians from his grandmother.

*MacLachlan, Patricia. (1999). *All the Places to Love.* (M. Wimmer, Illus.). New York: HarperCollins.
A view of all the special places on a farm from the point of view of a three-generation family.

Martin, Bill, Jr. (1989) *Chicka Chicka Boom Boom.* New York: Scholastic.
Rhythmic sounds and verse about the ABCs.

Martin, Bill, Jr. (1992). *Polar Bear, Polar Bear, What Do You Hear?* (E. Carle, Illus.). New York: Scholastic.
A story about animals and sounds.

Martin, Bill, Jr. (1997) *Brown Bear, Brown Bear, What Do You See?* (E. Carle, Illus.). New York: Henry Holt & Co.
A much-loved classic about animals and colors and much more!

McDonough, Yona Zeldis. (2003). *Who Was Wolfgang Amadeus Mozart?* (J. O'Brien and N. Harrison, Illus.). New York: Grosset & Dunlap.
A chapter book about Mozart plus a few "extras" on opera and the evolution of musical instruments, and a timeline.

McDonough, Yona Zeldis. (2004). *Who Was Louis Armstrong?* (J. O'Brien and N. Harrison, Illus.). Grosset & Dunlap.
A chapter book about Louis Armstrong.

McKissack, Patricia C. (1997). *Mirandy and Brother Wind.* (J. Pinkney, Illus.). New York: Dragonfly Books.
Caldecott winner, story includes a cakewalk.

McKissack, Patricia and McKissack, Frederick L. (1994). *Christmas in the Big House, Christmas in the Quarters.* New York: Scholastic.
Describes Christmas for the slaves and for the owners. Includes a cakewalk.

McPhail, David. (2001). *Mole Music.* New York; Henry Holt and Co.
Story of a mole learning to play violin and affecting others.

Meyrick, Kathryn. (2006). *The Musical Life of Gustav Mole.* New York: Child's Play International.
Gustav is a mole who was born into a musical family. He shares his experiences with individual instruments, and performing groups such as the orchestra, jazz band, and opera. CD included.

Miller, J. J. Phillip and Greene, Sheppard M. (2005). *We All Sing with the Same Voice* (P. Meisel, Illus.). New York: HarperCollins.
Illustrations of Sesame Street songs. CD included.

Moss, Lloyd. (2000). *Zin! Zin! Zin! A Violin.* (M. Priceman, Illus.). Aladdin.
An exuberant tribute to classical music and musicians.

Moss, Marissa. (2006). *Amelia's Notebook.* New York: Simon & Schuster.
A nine-year-old girl writes about moving, going to school, and making friends.

Music Educators National Conference. (1997). *Get America Singing. . .Again!* Milwaukee, WI: Hal Leonard.
Collection of common song repertoire for singing.

*Myers, Walter Dean. (2003). *Blues Journey.* (C. Myers, Illus.). New York: Holiday House.
Call-and-response blues-inspired poetry for older students.

Nelson, Kadir. (2005). *He's Got the Whole World in His Hands.* New York: Dial Books for Young Readers.
Illustrations of the familiar African American spiritual.

Nichol, Barbara. (1999). *Beethoven Lives Upstairs.* (S. Cameron, Illus.). New York: Orchard Books.
Nichol chronicles a slice of the composer's life through the point of view of a boy, Christoph, who lives
    downstairs from Beethoven.

*Pattou, Edith. (2001). *Mrs. Spitzer's Garden.* (T. Tusa, Illus.). San Diego: Harcourt.
A story of a teacher tending her garden.

Paxton, Tom. (1996). *Going to the Zoo.* (K. L. Schmidt, Illus.). New York: HarperCollins.
Colorful illustrations and rhythmic text.

Peek, Merle. (1981). *Roll Over.* New York: Houghton Mifflin/Clarion Books.
Great illustrations depicting the words of the song.

Pelham, David. (1991). *Sam's Sandwich.* New York: Dutton Children's Books.
Fold-out flap book with the look of a real sandwich and easy-to-say, rolling rhymes.

Pikey, Dav. (1990). *Twas the Night Before Thanksgiving Day.* New York: Scholastic.
Parody of the Clement Moore poem.

*Pinczes, Elinor J. (1995). *A Remainder of One.* (B. Mackain, Illus.). New York: Scholastic.
Division presented through rhyming text and illustrations.

Pinkney, Andrea Davis. (1999). *Duke Ellington.* (B. Pinkney, Illus.). New York: Hyperion Books.
A view into who Duke Ellington was and what he did for the musical world.

Pinkney, Andrea Davis. (2002). *Ella Fitzgerald: The Tale of a Vocal Virtuosa.* (B. Pinkney, Illus.). New
    York: Hyperion Books.
A cat tells the story of The First Lady of Song with a rhythmical beat.

Prince, Leontyne. (1997). *Aida.* San Diego, CA: Voyager Books.
A retelling of Verdi's opera.

Reich, Susanna. (1999). *Clara Schumann: Piano Virtuoso.* New York: Clarion Books.
A biography of the child prodigy.

Robinson, Sandra Chisholm. (1994). *The Rainstick, A Fable.* Guilford, CT: TwoDot.
History, myths, and traditions of West Africa come to life in this book.

Rosen, Michael. (2003). *We're Going on a Bear Hunt.* (H. Oxenbury, Illus.). New York: Margaret K. McElderry.
Based on the old camp chant, a father and children go out to hunt a bear and get chased all the way back
    home.

Ryan, Pam Munoz. (2002). *When Marion Sang.* (B. Selznick, Illus.). New York: Scholastic.
Tells the poignant story of Marian Anderson.

San Souci, Robert D. (1989). *Talking Eggs.* (J. Pinkney. Illus.). New York: Dial Books for Young Readers.
Creole folk tale with a strong heroine and magic.

Schulman, Janet. (2004). *Sergei Prokofiev's Peter and the Wolf.* (P. Malone, Illus.). New York: Knopf Books
    for Young Readers.
Excellent way to introduce children to classical music and the instruments of the orchestra. CD included.

*Scieszka, Jon. (1995). *Math Curse.* New York: Viking.
After being told that you can think of almost anything as a math problem, a girl starts thinking of everything in that way.

Scieszka, Jon. (1996). *The True Story of the Three Little Pigs.* (L. Smith, Illus.). New York: Puffin.
An impudent new version of the old story from the wolf's point of view.

Sendak, Maurice. (1988). *Where the Wild Things Are.* New York: HarperCollins.
Caldecott winner, story of Max who takes a journey from his very own bedroom.

Sherr, Lynn. (2001). *America the Beautiful: The Stirring True Story Behind Our Nation's Favorite Song.* New York: Public Affairs.
A history of Katherine Lee Bate's life, and what led her to write the poem.

Showers, Paul. (1993). *The Listening Walk.* (Aliki, Illus.). New York: HarperCollins.
Great as a story about sound and as a jumping-off point for taking your own walks.

Sis, Peter. (2006). *Play, Mozart, Play.* New York: HarperCollins.
The book follows Mozart's childhood.

Spier, Peter. (1988). *People.* (P. Spier, Illus.). Garden City, NY: Doubleday Books for Young Readers.
Exquisite paintings of human beings on four continents.

Spier, Peter. (1992). *Noah's Ark.* (P. Spier, Illus.). New York: Dragonfly Books.
Illustrations of the story of Noah's Ark.

Spier, Peter. (1992). *The Star Spangled Banner.* (P. Spier, Illus.). New York: Dragonfly Books.
Illustrated version of the writing of the American national anthem.

Spinelli, Eileen. (1996). *Someone Loves You, Mr. Hatch.* New York: Simon & Schuster Children's Publishing.
Looks at the effect that friendship and love can have.

Stott, Carole.(2003). *I Wonder Why Stars Twinkle.* New York: Kingfisher Books.
Questions and answers about space.

Swain, Gwenyth. (2005). *I Wonder As I Wander.* (R. Himler, Illus.). Grand Rapids, MI: Eerdmans Books for Young Readers.
A story of hope and love woven around a Christmas carol.

Thuswaldner, Werner. (2005). *Silent Night, Holy Night.* (R. Ingpen, Illus.). New York: Minedition.
Illustrated history of the popular Christmas carol.

Tripp, Paul. (2006). *Tubby the Tuba.* (H. Cole, Illus.). New York: Dutton Juvenile.
The orchestra's tuba gets tired of repeating "oompah" and learns a melody from a bullfrog. CD included.

Turner, Ann. (1997), *Shaker Hearts.* New York: HarperCollins.
Information concerning the Shaker movement in America.

Tyrrell, Frances. (2003). *Huron Carol.* Grand Rapids, MI: Eerdmans Books for Young Readers.
Translation and musical arrangement of an early 1600s Christmas carol (includes lyrics in Huron, French, and English).

*Van Allsburg, Chris. (1988). *Two Bad Ants.* Boston: Houghton Mifflin.
Two ants go through a lot in a kitchen in search of sugar.

Warren, George. (2004). *Shake, Rattle, & Roll.* New York: Sandpiper.
Short biographies of the founders of rock and roll.

Weiss, George David and Thiele, Bob. (2005). *What a Wonderful World.* (A. Bryan, Illus.). New York: Atheneum Books for Young Readers.
Illustrations of the song.

Williams, Linda. (1988). *Little Old Lady Who Was Not Afraid of Anything.* (M. Lloyd, Illus.). New York: Harper Collins.
Catchy refrain and rhythmic text brings a Halloween story to life.

Winter, Jeanette. (1992). *Follow the Drinking Gourd.* New York: Dragonfly Books.
Shows how the song holds directions for following the Underground Railroad to freedom.

Yarrow, Lipton and Purbaret. (2007). *Puff, The Magic Dragon.* New York: Sterling.
Wonderful illustrations bring the song to life.

Zanes, Dan. (2004). *Hello Hello.* (D. Saaf, Illus.). New York: Little, Brown.
Song-and-picture book about animals saying hello to each other.

Zelinsky, Paul. (1990). *The Wheels on the Bus.* New York: Dutton Children's Books.
Adaptation of the traditional song with parts that move.

Recommended DVDs

Fantasia (1940) Walt Disney Productions. 116 min.
All grades. The original 1940 Disney animated classic that artfully blends animation and classical music in *The Sorcerer's Apprentice*, *The Nutcracker Suite*, *Rite of Spring*, *Night on Bald Mountain*, and more.

Fantasia 2000 (1999) Walt Disney Productions. 90 min.
All grades. Sixty years later, Fantasia 2000 begins where the original left off, with seven new animations including Stravinsky's *Firebird Suite* and Gershwin's *Rhapsody in Blue*.

Isaac Asimov-Voyage To The Outer Planets (2003)
(DVD available from Music in Motion.) Gustav Holst's orchestral suite *The Planets* (1917) has been choreographed with live NASA footage of the moon landing and space probes, with added computer animation. Subtitles silently convey information on the planets and other space phenomena, so as not to disrupt the music.

Make Mine Music (1946) Walt Disney Productions. 67 min.
Primary grades. Disney's collection of imaginative animations of musical stories. Includes *Peter and the Wolf*, *Willie the Operatic Whale*, *The Silly Symphony*, and *Casey at the Bat*. Available through Music in Motion, www.musicinmotion.com.

Melodytime (1948) Walt Disney Productions. 75 min.
Primary grades. Music, fun, and fantasy in Disney's Johnny Appleseed, Little Toot, Pecos Bill, and four others.

Pulse: A Stomp Odyssey (2002) Honda. 40 min.
Accompanying audio CD also available.

Pulse: A Stomp Odyssey is a celebration of the global beat, an exploration of the sights and sounds of continents and cultures, guided by the internationally acclaimed performers of the sensational stage show *STOMP*.

Classical Music With Structured Movement

Classical Moves by Barb Stevanson.
Available from aeIDEAS.com. CD, DVD, and a book of instructions. Seven classical pieces have simple moves choreographed to the music.

Move It! Expressive Movements with Classical Music for All Ages by John Feierabend.

Move It! 2 Expressive Movements with Classical Music for All Ages by John Feierabend.
Available from GIA Publishing, Inc.

Recommended Teaching Books

Abraham, K. Adzenyah, Dumisani Maraire, and Cook Tucker, Judith. (1997). *Let Your Voice Be Heard! Songs from Ghana and Zimbabwe.* Danbury: World Music Press.
Book and CD with songs and games.

Amidon, Peter, David, Andy, and Brass, Mary Cay. (1990). *Chimes of Dunkirk: Great Dances for Children.* Brattleboro, VT: New England Dancing Masters Productions.
Book and CD set.

Amidon, Peter, David, Andy, and Brass, Mary Cay. (1990). *Listen to the Mockingbird: More Great Dances for Children.* Brattleboro, VT: New England Dancing Masters Productions.
Book and CD set.

Berenstain, Stan and Berenstain, Jan. (1985). *The Berenstain Bears and Too Much Junk Food.* New York: Random House.

Campbell, Patricia Shehan. (2008). *Tunes and Grooves for Music Education.* Upper Saddle River, NJ: Pearson Prentice Hall.

Chernaik, Judith (ed.). *Carnival of the Animals: Poems Inspired by Saint-Saëns' Music.* Cambridge, MA: Candlewick Press.
Book & CD set. Engaging poems written to match the music are in the book and read on the CD before the each music selection.

Hughes, Langston. (2003). *Works for Children and Young Adults: Poetry, Fiction, and Other Writing.* (D. Johnson, ed.). Columbia, MO: University of Missouri Press.

Komlos, Katalin (composer) and Erdei, Peter (ed.). (1974). *150 American Folk Songs: To Sing, Read and Play.* New York: Boosey & Hawkes.

Kriske, Jeff and DeLelles, Randy. (1992). *Highlighting the Holidays.* Kid Sounds.

Locke, Eleanor (composer). (2004). *Sail Away: 155 American Folk Songs to Sing, Read and Play.* New York: Boosey & Hawkes.

Longden, Sanna Hans. (2006). *More Folk Dance Music for Kids and Teachers.* Evanston, IL: FolkStyle Productions.
CD with instruction book.

Music Memory Bulletin, CDs—aeIDEAS.com
Classical music listening program for elementary students. The Bulletin includes listening maps, lesson plans, custom CDs of the 16 selections, and the Animated VideoMaps DVD.

Orozco, Jose-Luis. (2002). *Diez Deditos and Other Play Rhymes and Action Songs from Latin America* (E. Kleven, Illus.). New York: Puffin.

Saint-Saëns, Camille and Turner, Barrie C. (1999). *Carnival of the Animals: Classical Music for Kids.* (S. Williams, Illus.). New York: Holt.

Seeger, Ruth Crawford. (2002) *American Folksongs For Children.* New York: Music Sales Corporation.

Weikart, Phyllis S. (2006), *Teaching Movement & Dance: A Sequential Approach to Rhythmic Movement.* Ypsilanti, MI: High/Scope Press.

With Rhythmically Moving CDs 1–9.

National Standards For Music Education

Content Standards

1. Singing, alone and with others, a varied repertoire of music.
2. Performing on instruments, alone and with others, a varied repertoire of music.
3. Improvising melodies, variations, and accompaniments.
4. Composing and arranging music within specified guidelines.
5. Reading and notating music.
6. Listening to, analyzing, and describing music.
7. Evaluating music and music performances.
8. Understanding relationships between music, the other arts, and disciplines outside the arts.
9. Understanding music in relation to history and culture.

Grades K–4

1. **Content Standard:** *Singing, alone and with others, a varied repertoire of music.*

    a. Students sing independently, on pitch and in rhythm, with appropriate timbre, diction, and posture, and maintain a steady tempo.
    b. Students sing expressively, with appropriate dynamics, phrasing, and interpretation.
    c. Students sing from memory a varied repertoire of songs representing genres and styles from diverse cultures.
    d. Students sing ostinatos, partner songs, and rounds.
    e. Students sing in groups, blending vocal timbres, matching dynamic levels, and responding to the cues of a conductor.

2. **Content Standard:** *Performing on instruments, alone and with others, a varied repertoire of music.*

    a. Students perform on pitch, in rhythm, with appropriate dynamics and timbre, and maintain a steady tempo.
    b. Students perform easy rhythmic, melodic, and chordal patterns accurately and independently on rhythmic, melodic, and harmonic classroom instruments.

    c.   Students perform expressively a varied repertoire of music representing diverse genres and styles.

    d.   Students echo short rhythms and melodic patterns.

    e.   Students perform in groups, blending instrumental timbres, matching dynamic levels, and responding to the cues of a conductor.

    f.   Students perform independent instrumental parts while other students sing or play contrasting parts.

3. **Content Standard:** *Improvising melodies, variations, and accompaniments.*

    a.   Students improvise "answers" in the same style to given rhythmic and melodic phrases.

    b.   Students improvise simple rhythmic and melodic ostinato accompaniments.

    c.   Students improvise simple rhythmic variations and simple melodic embellishments on familiar melodies.

    d.   Students improvise short songs and instrumental pieces, using a variety of sound sources in their improvisations, including traditional sounds, nontraditional sounds available in the classroom, body sounds, and sounds produced by electronic means.

4. **Content Standard:** *Composing and arranging music within specified guidelines.*

    a.   Students create and arrange music to accompany readings or dramatizations.

    b.   Students create and arrange short songs and instrumental pieces within specified guidelines.

    c.   Students use a variety of sound sources when composing.

5. **Content Standard:** *Reading and notating music.*

    a.   Students read whole, half, dotted half, quarter, and eighth notes in $\frac{2}{4}$, $\frac{3}{4}$, $\frac{4}{4}$, and $\frac{6}{8}$ meter signatures.

    b.   Students use a system (i.e. syllables, numbers, or letters) to read simple pitch notation in the treble clef in major keys.

    c.   Students identify symbols and traditional terms referring to dynamics, tempo, and articulation and interpret them correctly when performing.

    d.   Students use standard symbols to notate meter, rhythm, pitch, and dynamics in simple patterns presented by the teacher.

6. **Content Standard:** *Listening to, analyzing, and describing music.*

    a.   Students identify simple music forms when presented aurally.

    b.   Students demonstrate perceptual skills by moving, by answering questions about, and by describing aural examples of music of various styles representing diverse cultures.

    c.   Students use appropriate terminology in explaining music, music notation, music instruments and voices, and music performances.

    d.   Students identify the sounds of a variety of instruments, including many orchestra and band instruments and instruments from various cultures, as well as children's voices and male and female adult voices.

    e.   Students respond through purposeful movement to selected prominent music characteristics or to specific music events while listening to music.

7. **Content Standard:** *Evaluating music and music performances.*

    a. Students devise criteria for evaluating performances and compositions.
    b. Students explain, using appropriate music terminology, their personal preferences for specific musical works and styles.

8. **Content Standard:** *Understanding relationships between music, the other arts, and disciplines outside the arts.*

    a. Students identify similarities and differences in the meanings of common terms used in the various arts.
    b. Students identify ways in which the principles and subject matter of other disciplines taught in the school are interrelated with those of music.

9. **Content Standard:** *Understanding music in relation to history and culture.*

    a. Students identify, by genre or style, aural examples of music from various historical periods and cultures.
    b. Students describe in simple terms how elements of music are used in music examples from various cultures of the world.
    c. Students identify various uses of music in their daily experiences and describe characteristics that make certain music suitable for each use.
    d. Students identify and describe roles of musicians in various settings and cultures.
    e. Students demonstrate audience behavior appropriate for the context and style of music performed.

    From *National Standards for Arts Education.* Copyright © 1994 by Music Educators National Conference (MENC). Used by permission. The complete National Arts Standards and additional materials relating to the Standards are available from MENC: The National Association for Music Education, 1806 Robert Fulton Drive, Reston, VA 20191; www.menc.org.

The Little Red House With No Doors and No Windows and a Star Inside

Reader 1: There was once upon a time a little boy who was tired of playing with his toys and tired of his books and puzzles. So he asked his mother.
Boy: "What shall I do?"
Reader 2: His mother, who always knew fun things for little boys to do, said—
Mother: "Why not go and find a little red house with no doors and no windows and a star inside."
Reader 1: This really made the little boy wonder. Usually his mother had good ideas, but he thought that this one was very strange.
Boy: "Which way shall I go? I don't know where to find a little red house with no doors and no windows."
Mother: "Go down the lane past the farmer's house and over the hill, and then hurry back as soon as you can and tell me all about your journey."
Reader 2: So the little boy put on his hat and his jacket and started out. He had not gone very far down the lane when he came to a merry little girl dancing along in the sunshine. Her cheeks were like pink blossom petals and she was singing like a robin.

Boy: "Do you know where I shall find a little red house with no doors and no windows and a star inside?"

Girl: "Ask my father the farmer. Perhaps he knows."

Reader 1: So the little boy went on until he came to the great brown barn where the farmer kept barrels of fat potatoes and baskets of yellow squashed and golden pumpkins. The farmer himself stood in the doorway looking out over the green pastures and yellow grain fields.

Boy: "Do you know where I shall find a little red house with no doors and no windows and a star inside?"

Farmer (chuckles): "I've lived a great many years and I never saw one, but ask Granny who lives at the foot of the hill . . . She knows how to make homemade cookies, taffy, and popcorn balls . . . and red mittens! Perhaps she can tell you."

Reader 2: So the little boy went on farther still, until he came to the Granny sitting in her rocker on her front porch. She had lots of wrinkles and a big smile on her sweet face.

Boy: "Please, dear Granny, where shall I find a little red house with no doors and no windows and a star inside?"

Reader 1: The granny was knitting a red mitten and when she heard the little boy's question, she laughed so cheerily that the wool ball rolled out of her lap and down to the little stone path.

Granny (laughing): "I should like to find that little house myself! It would be warm when the frosty night comes and the starlight would be much prettier than a candle. But ask the wind that blows about so much and listens at all the chimneys. Perhaps the wind can tell you."

Reader 2: So the little boy took off his cap politely to the granny and went on up the hill rather sadly. He wondered if his mother, who usually knew almost everything, had perhaps made a mistake. The wind was coming down the hill as the little boy climbed up. As they met, the wind turned about and went along, singing beside the little boy. It whistled in his ear, and pushed him along and dropped a pretty leaf into his hands.

Boy: "I wonder if the wind *could* help me find a little red house with no doors, and no windows and a star inside."

Reader 1: The wind cannot speak in our words, but it went singing ahead of the little boy until it came to an orchard. There it climbed up in the apple tree and shook the branches. When the little boy caught up, there, at his feet, laid a big red apple.

Reader 2: The little boy picked up the apple. It was as much as his two hands could hold. It was as red as the sun had been able to paint it, and the thick brown stem stood up as straight as a chimney.

Reader 1: And it had no doors and no windows. Was there a star inside?

Boy: "Wind, thank you! Thank you so much!"

Reader 2: The wind whistled back, as if it were saying, "You're welcome."

Reader 1: The little boy hurried back down the lane with the big, red apple in his hand. When he reached his house the little boy gave the apple to his mother.

Mother: "You have found a house with no doors and no windows, but where is the star?"

Reader 2: His mother took a knife (at this point, Mother starts cutting an apple crosswise) and cut the apple through the center. Oh, how wonderful! There inside the apple, lay a star holding five brown seeds.

Boy: "It is too wonderful to eat without looking at the star, isn't it?"

Mother: "Yes indeed, son, it is!"

Have the class sing some apple songs after performing the play.

Adapted from a story by Carolina Sherwin Bailey
North Carolina, Department of Agriculture and Consumer Services

Recommended Websites

Music

www.musick8kids.com
www.preschoolexpress.com
www.karenandkids.com
www.bussongs.com
www.scoutsongs.com
www.suzyred.com
www.americanfolksongs.com
www.lessonplanspage.com
www.mrsjonesroom.com
artsedge.kennedy-center.org/teach/les.cfm
lessonplanet.com
www.KIDiddles.com (song lyrics and recorded melodies)

Jazz Websites for Kids

www.pbskids.org/jazz
www.smithsonianjazz.org
www.jalc.org/jazzED/j4yp_curr

The History of Spirituals

www.spiritualsproject.org
www.negrospirituals.com

Orchestral Instruments

www.dsokids.com
www.datadragon.com/education/instruments

For Students and Teachers

www.classicsforkids.com/index.asp
www.pasadenaisd.org/sailon/musick_5.htm
www.artsalive.ca/en/mus/activitiesgames/index.html
www.playmusic.org
www.childrensmusic.org
www.funbrain.com/notes/index.html
http://library.thinkquest.org/15413/instruments/instruments.htm?tqskip1=1
www.achievement.org/autodoc/halls/art

www.creatingmusic.com
http://pbskids.org/mayaandmiguel/english/games/globalgroovin/game.html

Literature

www.books4teachers
www.amazon.com
www.readingonline.org
www.readinga-z.com
www.junebox.com
www.schoolspecialtyonline.com
www.carolhurst.com
www.readinglady.com
www.scholastic.com

U.S.

www.50states.com
www.texasteachers.net
www.nasa.gov
www.wildflower.org
www.americasstory.com

Science

www.songsforteaching.com/sciencesongs.htm
http://faculty.washington.edu/chudler/songs.html
www.youtube.com/watch?v=05ip-N0H1Ig

Arts and Crafts

http://familyfun.go.com
www.amazingmoms.com
www.seaworld.org
www.abcteach.com
www.kinderart.com
www.cutecolors.com
www.kidsrcrafty.com
www.coloring.ws
www.crayola.com
www.crest.com
www.dole.com
www.smokeybear.com
http://disney.go.com

www.kaboose.com
www.shindigz.com
www.orientaltrading.com
www.discountschoolsupply.com

Games

www.gamesquarium.com
www.gameskidsplay.net

Classroom Management and Forms

www.canteach.ca
www.lauracandler.com

General Teaching Tips/Ideas

www.sitesforteachers.com
www.edhelper.com
www.marcias-lesson-links.com
www.hummingbirded.com
www.teacherplanet.com
www.theteachersguide.com
www.preschooleducation.com
www.kindergartentreehouse.com
www.mrsjonesroom.com
www.lessonplanspage.com
www.teachme2.com
www.teacherspot.com
www.teacher2teacher.com
www.lessonplanz.com
www.eduplace.com
www.units4teachers.com
www.enchantedlearning.com
www.teachers.net
www.childfun.com
www.dltk-teach.com
www.abcteach.com
www.123child.com
www.learningpage.com
www.earlychildhood.com
www.alphabet-soup.net
www.howtolearn.com
www.preschoolexpress.com
www.teachervision.com

www.resourcefulclassroom.com
www.learningplanet.com
www.makinglearningfun.com
www.earlychildhoodlinks.com
www.poetry4kids.com
www.gigglepoetry.com
www.thekids.com
www.educationalscience.com
www.scicentral.com
www.cloroxclassroom.com
www.pearsonschool.com
www.kiddyhouse.com
www.kaboose.com
www.hubbardscupboard.org

APPENDIX 4 | **SAMPLE ASSIGNMENTS**

Connection Lesson Example: Math with Music

Hunter lesson plan model

Grade level: Kindergarten

Shape Song (Excerpt)

(Sung to the tune of London Bridge)
Two sides short and two sides long,
Two sides short, two sides long,
Two sides short and two sides long,
We're a rectangle.
Our four sides are just the same.
Just the same, just the same,
Our four sides are just the same,
We're a square.

When switching dynamics, I suggest that lines in bold be sung louder (*forte*), and the other lines softer (*piano*).

Source: www.perpetualpreschool.com/preschool_themes/shapes/shapes_songs.htm.

Math Objective

The student will identify four basic shapes by name and learn their differences.

Music Objective

The student will learn that dynamics refers to "the different degrees of loudness and softness of sound." He or she will identify and/or perform two contrasting dynamic markings in the music.

Soft (*p*-*piano*)   Loud (*f*-*forte*)

Materials

Classroom where triangular, square, rectangular, and circular objects can be found; shapes poster; coloring utensils and paper for each student.

Procedure

Anticipatory Set

The teacher will initiate a short game of "I Spy," using shape characteristics as clues (e.g. "I spy an object that is round," or " I spy an object that has two long sides and two short sides.") Students will name objects in the room, and the teacher will explain that the objects are similar to basic shapes because of the kind and number of their sides.

State the Objectives

The teacher will tell students that they will be learning about shapes and what makes them different from each other. They will also be told that they will experience singing in both their loud and soft singing voices.

Teacher Input

The teacher will show the shapes poster and give definitions and examples of triangles, circles, rectangles, and squares:

- Rectangle—has four sides. There are two long sides that are the same and two shorter sides that are the same (e.g. a door).
- Square—has four sides. All four sides are the same (e.g. a cracker).
- Triangle—has three sides. A triangle also has three corners (e.g. a pizza slice).
- Circle—has no straight sides. Circles are round (e.g. a ball).

The teacher will also explain the difference between loud and soft singing voices, when they are appropriate to use, and that the difference in volume is called *dynamics*.

Modeling

The teacher will sing the "Shape Song" using both a soft (*piano*) and a loud (*forte*) singing voice, while pointing out the shapes on the shape poster. She will teach the song to the students by rote.

Check for Understanding

The teacher will point out an object in the room and ask what shape it is. Students will answer by holding up finger(s) under their chins: one finger for a triangle, two fingers for a square, three fingers for a rectangle, and four fingers for a circle.

Guided Practice

The class will sing the "Shape Song" together. The teacher may choose alternate places in the song for the class to use *piano* or *forte* singing voices. The class will then have a class scavenger hunt around the room, pointing out objects that are a specific shape.

Independent Performance

The students will draw pictures of specific items that are in the shape of a circle, triangle, square, or a rectangle and label it.

Review/Closure

The class will sing the song again, changing dynamics at specific parts, and hold up the pictures that they drew when that shape is mentioned in the song.

Visual Aid: Shapes Poster

A poster with pictures of a square, triangle, rectangle, and a circle, drawn and labeled correctly.

Courtesy of Abianna Smith, Texas State University

Listening with Movement Lesson #1: "Viennese Musical Clock" from *Háry János Suite* by Zoltan Kodály

Composer

Zoltan Kodály (1882–1967) was born in what is now Slovakia. He died in Budapest, Hungary after a long and very productive life. His compositions are part of the early 20th-century Contemporary period.

In 1900, Kodály began to study music at the Franz Liszt Academy of Music in Budapest, Hungary. Because his father worked with the Hungarian Railway System, he was easily able to travel and learn about the music of his country. He began to collect the melodies of traditional Hungarian folk music, which he often used in his compositions. Kodály lived most of his life in Budapest, even during the difficult war times. He composed music for orchestra, chamber ensembles, and voice, but the suite from his folk opera *Háry János* is the best known and most widely performed of all of his compositions.

Instruments Heard

Full orchestra.

Subject Incorporation

This selection could be connected in several different ways to the classroom curriculum. Have students choose a group based on interest in the following assignments:

- A scientific review of timepieces (how they have been made through history).
- A study of the wars that would have affected Kodály's life in Budapest.
- Researching and drawing the musical clock that still stands and operates in front of the Imperial Palace in Vienna.

Have the group share their reports/pictures with the class.

Movement Activity

Form	Introduction A B A C A D A Coda (rondo).
Introduction	Like a clock face, begin with both arms at 12:00, move right arm clockwise with the beat from there back around to 12:00, making a full circle.
A Section	March in place to the beat using stiff arms and legs like the mechanical movements of figures moving on a clock.
B Section	With arms at sides, rock left and right on the accented beat.
C Section	Tap a pretend watch on the beat, first on one arm, then on the other, changing arms/ watches as you wish.
D Section	Clasp hands in front and swing them left and right like a pendulum on the accented beat.
Coda	Like a clock face, begin with both arms at 12:00, move right arm clockwise with the beat from there back around to 12:00, making a full circle.

Source: *Music Memory Bulletin*, Mollie Tower, Senior Author. Published by aeIDEAS.com.

Listening with Movement Lesson #2: "Wild Horseman" by Robert Schumann

Composer

Robert Schumann (1810–56) was born in Germany, and became one of the greatest composers of the Romantic period. Schumann began to compose at the young age of 7, and hoped to one day be a great pianist. When Schumann was 16, his father, who had supported Schumann's interest in music, died. His mother, who hadn't supported a musical career, pushed Schumann into law school. Very quickly, he found he was not interested in the study of law, and returned to his piano studies. A hand injury that might have been caused by a hand-strengthening device he invented prevented Schumann from pursuing his dream of becoming a professional pianist, so he concentrated on composing. Later in life, Schumann married Clara Weik, who was the daughter of his former piano teacher. Schumann's compositions include many works for piano, one opera, vocal solos, four symphonies, and many selections for orchestra, choir and chamber music groups.

Instrument Heard

Piano.

Subject Incorporation

A teacher may use Schumann's "Wild Horseman" to have students research and discuss how horses have been important through history. Divide the students into several groups and assign each group to draw and write about the use of horses in a specific period in the past. Have students share with the class what they drew and how horses were used. Compare and contrast the use of horses in different eras of the past, and in the present.

Movement Activity

Form	A A B A
Section A	Hold a scarf and swing right arm from right to left in front of the body while bouncing on feet to the beat.
Section A	Hold a scarf and swing right arm from right to left while bouncing on feet to the beat.
Section B	Hold scarf with both hands and twirl it to the left for two counts, then to the right for two counts while still bouncing on feet.
Section A	Hold a scarf and swing right arm from right to left while bouncing on feet.

Courtesy of Emily Cooper, Dahlia Figueroa,
and Caitlin Hodge, Texas State University

Correlation Lesson Example: "Dusty Locks" and Music

Level: Grade 4

Language Arts Objective

Students develop language for the purpose of effectively communicating though listening, speaking, viewing, and presenting.

Materials

Dusty Locks and the Three Bears by Susan Lowell and Randy Cecil; Narrator script; individual character parts written on cards; scarves or streamers for "the wind" actors; minimum costuming for the characters.

Procedure

The teacher will begin by brainstorming with the students what fairy tales have been set in a forest. Then the teacher will read *Dusty Locks and the Three Bears*. Next, the teacher will talk with the students about how to perform a play based on the book. She will teach "The Three Bears" song by rote. Provide reminders on: projecting your voice, looking up from your card as much as possible, remaining in character throughout the play. The students will then be assigned or volunteer for parts. The teacher needs to assign roles for: Narrator, Dusty Locks, Mama Bear, Papa Bear, Baby Bear, and Dusty Locks's mother.

Most of the remaining students will be the trees in the forest, and the rest will be the wind. The teacher will give the characters with speaking parts cards with their lines. The "wind" students will be instructed to "become" the wind any time Dusty Locks runs through the forest. When the wind students are not being "the wind," they are to hide. The tree students will sway when the wind blows through, and when any of the characters are walking through the forest. Anytime the wind or tree students hear sound words (e.g. stomp, thunder, etc.) they will make those sounds with vocal sounds or body percussion. One student will read from the Narrator script while the students perform the play.

The teacher should lead a rehearsal, including the appropriate sections of the song as that action occurs in the play. The trees and wind groups are the chorus. Present the play for another classroom.

On a following day, discuss and listen to other pieces of music written as incidental music for plays (e.g. Mendelssohn's overture and incidental music written for Shakespeare's *Midsummer Night's Dream*).

Source

www.calicocookie.com/bears.html

Music Correlation

Sing "The Three Bears Song" with the melody of "Pop Goes the Weasel" as incidental music during the play. Learn about other types of incidental music that have been composed.

The Three Bears Song (Excerpt)

(Sung to the tune of "Pop Goes the Weasel")

Dusty came to a house in the woods
inside all was quiet.
She saw cereal in three different bowls
and said, "I think I'll try it!"

"The first bowl is much too hot!
The second's too cold—I hate it!
But the third bowl tastes just right!"
So Dusty quickly ate it.

Courtesy of Emilee Birdsong, Texas State University

Integrated Unit Table of Contents, Example #1: The Four Seasons

Level: Grade 1

Monday: Introduction of the Four Seasons

Science: weather match game, and "The Seasons Song" (piggyback song)
Music: "The Four Seasons" (rhythmic activity #1)
Language Arts: reading, and "The Seasons Song" (Hap Palmer)

Tuesday: Spring

Math: addition and subtraction, and "See the Giant Sunflower" (piggyback song)
Music: "De Colores" (song map)
Language Arts: poetry, and "I'm a Little Watering Can" (piggyback song)

Wednesday: Summer

Language Arts: writing, and "Shells on the Seashore" (piggyback song)
Music: "Blue Skies" (song map)
Language Arts: poetry, and "To the Beach" (piggyback song)

Thursday: Fall

Art: coloring, and "Falling Leaves" (piggyback song)
Music: Vivaldi's "Four Seasons: Autumn" (YouTube Lesson) (listening activity with structured movement)
Language Arts: literature (correlation lesson), and "Pretty Leaves are Falling Down" (piggyback song)

Friday: Winter

Science: experiment, and "Snowflakes" (piggyback song)
Music: "The Winter Song" (rhythmic activity #2)
Language Art: spelling, and "Winter's Coming" (piggyback song)
> Courtesy of Kristina Goehring, Holly Henderson, and Dru Marshall, Texas State University

Integrated Unit Table of Contents, Example #2: Major Land Biomes

Level: Grade 4

Day 1: Tundra

Music: listening activity and composer study: Tchaikovsky (Listening Map for "Russian Dance" from *The Nutcracker*)
Language Arts: creative writing on animals of the Arctic and "The Snow Maiden" by Tchaikovsky (writing inspiration)
Science: Tundra temperatures and "It is Snowing" (piggyback song)

Day 2: Coniferous and Deciduous Forests

Music: a squirrel song (rhythmic activity #1—piggyback song with motions)
Language Arts: *Dusty Locks* (correlation lesson)
Math: graphing neighborhood deciduous trees and "Grapharena" (piggyback song)

Day 3: Desert

Music: "I Have a Ball" (song map) (YouTube)
Language Arts: Sonora Desert activity pages and "Saguaro Cactus Song" (piggyback song)
Science: survival game and "Deep in the Canyon"" (piggyback song)

Day 4: Rainforest

Music: women yodelers and singing from Epirus (*YouTube*)
Language Arts: reporting from Madagascar and "The Rainforest Song" (piggyback song)
Art: making and using a rain stick and "Do You Know the Jungle Animals" (rhythmic activity #2—adding instruments to a song)

Day 5: Grasslands

Music: "Home on the Range" (song map)
Language Arts: a biome "I" poem (children's song, "Biomes" by Eldon)
Science: grasslands scientific travel guide and "Scientific Method Blues"
   Courtesy of Emilee Birdsong, Kaitlyn Gregory, and Mallory Thompson, Texas State University

Integrated Unit Lesson Example #1: "I Have a Ball"— Major Land Biomes Unit

Day 3: Music Lesson/Desert

YouTube Lesson
Song Map Lesson
Level: Grade 4

Music Objectives

1. The student will learn to sing the Tunisian children's song, "I Have a Ball," and sing with a YouTube sound clip while using a Key Phrase Song Map.
2. The student will demonstrate the steady feeling in a song by tapping on each picture as he or she sings the song. This steady feeling is called *steady beat* or *pulse*.
3. As an added challenge, the student will demonstrate that there are many more sounds (e.g. taps or claps) for the rhythm than there are for the steady beat by clapping the rhythm of the song as it is sung.

Social Studies Objective

The student will explore cultural aspects (language, music) of the desert biome in Tunesia.

State Learning Standards in Music

§117.15. Music, Grade 4
    (4.3) Creative expression/performance
        B) Incorporate basic rhythmic patterns in simple meters in musical compositions

Materials

- "I Have a Ball" song map handout
- A pencil or something similar to use while tapping
- Sound clip of the song from the provided website
- Reference materials about Tunisia

Procedure

1. Briefly describe Tunisia and its location in the Sahara Desert. Provide pictures and other reference materials, and tell the students that in Tunisia, Arabic is spoken.
2. Explain to students that they are going to learn a Tunisian children's song in Arabic. Pass out the song map handout.
3. Have students listen to the YouTube sound clip once. Then teach the song by rote. It is a fairly difficult song to learn.
4. Once everyone is comfortable with the song, have each student take out a pencil. Explain the term "steady beat" and demonstrate with a familiar children's song. Using the song map, have each student use the eraser end of the pencil to tap the steady beat on each picture as they sing the new song they have learned.
5. Monitor to be sure everyone is tapping out the steady beat. For a challenge, have the students tap out the rhythm of the words as well.

Source

www.mamalisa.com/?t=es&p=2235&c=16

I Have a Ball

(Excerpt of Tunisian children's song sung in Arabic)

    En'a—endi kura
    Maj mal—aha
    Tej—ri kel—os—fura
    Kur—a—ti aha

    English translation:
    I have a ball
    It's the finest.

It flies like a bird,
My ball. Ah! Ah!
Courtesy of Mallory Thompson,
     Texas State University

"I Have a Ball" – Song Map

En'a—endi kura

Maj mal—aha

Tej—ri kel—os—fura

Kur—a—ti aha

Integrated Unit Lesson Example #2: Personal Percussion— The Five Senses Unit

Day 2: Music Lesson/Hearing

Rhythmic Activity Lesson
Level: Grade 3

Music Objective

The student will enhance music by adding appropriate body percussion or instrumental percussion sounds.

Science Objective

The student will explore sounds using their sense of hearing, and make observations of sounds by listening carefully.

State Learning Standards in Music

§117.12. Music, Grade 3
    (2) Creative expression/performance. The student performs a varied repertoire of music. The student is expected to:

A) sing or play a classroom instrument independently or in groups; and

B) sing songs from diverse cultures and styles or play such songs on a musical instrument.

Materials

Cool whip bowl for drum for each student; two pencils for each student to use as drum sticks; paint and glitter to decorate drums; recording of "Feliz Navidad"; materials and pictures of Christmas celebrations in Mexico

Procedure

The students will explore the sounds in the classroom to utilize their sense of hearing. Taking turns in small groups, the students will tap different items in the classroom to hear the differences in the sound. Categorize sounds by terms such as metal, plastic, wood, and so forth. Then the students will decorate their own cool whip bowls with the supplies provided.

While bowls dry, talk to the children about the culture of Mexico. Children will learn that a traditional Mexican Christmas is both similar and different from an American Christmas in many ways. Provide a few facts on a traditional Mexican Christmas. Teach the students how to say "Merry Christmas" in Spanish—*Feliz Navidad.*

Have students listen to "Feliz Navidad," a Christmas song written in 1970 by José Feliciano, a Puerto Rican singer-songwriter. (It is popular in America and throughout the Spanish-speaking world.) Next, have students sing with the recording while playing the rhythmic patterns in the music on their drums.

"Feliz Navidad" Song (Excerpt)

Feliz Navidad.
Feliz Navidad.
Feliz Navidad.
Prospero Año y Felicidad.

Sources

www.lyricsmode.com/lyrics/j/jose_feliciano/feliz_navidad.html
http://gomexico.about.com/od/festivalsholidays/p/christmas.htm

Courtesy of Sara Vaughn, Texas State University

Integrated Unit Lesson Example #3: Zipping Off to Mercury—The Planets Unit

Day 1: Science Lesson/Mercury and Venus

Song Map Lesson
Level: Grade 3

Science Objective

Students will learn about the first two planets closest to the sun. The class will compare and contrast the two planets, and the students will learn about the gravity of each planet.

Music Objective

The students will demonstrate the steady feeling in a song. This steady feeling is called *steady beat* or *pulse*.

State Learning Standards in Science

§112.5. Science, Grade 3
    (b) Knowledge and Skills
        (11) Science Concepts. The student knows that the natural world includes earth materials and objects in the sky. The student is expected to:
        C) identify the planets in our solar system and their position in relation to the Sun; and
        D) describe the characteristics of the Sun.

Materials

Floating in Space by Franklin M. Branley, illustrated by True Kelley; large pieces of paper, one for each student; markers; two colors of paper; and glue.

Procedure

Start by going over some simple facts about Mercury and Venus and have the students compare the two planets. The class will give examples of how they are different and alike. Also, the class will compare the positions of the two planets in relation to the Sun and the earth. Read *Floating in Space* to the class.

Next have the students trace their bodies on large pieces of paper and ask them to add an astronaut suit. Once the class has completed the task, they will discuss what they would take with them to Mercury and Venus, what they would need, and where they would keep it in their astronaut suits. After they have made labels on two different colors of paper (one color for each planet), the class will then glue the labels onto their personal astronauts.

Ask the class the differences between the items that they are taking to each planet. Then pass around the song sheets and have the class sing "Zipping Off to Mercury," using a Tapping the Beat Song Map as they sing the song.

Sources

- *Floating in Space* by Franklin M. Branley, illustrated by True Kelley
- *Whole Language Sourcebook* by Jane Baskwill and Paulette Whitman
- http://ritter.tea.state.tx.us/teks/grade/Third_grade.pdf

Piggyback Song (Excerpt)

(Sung to the tune of "London Bridge is Falling Down")

Zipping off to Mercury,
Thrusting off to Mars,
Zooming off to Jupiter,
Flashing past the stars.

Song Map (Excerpt)

Moving from left to right, tap each picture on the steady beat as you sing.

Courtesy of Preslee Allen, Texas State University

Compare/Contrast Music Sheet

Name _____

Name of Composition _____

List at least 3 things that are the Same in these two musical selections:

List What is Different:
(try to name 3 or more differences)

Which version do you like best?   1st _____   2nd _____

Why?

List a descriptive adjective for #1 _____

          #2 _____

Music, Art and Writing Worksheet

As you listen to the music, write descriptive words.

_____   _____   _____

_____   _____   _____

As you listen again, draw a picture that reflects your descriptive words.

During the final listening time, write a descriptive paragraph about your picture.

_____

_____

_____

_____

_____

Courtesy of Glenda Carnes

Scales

The scale is one way melody is organized. Scales help us recognize steps and skips.

Major scales are arranged in a series of whole and half steps. On a piano keyboard, the half steps are next to each other. Be careful, sometimes a half step is a white key to a black key, but it may be a black key to a white key or a white key to a white key.

Listen as a major scale is played.

Major scales are formed using the following pattern: (— = whole step, ½ = half step)

Whole step-whole step-half step-   whole step-whole step-whole step-half step

—   —   ½   —   —   —   ½

Find the pattern for the C major scale on this piano keyboard. Watch for the whole and half steps:

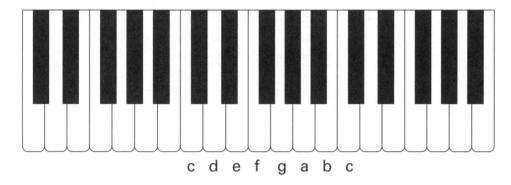

c d e f g a b c

The major scales often used in children's music are C, G, F, and D. Music written in one of these scales is said to be in the "key of C" or "key of G."

* Music in the key of C has no sharps or flats.
* Music in the key of G has one sharp, f-sharp.
* Music in the key of F has one flat, b-flat.

C major scale:

c   d   e   f   g   a   b   c

G major scale:

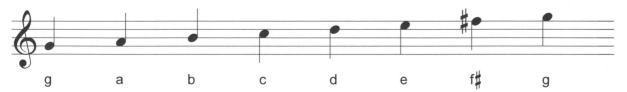

g   a   b   c   d   e   f♯   g

F major scale:

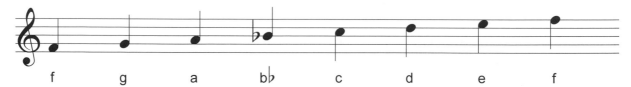

f g a b♭ c d e f

Tones arranged in certain patterns are called modes. *Major* and *minor* are the modes most often used in children's music.

Listen as a minor scale is played. A minor scale uses the following pattern of whole and half steps:

Whole step-half-step-whole step-whole step-half step-whole step-whole step

—   ½   —   —   ½   —   —

Find the pattern for the *a minor scale* on this piano keyboard. Watch for the whole and half steps:

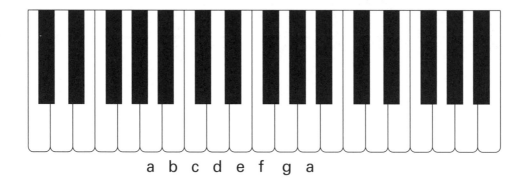

a b c d e f g a

Decide what key and mode (major or minor) each one of these songs uses.

Songbook Selections

Get America Singing. . .Again!

APPENDIX 6 | **GLOSSARY**

A cappella	Unaccompanied music. Italian term meaning "in chapel style."
Accent	A beat that is accentuated, stressed, made louder or accented.
Alto	The lower female voice category. The second part in four-part harmony.
Audiation	The process of mentally hearing and comprehending music, even when no physical sound is present.
Barline	A line drawn before the accented beat to group the steady beats into sets. It measures the music.
Bass	The lower male voice category. The fourth part in four-part harmony.
Coda	An ending. Literally, it means "tail" in Italian.
Composer	One who composes music.
Composition	A composed piece of music.
Compositional Formula	A system created to help children create music.
Crescendo	A dynamic marking meaning gradually getting louder.
Da capo	Often abbreviated to D.C. indicating that the performer should go back to the beginning and repeat the previous part of the music. Literally, it means 'from the head' in Italian.
Decrescendo	A dynamic marking meaning gradually getting softer.
Dotted Note	A dot follows a note, as in dotted half note. The dot adds half of the value of the note. A dotted half note would be held for 3 beats (2 for the half note + 1 for the dot). A dotted quarter note would be held for 1½ beats (1 for the quarter note + ½ beat for the dot).
Double Bar	A symbol at the end of music.
Double Bass	The large stand-up stringed instrument, often played in jazz quartets.
Double Dotted Bar	A repeat sign.
Dynamics	One of the musical elements, representing the softs and louds in music. In music, *p* means soft and *f* means loud.
Eighth Note	A type of musical note receiving half a beat in most children's music. Two eighth notes equal one quarter note. ♫ is the short-hand notation for two eighth notes that we call "te-te" in class. Division of the beat.
Fermata	An indication to hold or pause on a note or rest in a piece.
Form	One of the musical elements. A specific structure in music such as ABA.

Forte	An Italian term meaning loud. Used in music as a dynamic level, marked with an *f*, to indicate loud.
Fugue	A type of "follow-the-leader" or imitative form in music. One voice or section plays a melody or theme in the music then another voice enters and plays the same theme, but at a higher or lower pitch. This pattern is followed several times by different sections or voices.
Genre	A collection or grouping of something into a category, such as the genre of American folk music.
Half Note	A type of musical note receiving two beats in music where the quarter note equals one beat.
Harmony	Two or more notes sounding together. One of the musical elements. Accompaniments performed on guitar or piano can create harmony. Voices singing different pitches at the same time create harmony.
Improvisation	Music that is played without writing it out first. It is a section of original performed music, created during a solo part of a jazz composition. The performer must know much about music theory in order to do this type of music.
Introduction	Something that goes before, or at the beginning of a musical composition.
Lyrics	The words to a song or musical composition.
Measures	Grouped sets of beats created by the bar lines are called measures.
Melody	One of the elements of music. The tune of the music.
Meter	Grouping of beats in duple (2 beats), triple (3 beats) or quadruple (4 beats) meters; created by an accented first beat.
Meter Signature	Numbers appearing at the beginning of music. Top number indicates the number of beats in a measure, and the bottom number indicates the type of note that gets 1 beat. Sometimes called time signature.
Opera	A story told in singing. Includes soloists, costumes, orchestra, and sometimes chorus. A dramatic presentation where the story in song is acted out.
Oratorio	A musical setting of a text, usually sacred. Like an opera with soloists, orchestra and chorus included, but it isn't acted out.
Ostinato	An underlying repeating accompaniment. A short phrase that is rhythmic or melodic is persistently repeated. A boogie-woogie bass is a type of ostinato. Plural is Ostinati.
Piano	1) An Italian term meaning soft or quiet, and used in music as a dynamic level indicated by *p*. 2) A keyboard instrument with strings and hammers that hit the strings, causing the sound.
Pitch	Indicating the up and down movement of melody. Sometimes listed as an element, sometimes replaces "melody" as an element, especially with modern music which has no real melody, but does have "pitches" that move higher and lower.
Pizz.	Abbreviation of *pizzicato*. An Italian term indicating to string players that they should pluck, rather than bow, the strings of their instrument.
Programmatic	A type of music that tells a story in sound, using no words.
Quarter Note	A type of musical note receiving one beat in most children's music. It is one-fourth of the whole note, thus the name "quarter." For iconic notation we use the single line (l) and call it "tah."
Rhythm	An element of music, including the pulse or steady beat, rhythm patterns, rhythm of the words of the song, division of the beat, note values.

Rhythmic Composition	A composed piece of music made up of rhythm patterns which are performed on instruments or with sounds.
Rhythm Patterns	Combinations of different rhythms, sometimes can be found in the rhythm of the words. "｜◨◨｜" is a type of rhythm pattern.
Rondo	A type of ABACA form. The returning A section occurs three or four times.
Sforzando	An Italian term meaning suddenly loud (*subito forte*) and is usually marked as *sf*.
Soprano	The highest female voice classification. The first voice in four-part harmony.
Sound Composition	Sounds, either made by the children or played by instruments, replace the words of a story or book. The book can be told only in sounds as the pictures are shown.
Steady Beat	The pulse or "heartbeat" of music. Part of element rhythm, and is what makes us want to tap our toes to the music.
Symphony	A large orchestra, or a composition for a large orchestra.
Tenor	The higher male voice category. The third part in four-part harmony.
Tone Color	One of the musical elements meaning the sound source, or what is making the sounds in the music. Also called timbre.
Tutti	Often found after a solo section, this indicates that the ensemble will play all together.
Whole Note	A type of musical note receiving four beats in most children's music.

APPENDIX 7 | **THE LISTENING PROGRAM**

Listening Maps

Taken from the *Music Memory Listening Program*, Mollie Gregory Tower, senior author. http://www.aeideas.com/musicmem.cfm

The maps in this chapter can also be found in full color on the companion website www.routledge.com/textbooks/9780415878234

Track listing for the Listening Maps

1st Movement, "Spring", *The Four Seasons* by Vivaldi	Track 2
1st Movement, *Eine Kleine Nachtmusik* by Mozart	Track 5
"Hallelujah Chorus," *Messiah* by Handel	Track 3
"Russian Dance," *Nutcracker* by Tchaikovsky	Track 7
"Viennese Musical Clock," *Háry János Suite* by Kodaly	Track 15
"Variations on Simple Gifts," *Appalachian Spring* by Copland	Track 16
3rd Movement, *Symphony No. 1 ("Afro-American")* by Still	Track 17
"The Stars and Stripes Forever" by Sousa	Track 18
"Mars, the Bringer of War" *The Planets* by Holst	Track 19

1st Movement, "Spring", *The Four Seasons* by Vivaldi

Map by Debra Erck   computerized by Kay Greenhaw

263

1st Movement, *Eine Kleine Nachtmusik* by Mozart

Eine Kleine Nachtmusik: 1st Movement by Mozart (1756-1791)

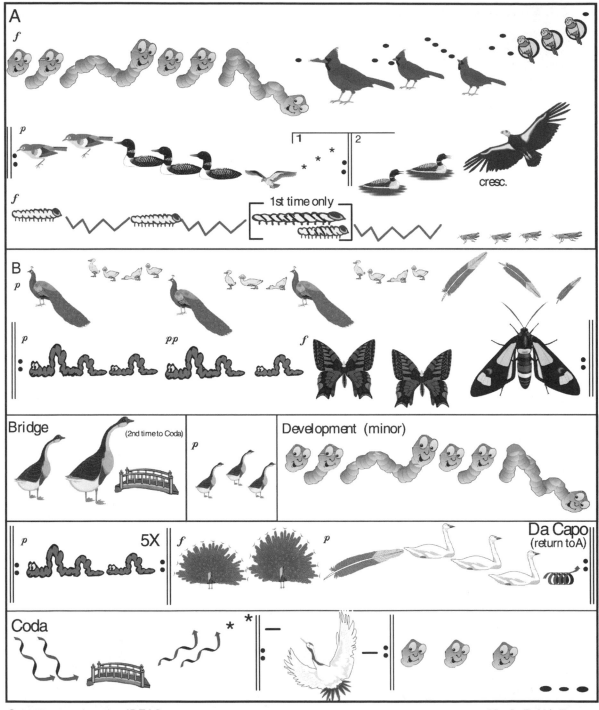

Map by Debbie Tannert

"Hallelujah Chorus," *Messiah* by Handel

Messiah: "Hallelujah Chorus"
by Handel (1685-1759)

Map by Kay Greenhaw © 1998

"Russian Dance," *Nutcracker* by Tchaikovsky

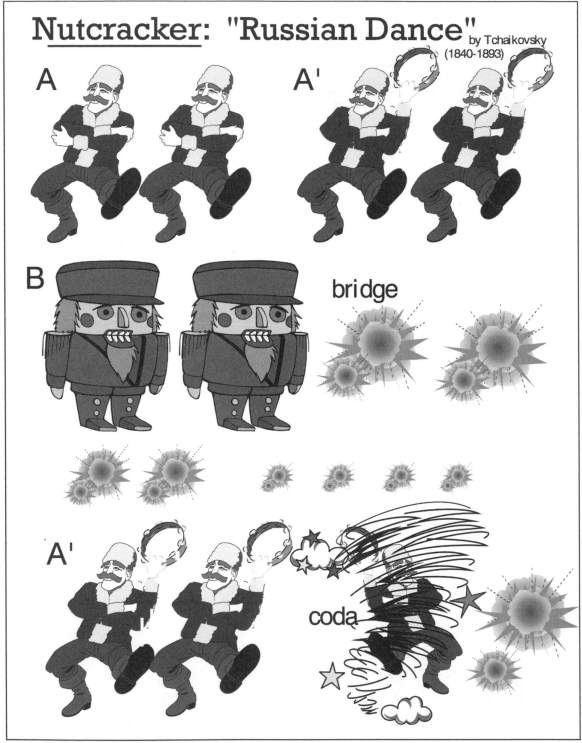

© 2003 arts education IDEAS   Map by Kay Greenhaw

"Viennese Musical Clock," *Háry János Suite* by Kodály

© 2006 arts education IDEAS

Map by Debbie Tannert

267

"Variations on Simple Gifts," *Appalachian Spring* by Copland

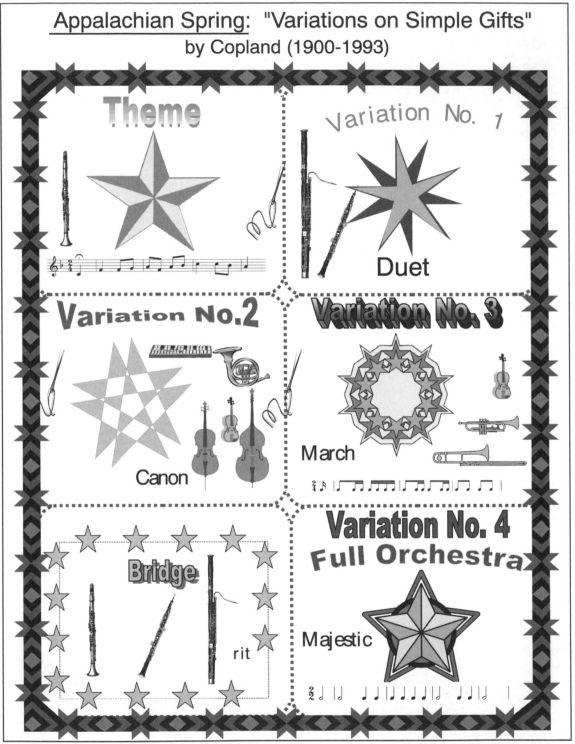

3rd Movement, Symphony No. 1 ("Afro-American") by Still

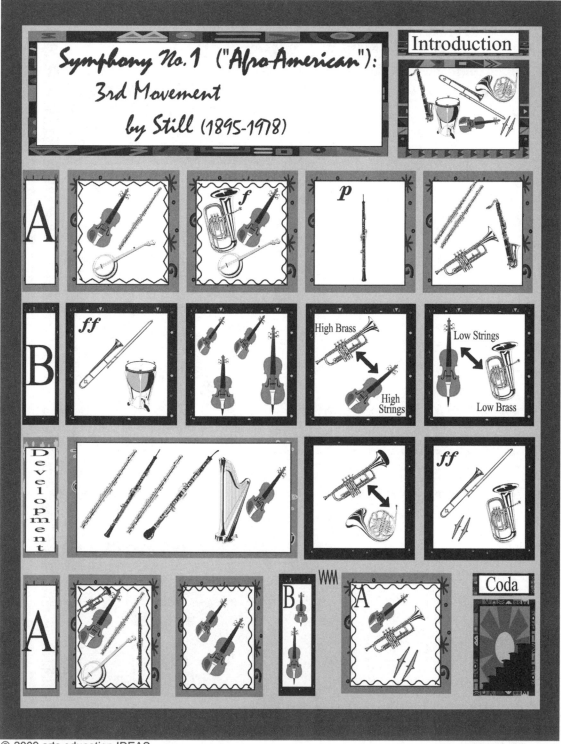

Map by Debbie Tannert

269

"The Stars and Stripes Forever" by Sousa

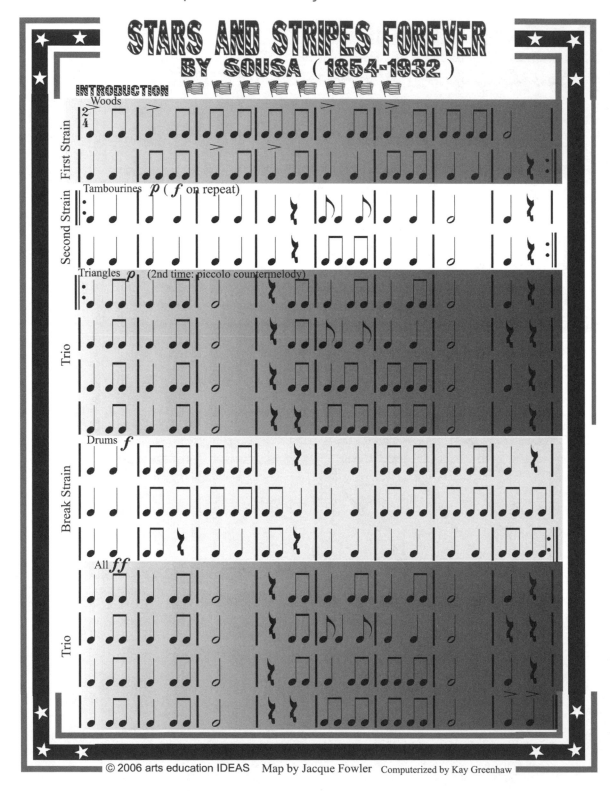

"Mars, the Bringer of War" *The Planets* by Holst

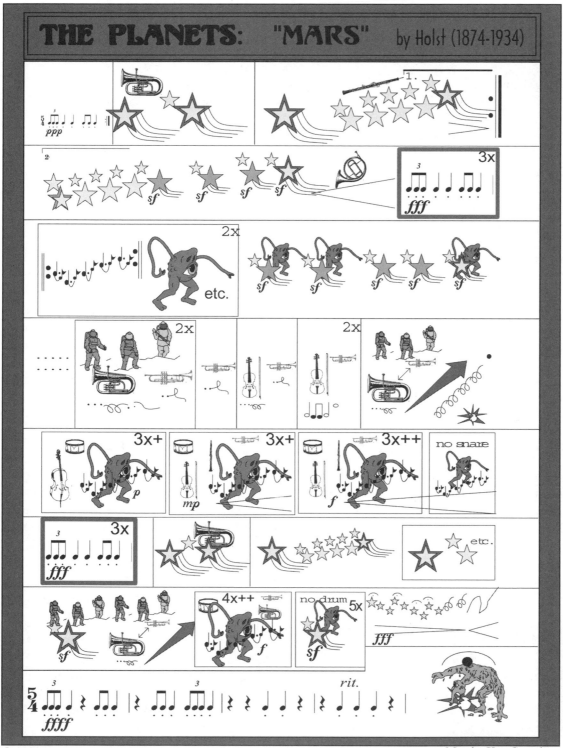

Map by Kay Greenhaw

271

How to Follow the Listening Maps

1st Movement, "Spring", *The Four Seasons* by Vivaldi (p. 263)

The piece is illustrated on the map in five large sections:

I. Opening theme—A.
II. Solo violins take turns depicting the singing of birds, followed by the repeat of the last half of the A theme.
III. A flowing stream, imitated by the strings, ending again with the last half of the A theme.
IV. The thunderstorm begins with everyone playing, then has alternating sections with solo violins and "lightning" played by the strings section.
V. Developmental section with theme and bird song fragments, beginning with solo violins, then full group, back to one violin solo with harpsichord, ending with the last half of the A theme, played twice (first loud, then soft).

This is a steady beat tapping map. Tap the beat twice on each symbol. Begin at the top left corner with the four flowers in section I, tapping twice on each petal. In section II, tap back and forth on the bird pictures and solo violin pictures, moving to the flower when the A theme is heard again. Next, tap twice on each picture of a fish or wave in section III, followed again by the flower petals. In section IV, tap twice on each lightning bolt and violin picture, followed once again by the flower petals. When the violin solo is heard in section V, start by pointing to the single violins in the final box. When a steady beat is heard, point to the crossed violin pairs in the arch shape. When the solo violin is again heard, point to the single violin pictures in the bottom arch shape, followed one last time by the flower petals (two taps per petal), first the *forte* one, then the *piano* flower. Point to the *fermata* (birds-eye) on the last note.

1st Movement, *Eine Kleine Nachtmusik* by Mozart (p. 264)

Follow the melodic direction along the top edge of the creatures' bodies and other images.

On the parrots at the end of the first line, point to the parrot then circle around on the swing clockwise. Be sure to notice the repeat signs, first and second endings and da capo as you follow the map. Notice the caterpillars in the A section marked "1st time only." In the B section, the moth is a longer phrase than the butterflies that precede it. Be sure to jump to the coda the second time after the bridge section.

Note: This piece is a useful introduction to sonata form, for those teachers who want to use it. The form is AB (Exposition), Development, and a return to AB (recapitulation) and Coda.

"Hallelujah Chorus," *Messiah* by Handel (p. 265)

The boxes have numbers indicating repeats.

In the third box, (rainbow with angels over it), point to the lone angel to the right for the hallelujahs after the omnipotent phrase each time.

The first box with the crown is used two and a half times. After the "Lord" symbol you will see a line. This is where you will skip to the "crown and Lord" box at the end of the row.

The figure eight on its side is the sign for *infinity* in math.

"Russian Dance," *Nutcracker* by Tchaikovsky (p. 266)

Follow this map from left to right, top to bottom. Each dancer on the map represents 16 beats. Listen for the tambourine in the sections where it is pictured (A'). The pictures in the "bridge" section and at the end of the coda represent actual sounds in the music.

"Viennese Musical Clock," *Háry János Suite* by Kodály (p. 267)

Follow the sections in order as notated at the top of the listening map. Tap two times on each of the icons that represent the strong beat (**1**—2) within each section.
   Notice:

- Flower icons in A represent the strong beat, the notation represents the rhythm.
- Instruments pictured in left-to-right order across top of the A clock (piccolo, oboe, flute, trumpet.) Each return of the A section features a different instrument.
- In the B section the trumpet plays first and then the piccolo.
- The oboe then trumpet is named at the top of the D section. The oboe plays first, the trumpet plays on the repeat of the top line of pictures. The flute and clarinet play the second line of icons in D.

"Variations on Simple Gifts," *Appalachian Spring* by Copland (p. 268)

This map represents a Shaker quilt. The dashed lines are stitches and each stitched section is one section of the piece.
   The first star is very plain to represent the unchanged theme. The first variation is a duet and the corresponding star shows a visual duet. The second variation is a round in three parts and the corresponding star is a triple star. The third variation music is fast, so the star also looks like quick movement. The bridge contains pieces of the theme in it, and the picture shows pieces of stars. Finally, the fourth variation sounds very stately and grand and the "stained glass" star demonstrates a stately and grand picture. The three needle and thread pictures represent short bridge sections.

3rd Movement, Symphony No. 1 ("Afro-American") by Still (p. 269)

0:00   Introduction Start at top right corner; follow boxes by listening for instruments shown.

Line 1
0:13   Theme A, Box 1
0:27   Box 2
0:41   Box 3
0:49   Box 4

Line 2
0:56   Theme B, Box 1
1:01   Box 2
1:09   Box 3
1:16   Box 4

Line 3

1:23	Development, Box 1
1:45	Box 2
1:52	Box 3

Line 4

2:03	Theme A, Box 1
2:18	Box 2
2:31	Theme B, Box 3
2:38	Theme A, Box 4
2:52	Coda. Follow stairs upward.

"The Stars and Stripes Forever" by Sousa (p. 270)

Tap one flag on each beat of the introduction. Tap the rhythm patterns along with the music for the four sections. The instrument names on the map represent the instruments students will play, not the instruments heard in the selection. The rhythm patterns follow, but do not always correspond exactly, to the rhythm being played by the band. Observe the repeat signs (‖: :‖) by repeating these sections.

"Mars, the Bringer of War" *The Planets* by Holst (p. 271)

0:00	Line 1	The A theme is represented by stars. Repeat, moving to second ending on—
0:45	Line 2	(A continued) Note rhythm in box that is repeated three times.
1:20	Line 3	The B theme is represented by Cyclops.
2:04	Line 4	The C theme is represented by astronauts.
2:31		Transition
2:39		C theme again
3:08	Line 5	B theme again
4:11	Line 6	A theme again
5:01	Line 7	C theme again
5:15		B theme again
6:02		Coda begins
6:38	Line 8	Coda (continued)

274

CD TRACK LIST

Track 1   II. Rondeau, *Overture (Suite) No. 2* in B minor, BWV 1067 by Bach

Track 2   I. Allegro, "Spring" (La primavera), Violin Concerto in E major, Op. 8, No. 1, RV 269, *Four Seasons* (Le quattro stagioni) by Vivaldi

Track 3   "Hallelujah Chorus," *Messiah*, HWV 56 by Handel

Track 4   Hornpipe, *Water Music*, Suite No. 1 in F major, HWV 348 by Handel

Track 5   I. Allegro, Serenade No. 13 in G major, *Eine Kleine Nachtmusik*, K. 525 by Mozart

Track 6   Variations in C major on *Ah, vous dirai-je, Maman*, K. 265 by Mozart

Track 7   "Russian Dance," Act II, *Nutcracker*, Op. 71a by Tchaikovsky

Track 8   "Chinese Dance," Act II, *Nutcracker*, Op. 71a by Tchaikovsky

Track 9   "The Elephant," *Carnival of the Animals*, by Saint-Saëns

Track 10   "The Swan," *Carnival of the Animals*, by Saint-Saëns

Track 11   "Flight of the Bumblebee," *The Tale of Tsar Saltan*, Op. 57 by Rimsky-Korsakov

Track 12   "Wild Horseman" (Wilder Reiter), *Album fur die Jugend*, Op. 68 by Schumann

Track 13   "The Moldau" (Vltava), from *Ma vlast* (excerpt) by Smetana

Track 14   Gymnopédie No. 1 by Satie

Track 15   II. "Viennese Musical Clock" (Becsi harangjatek), *Háry János Suite* by Kodály

Track 16   "Variations on Simple Gifts," *Appalachian Spring* by Copland

Track 17   III. Humor (Animato) *Symphony No. 1 ("Afro-American")* by Still

Track 18   March "The Stars and Stripes Forever," by Sousa

Track 19   I. "Mars, the Bringer of War," *The Planets* Op. 32 by Holst

Track 20   "What a Wonderful World," by Thiele and Weiss

Track 21   "Early Light," (for band) by Carolyn Bremer

Track 22   "Malagueña," *Andalucia Suite Espagnole* by Lecuona

NOTES

Section I: Getting Started

1 Personal correspondence with author, September 2006.
2 Based on idea from Dr. Robin Stein, Texas State University.

Chapter 1: Organizing for Successful Teaching

1 Source: http://www.quotegarden.com/teachers.html.
2 Source: http://quotationsbook.com/quote/38350/.
3 Source: http://quotationsbook.com/quote/38127/.
4 Source: http://clinton3.nara.gov/WH/Work/061600.html.
5 Source: http://www.pdxmetroarts.org/welcome.html.
6 Letter to School and Education Community Leaders, August 2009.
7 *Learning Sequences in Music: Skill, Content, and Patterns* (1997) by Edwin E. Gordon. Published by GIA Publications.
8 Based on idea from Glenda Carnes, Texas State University.
9 "The Effects of Background Music on Studying" by Susan Hallam. Unpublished paper, School of Education, Oxford Brookes University, Oxford, UK.
10 *My Many Colored Days* (1996) by Dr. Seuss (Steve Johnson and Lou Fancher, Illus.). Published by Knopf Books for Young Readers.
11 "Reducing Aggression With Touch" (2006) by Frances M. Carlson and Bryan G. Nelson. Published by Southern Early Childhood Association, Vol. 34 # 3, Fall 2006.
12 Source: http://drjean.org.

Chapter 2: Framework for Teaching and Learning

1 *Frames of Mind: The Theory of Multiple Intelligences* (1983) by Howard Gardner. Published by Basic Books.

2   "Recognizing the Role of Artistic Intelligences" (1990) by Charles Fowler. Published in the September issue of the *Music Educators Journal*.

3   ERIC Clearinghouse on Assessment and Evaluation. Source: http://www.eric.ed.gov/.

4   *Eight Ways of Knowing: Teaching for Multiple Intelligence* (1999) by David Lazear. Published by Corwin Press.

5   Personal correspondence, Mary Ellen Titus, multiage elementary classroom teacher, Manhattan School district, Kansas (2000).

6   *The Swassing-Barbe Modality Index: Zaner-Bloser Modality Kit* (1979) by R. H. Swassing, W. B. Barbe, & M. N. Milone. Published by Zaner-Bloser.

7   *The Process of Education* (1977) by Jerome Bruner. Published by Harvard University Press.

8   *The Process of Education* (1977) by Jerome Bruner. Published by Harvard University Press.

9   *Learning and Teaching the Ways of Knowing* (1985) by Elliot Eisner (ed.). Published by Yale University Press.

10 *Re-Imagining Schools: The Selected Works of Elliot Eisner* (2005) by Eliot Eisner. Published by Routledge.

11 *The Arts and the Creation of Mind* (2002) by Elliot Eisner. Published by Yale University Press.

12 *Science of Education and the Psychology of the Child* (1970) by Jean Piaget. Published by Viking Press.

13 *Science of Education and the Psychology of the Child* (1970) by Jean Piaget. Published by Viking Press.

14 Based on idea from Dr. Robin Stein, Texas State University.

15 *The Dreamkeepers: Successful Teachers of African American Children* (1994) by Gloria Ladson-Billings. Published by Jossey-Bass Publishers.

16 Source: http://rethinklearningnow.com/stories/story/?storyId=29292.

17 MENC: Opportunity-to-Learn Standards for Music Instruction, 1994. Source: http://www.menc.org/resources/view/opportunity-to-learn-standards-for-music-instruction-grades-prek-12.

Chapter 3: Inside the Music: The Basic Elements of Music

1   'Jerome S. Bruner and the Process of Education' by M. K. Smith. Published in *the encyclopedia of informal education* (2002) Source: http://www.infed.org/thinkers/bruner.htm.

2   *Integrating the Arts into the 4th and 5th Grade Classroom: A Primer for Classroom Teachers* by Dr. Sue Snyder. Published by Arts Education Ideas. Source: www.acideas.com/text/articles/integrating thearts.cfm.

3   Based on idea from Dr. Robin Stein, Texas State University.

4   This activity is adapted from a process taught by Barbara Grenoble, an outstanding music teacher from Denver, Colorado.

5   Concert notes for the Brandon Hill Chamber Orchestra in Bristol, UK. Source: http://bhco.co.uk/pages/node/129.

6   Source: www.carolynbremer.com.

7   Based on notes from Austin Symphonic Band program, "Music for All Seasons."

8   "Just like Dancing, with Sousaphones" (2009) by Gia Kourlas. Published December 22, 2009 in *The New York Times*.

Section II: *Somos Músicos*: Doing What Musicians Do

1 *Learning, Arts, and the Brain* (2008) The Dana Consortium Report on Arts and Cognition. Published by Dana Press, New York.

Chapter 4: Listening

1 Source: http://www.xpdl.org/nugen/p/whyismusicimportant/.
2 Source: http://sites.google.com/a/ocalayouthsymphony.org/www/whymusic.
3 Source: http://www.soundpiper.com/mln/emotion.htm.
4 *What to Listen for in Music* (2009) by Copland and Slatkin. Published by Penguin Group (USA).
5 *The Biological Foundation of Music* (2001) by Robert J. Zatorre and Isabelle Peretz. Published by New York Academy of Sciences.
6 *Creative Music Education: A Handbook for the Modern Music Teacher* (1976) by R. Murray Schafer. Published by Macmillan.
7 *What Works: Instructional Strategies for Music Education* (1989) by Margaret Maerrion (ed). Published by Music Educators National Conference.
8 "Confidence in the Classroom: Ten Maxims for the Teachers" (1990) by James Eison. Published in *College Teaching*, Winter 1990.
9 *Peter and the Wolf* (1987) by Sergei Prokofiev and Warren Chappell. Published by Schocken Books.
10 *Hush* (1992) CD by Yo-Yo Ma and Bobby McFerrin. Sony.
11 Source: http://www.xpdl.org/nugen/p/whyismusicimportant/.
12 Source: http://sites.google.com/a/ocalayouthsymphony.org/www/whymusic.

Chapter 5: Performing

1 Researched and written by Carolyn Phillips while she was executive director of the Norwalk Youth Symphony, Connecticut (see Appendix 3).
2 Source: http://thinkexist.com/quotation/i_don_t_sing_because_i-m_happy-i-m_happy_because/331094.html.
3 Othello Act IV, scene 1
4 Source: http://www.lessonsense.com/general/singing.html.
5 "A Comparison on the Effect of Pitch Accuracy of Group and Individual Singing in Young Children" by Mary Goetze. Published in the *Bulletin for the Council for Research in Music Education*, Winter, 1989.
6 *The Musical Classroom* (2007) by Patricia Hackett and Carolyn Lindeman. Published by Pearson Education.
7 "Singing with TREBLEMAKERS, Songs for Young Singers" (2002) and "Singing with TREBLEMAKERS, Our Favorite Folk Songs" (2002). Mejunda label.
8 Source: http://www.brainyquote.com/quotes/quotes/w/williamchr366306.html.
9 Source: http://thinkexist.com/quotation/when_the_music_changes-so_does_the/186986.html.
10 Source: http://lyrics-a-plenty.com/d/drift_away.lyrics.php.
11 Source: www.dancingmasters.com.
12 *Move Folk Dance Music for Kids and Teachers* by Sanna Langden. Published by Silver Burdent.

13 *Movement in Steady Beat* (2002, 2nd edition) by Phyllis Weikart. Published by High Court Press.

14 *Movement in Steady Beat* (2002, 2nd edition) by Phyllis Weikart. Published by High Court Press.

15 *Teaching Movement and Dance: Sequential Approach to Rhythmic Movement* (1989, 6th edition) by Phyllis Weikart. Published by The High/Scope Press. Text and CDs.

Chapter 6: Creating

1 Researched and written by Carolyn Phillips while she was executive director of the Norwalk Youth Symphony, Connecticut (see Appendix 3).

2 Source: http://www.creativityatwork.com/articlesContent/Quotes/quotes3business-creativity.htm.

3 Source: http://www.great-inspirational-quotes.com/art-quotes.html.

4 *Creative Problem Solving: A Step-by-Step Approach* (2002) by Robert A. Harris. Published by Pyrczak Publishing.

5 *Brain-Based Learning: The New Paradigm of Teaching* (2008, 2nd edition) by Eric Jensen. Published by Corwin Press.

6 Based on idea from Dr. Robin Stein, Texas State University.

7 *A Whole New Mind: Why Right-Brainers Will Rule the Future* (2006) by Daniel H. Pink. Published by Riverhead Trade.

8 *Examining Intelligence* by Robert Sternberg. Source: www.aacsb.edu/publications/Archives/JanFeb06/p22-27.pdf.

9 Source:http://www.artsactionfund.org/page/-/AAF/pdf/50-states-50-days/Research%20Arts%20Ed%20Drop%20Out.pdf.

10 *Creative Process Vs Product* by Audette Sophia. Source: www.catalystarts.wordpress.com.

11 Dr. Torrance's updated biography, *E. Paul Torrance: The Creativity Man* (2007) by Garnet Millar. Published by Scholastic Testing Service.

12 *Music Ace Deluxe (or Music Ace 2)* (2003). Published by Harmonic Vision.

Section III: Integrating Music Into the Curriculum

1 *Integrate With Integrity: Music Across the Curriculum* (1996) by Dr. Sue Snyder. Published by IDEAS Publishing.

2 Source: http://professionals.collegeboard.com/data-reports-research/sat/cb-seniors-2008.

3 Source: www.aep-arts.org/publications/info.htm?publication_id=10.

4 "Learning Through the Arts: Curriculum Implications" (1999) by J.Burton, R. Horowitz, and H. Abeles. In E. Fiske (ed.) *Champions of Change: The Impact of the Arts on Learning* (pp. 35–46). Published by The Arts Education Partnership.

5 Based on idea from Dr. Robin Stein, Texas State University.

Chapter 7: Using Music to Enhance Learning in Language Arts

1 Source: http://onlinelibrary.wiley.com/doi/10.1111/j.1749-6632.2009.04417.x/full.

2 Researched and written by Carolyn Phillips while she was executive director of the Norwalk Youth Symphony, Connecticut (see Appendix 3).

3 Source: http://www.quotationspage.com/quote/30291.html.

4 Source: http://www.elementalmuzic.com/.

5 Proceedings of the National Academy of Sciences 2002. Source: 10.1073/pnas.162368599.

6 *Learning, Arts, and the Brain* (2008) The Dana Consortium Report on Arts and Cognition. Published by Dana Press.

7 *A Whole New Mind: Why Right-Brainers Will Rule the Future* (2006) by Daniel H. Pink. Published by Riverhead Trade.

8 Based on idea from Dr. Robin Stein, Texas State University.

9 *Home Place* (1993) by Crescent Dragonwagon. Published by Aladdin.

10 *Chicka Chicka Boom Boom* (2000) by Bill Martin, Jr. and John Archambault. Published by Beach Lane Books.

11 *Noah's Ark* (1992) by Peter Spier. Published by Dragonfly Books.

12 *People* (1988) by Peter Spier. Published by Doubleday Books for Young Readers.

13 *The Very Busy Spider* (1995) by Eric Carle. Published by Philomel Publishing.

14 "The Effect of the Incorporation of Music Learning into the Second-Language Classroom on the Mutual Reinforcement of Music and Language" by Anne S. Lowe. Unpublished doctoral dissertation, 1995, Urbana-Champaign, University of Illinois.

15 "Enhancing Acquisition through Music" by Robert Lake. Published by *The Journal of the Imagination in Language Learning and Teaching*, volume VII, 2002–2003.

16 *New Shoes for Silvia* (1993) by Johanna Hurwitz. Published by HarperCollins.

Chapter 8: Using Music to Enhance Learning in Science

1 Researched and written by Carolyn Phillips while she was executive director of the Norwalk Youth Symphony, Connecticut (see Appendix 3).

2 Source: http://www.heartquotes.net/music-quotes.html.

3 Source: http://www.sayingsnquotes.com/quotations-by-subject/art-quotes-and-sayings/.

4 Source: http://www.childrensmusicworkshop.com/advocacy/toptenquotes.html.

5 Source: www.science.tamu.edu/CMSE/activities/PalmPipesChimesHints.doc.

6 Source: www.baroque-music-club.com/vivaldiseasons.html.

Chapter 9: Using Music to Enhance Learning in Math

1 Researched and written by Carolyn Phillips while she was executive director of the Norwalk Youth Symphony, Connecticut (see Appendix 3).

2 Source: http://hubpages.com/hub/The-Importance-of-Music-Education-in-Public-Schools

3 Source: http://www.quotegarden.com/music.html

4 Source: www.happalmer.com.

5 "Musical Mnemonics as an Aid to Retention with Normal and Learning Disabled Students." (1983) K. Gfeller. Published in *Journal of Music Therapy*, 20(4), 179–89. "Music and Vocabulary Learning." (1982) D. Schuster and D. Mouzon. Published by *Journal of the Society for Accelerative Learning and Teaching*, 7(1), 82–106.

6 *Music: A Mathematical Offering* (2008) by Dave Benson, Department of Mathematics, University of Aberdeen. Source: http://www.maths.abdn.ac.uk/~bensondj/html/music.pdf

7 *Percussion Fast and Cheap* by Catherine Schmidt-Jones. Source: http://cnx.org/content/m11889/latest.

8 *Music with the Brain in Mind* (2000) by Eric Jensen. Published by Corwin Press.

Chapter 10: Using Music to Enhance Learning in Social Studies

1 Researched and written by Carolyn Phillips while she was executive director of the Norwalk Youth Symphony, Connecticut (see Appendix 3).

2 Source: http://www.iwise.com/O6JTK.

3 Source: http://www.toddgreen.com/quotes.html.

4 Source: http://artsedge.kennedy-center.org/quotes.aspx.

5 "Engaging Community Resources for Experiencing Brazilian Music" (2009) by Elisa Macedo Dekaney and Deborah A. Cunningham. Published in the December 2009 *Music Educators Journal.*

6 *National Standards for Arts Education* (1994) Reston VA: Music Educators National Conference.

7 "Music Education in Our Multimusical Culture" (1993) by Bennett Reimer. Published in the *Music Educators Journal.*

8 *If America Were a Village: A Book about the People of the United States* (2009) by David J. Smith. Published by Kids Can Press.

9 *Music Memory Bulletin, 2009–2010* (2009) Mollie Tower, senior author. Published by Arts Education Ideas.

10 *Music Memory Bulletin, 2009–2010* (2009) Mollie Tower, senior author. Published by Arts Education Ideas.

11 *Listen to Learn: Using American Music To Teach Language Arts and Social Studies* (2004) by Teri Tibbett. Published by Jossey-Bass.

12 *Music Memory Bulletin, 2006–2007* (2006) Mollie Tower, senior author. Published by Arts Education Ideas.

13 *Music Memory Bulletin, 2006–2007* (2006) Mollie Tower, senior author. Published by Arts Education Ideas.

14 Source: www.pbs.org/wnet/slavery/experience/education/feature.html.

15 *Fifty Nifty United States* CD. Published by Shawnee Press.

16 Source: www.musick8.com.

Chapter 11: Relating Music to the Other Arts

1 Source: http://www.campaign800.org/aboutcampaign-800.html.

2 Researched and written by Carolyn Phillips while she was executive director of the Norwalk Youth Symphony, Connecticut (see Appendix 3).

3 Source: http://www.quotegarden.com/music.html.

4 Source: http://www.great-quotes.com/quote/919984.

5 Source: http://www.saidwhat.co.uk/keywordquotes/performance.

6 *The Philosophy of Music Education: Advancing the Vision* (2002) by Bennett Reimer. Published by Prentice Hall.

7 *Third Space: When Learning Matters* (2005) by Lauren M. Stevenson and Richard J. Deasy. Published by Art Education Partnership.

8   *Works for Children and Young Adults: Poetry, Fiction, and Other Writing* (2003) by Langston Hughes (Dianne Johnson, ed.). Published by University of Missouri Press.

9   *Cool Daddy R*at (2008) by Kristen Crow. Published by Putnam Juvenile.

Chapter 12: Favourite Teaching Tips

1   Source: http://www.artsactionfund.org/page/-/AAF/pdf/50-states-50-days/Research%20Arts%20Ed%20Drop%20Out.pdf.

INDEX